A Tale Told

Shakespeare's *The Winter's Tale* and Hidden Catholic England

Robert T. Morrison

Copyright © 2020 by Robert T. Morrison.

All rights reserved. No part of this publication may be reproduced, distributed or transmitted in any form or by any means, including photocopying, recording, or other electronic or mechanical methods, without the prior written permission of the publisher, except in the case of brief quotations embodied in critical reviews and certain other noncommercial uses permitted by copyright law.

Picture Acknowledgment and Credit: pages 18, 29, 93, 109, 177, 183 and 186 (Mary Evans Picture Library); page 45 (Grosvenor Prints/Mary Evans Picture Library); page 119 (Mary Evans Picture Library/Charles Folkard); and page 221 (Michelle De Castro)

Cover art by Michelle De Castro

Book Layout © BookDesignTemplates.com

A Tale Told Softly: Shakespeare's *The Winter's Tale* and Hidden Catholic England/ Robert T. Morrison. —7th ed.
ISBN 978-1490569420

Contents

Introduction 3

Sounding the Walls 9

    Camillo and Paulina 11

    Camillo as Pope 15

    Pope Paul V and James I 27

    Hermione, Leontes, and Their Offspring 34

    Polixenes, Sicilia, and Bohemia 47

    The Oracle and Rome 51

    Dramatis Personae 55

The Catholic Tragedy: Acts I - III 63

    Common Beginnings and Hope 63

    The Madness of Leontes 68

    Plots and Oaths 74

    Accusations of Treason 79

    Tyranny and Heresy 85

    Antigonus's Decision 92

  Time 112

The Catholic Comedy: Acts IV & V 117

  Penance 124

  Leontes's Decision 132

  The Mass 136

  Perdita's Anointing 144

  Saints Peter and Paul 149

  English Heirs in Heaven 154

Hiding Spots and Disguises 163

  Hermione as the Mystical Body of Christ 164

  Flora, The Blessed Virgin Mary, and Florizel 175

  The Oracle and Providence 197

  Hermione's Yoke (and *Agnus Dei*) 204

  Catholic Englishman's Tale 209

  A Tale Told Boldly 215

  A Tale Told Softly 218

Bibliography 227

+
AMDG

To my beautiful wife and best friend, Becky Morrison

Regina sacratissimi Rosarii, ora pro nobis

*That she is living,
Were it but told to you, should be hooted at
Like an old tale*

— Paulina, *The Winter's Tale*

Introduction

To best understand the tale that follows, one must appreciate the lengths to which Catholics in Shakespeare's England went to conceal their religion. And to get a sense of that, it helps to have some familiarity with a great, but little known saint. In 1970, the Catholic Church canonized St. Nicholas Owen among the Forty Martyrs of England and Wales. We do not have much information on the saint but know that he became a lay brother in the Society of Jesus (the Jesuits) as a young man and showed his remarkable skill primarily in constructing hiding places for Catholics, especially priests. Shortly after the discovery of the Gunpowder Plot (with which the saint had no involvement, despite accusations), English authorities captured St. Nicholas. His captors tortured him to death during the course of interrogation in the Tower of London in 1606.

Fr. John Gerard knew St. Nicholas and wrote of his martyrdom in *The Condition of Catholics under James I*:

> But the man that was most extremely used and with extremities brought unto the last extremity, which is death itself, was one Nicholas Owen, commonly called and most known by the name of Little John. By which name he was so famously and so much esteemed by all Catholics, especially those of the better sort, that few in England, either Priests or others, were of more credit. This man did for seventeen or eighteen years continually attend upon Father Garnett, and assist him on many occasions. But his chief employment was in making of secret places to hide Priests and Church stuff in from the fury of searches; in which kind he was so skillful both to devise and frame the places in the best manner, and his help therein desired in so many places, that I verily think no man can be said to have done more

> good of all those that laboured in the English vineyard. For, first, he was the immediate occasion of saving the lives of many hundreds of person, both ecclesiastical and secular, and of the estates also of those seculars, which would have been lost and forfeited many times over if the Priests had been taken in their houses.[1]

The saint did tremendous work "in the English vineyard," saving many hundreds of lives.[2] Thus, St. Nicholas built humble masterpieces to hide priests who suspected they might have only a limited time in England before they were caught and executed. He generally crafted these hiding places within the homes of relatively wealthy Catholic sympathizers. The homes were grand in many cases, while the hiding places were purely functional. Yet from the perspective of eternity, his humble works were infinitely more valuable than the most regal and luxurious dwellings.

If, as many have argued, Shakespeare was a Catholic, he too might have benefitted from the sacraments and guidance of priests whose work in England was facilitated by the efforts of St. Nicholas Owen. He would have had to conceal his faith just as others did, which perhaps explains why we do not have overt testaments to his beliefs. And yet this book makes the argument that there is a complete and devout Catholic allegory within Shakespeare's *The Winter's Tale*. Whereas St. Nicholas Owen designed his masterpieces to conceal Catholic priests, the pages that follow attempt to demonstrate that Shakespeare designed a masterpiece to conceal a tale of the beliefs, struggles and hopes of the Catholics in England who relied upon those priests.

Skeptics generally make one or both of two arguments to suggest the virtual impossibility of finding a hidden Catholic allegory in Shakespeare's plays: (i) Shakespeare would not have written such an allegory because he would have risked too much in doing so, or (ii) because we do not have evidence that Shakespeare wrote a Catholic allegory he never wrote one. Of course the counter to both arguments is that Shakespeare was as skilled in concealing an allegory as St. Nicholas Owen was in concealing priests – he minimized the risk by hiding it masterfully, and we do not see it because he hid it masterfully. It is true that some of St. Nicholas Owen's hiding places were discovered. But these hiding places were found only after authorities tore apart a house, often over the span of several days, following reports of a priest inside. If authorities did not suspect a Shakespeare play had forbidden Catholic elements, there is no reason to suspect they would have scrutinized it to the extent necessary to discover a well-hidden allegory.

Even so, acknowledging that Shakespeare could have written a Catholic allegory does not necessarily mean that he did in fact write one. The burden of proof on anyone suggesting that such an allegory exists should be relatively high. The pages that follow attempt to meet that burden by presenting a case that relies upon surprisingly numerous and straightforward correlations between the language, themes, and plots in the play and the generally unambiguous and well-documented political realities of religious life in Shakespeare's England.

The allegory generally follows the sequence of the play and consists of two parts: first, the dire circumstances that Catholics in Shakespeare's England faced at the time the play was written and first performed and, second, a vision of what such Catholics hoped for as a remedy. After seeing the basic sketch of the allegory, one can more easily see that Shakespeare intended to link many of the themes, characters and even wording nuances of the play to the religious events taking place in his England.

The Winter's Tale is a play of moral certainties: of the two characters that face the play's most crucial moral dilemmas, one (Leontes) undergoes sixteen years of penance in reparation for his bad deeds while the other (Antigonus) is eaten by a bear. The religious viewpoints cited in this book are equally stark and come from the principal figures shaping the debates at the time the play was written. For the allegory to be plausible, there needs to be fairly close correlation between the supposed allegorical drama and the literal drama. For instance, if we find ourselves wondering why a character who is clearly virtuous in the play is a villain in the allegory, we would know something is amiss. The allegory described in this book aligns the moral certainties of *The Winter's Tale* with the perspective of Catholics in Shakespeare's England. Astonishingly, the fit is virtually exact.

Something would also be amiss if the correlations between the allegorical and literal meanings required us to see connections that no reasonable member of Shakespeare's audience would have considered real. Without a doubt, the allegory is hidden and disguised; but it is eminently reasonable once we see it. So, for instance, "oath" in the play matches what "oath" meant in Shakespeare's England. So too with "priest," "allegiance," "oracle," "heretic," "plot," "holy father," "keys," "authority," "adulterous," "queen," and many other concepts – I take it for granted that Shakespeare understood that what he wrote resonated with the most salient ideas of his day, and that he intended the clear meanings such associations have in the play.

The first chapters establish Paulina and Camillo as figures for Saints Paul and Peter. This allegorical connection is complete in itself – one can appreciate the parallels between the characters and the saints without any particular appreciation for the events in Shakespeare's England under James I.

After seeing Camillo and Paulina in their allegorical roles, the next chapters look to historical connections to see how the remaining key characters fit within the allegory. With the allegorical "list of actors," the book turns to seeing how to read *The Winter's Tale* as an allegory from first scene to last, pairing the actions of the play to the relevant theological and historical realities in Shakespeare's England. Finally, the last chapters explore certain nuances of the allegory that are so rich and important that they deserve special consideration beyond the narration of the allegory based on the play's chronology.

As we should expect, not every line in the play fits within the allegorical meaning.[3] Indeed, it might have stretched even Shakespeare's unique talents to write a play that worked extraordinarily well throughout both literally and in its hidden allegorical sense. Moreover, Shakespeare had to work within the censorship regulations in place, including the Abuses of Players Act of 1606. As Ian Wilson notes, Shakespeare was left to "sticking with pagan themes" for the most part in his later plays.[4] These censorship constraints effectively required Shakespeare to use allegory to comment on the religious issues of his England and limited the material with which he could work. The pages that follow show that, despite these limitations, *The Winter's Tale* is a far more complete religious allegory than we might have imagined Shakespeare, or anyone else, could write under King James I's anti-Catholic reign.

As enjoyable as *The Winter's Tale* is to read in its literal meaning, the allegory described in these pages might help many readers have a greater appreciation for one of Shakespeare's last public plays. G. Wilson Knight, who had much praise for the play, wrote:

> *The Winter's Tale* may seem a rambling, perhaps an untidy, play; its anachronisms are vivid, its geography disturbing. . . . The more profound passages are perhaps rather evidence of what is beating behind or within the creative genius at work than wholly successful ways of printing purpose on an average audience's, or average reader's, mind.[5]

If, as this book attempts to demonstrate, Shakespeare intended not only the literal meaning but also a well-developed and thorough allegory for the religious events of his day, the play may seem tidier, less rambling, and altogether more refined than the late Professor Knight suggested. And though I am biased, I think that seeing the allegorical meaning might prompt some readers to consider that *The Winter's Tale* may well be one of the greatest works of genius in the English language.

Notes

[1] Fr. John Gerard, S.J., *The Condition of Catholics under James I*, 182.

[2] Like all saints, St. Nicholas had a fruitful spiritual life. As Fr. Gerard relates, it seems unlikely that he could have achieved his results from natural skill alone (regardless of such skill): "Yea, he did much strive to make them of several fashions in several places, that one being taken might give no light to the discovery of another. Wherein he had no doubt great aid from Almighty God, for his places were exceeding fortunate (if so we may term the providence of God) and no marvel, for he ever began his work with communicating [receiving Holy Communion at Mass] that day he entered upon it, and, as much as his labour would give him leave, did continually pray whilst he was working." Ibid. 184.

[3] J.A. Bryant, Jr. wrote in his essay about the allegory of *The Winter's Tale* that, "The kind of absolute correspondence, traceable point by point through every line of a poem, that is sometimes used as a criterion by academic allegory hunters is not a characteristic of this play – or, for that matter, of any really respectable literary work." J.A. Bryant, Jr., *Shakespeare's Allegory: The Winter's Tale*.

[4] Ian Wilson, *Shakespeare the Evidence*, 341.

[5] G. Wilson Knight, *The Crown of Life: Essays in Interpretation of Shakespeare's Final Plays*, 128.

SECTION ONE

Sounding the Walls

To set the stage for seeing *The Winter's Tale* as an allegory for Catholic life under King James I, it is worth considering two skill sets in Shakespeare's England that had far greater importance than they do in Western culture today: hunting priests (practiced by the pursuivants), and building hiding places for Catholic priests. In his *Autobiography of a Hunted Priest*, Fr. John Gerard, S.J.,[1] relates one of his many experiences in which the competing skill sets were put to the test:

> I was hardly tucked away when the pursuivants broke down the door and burst in. They fanned out through the house, making a great racket. The first thing they did was to shut up the mistress of the house in her room with her daughters, then they locked up the Catholic servants in different places in the same part of the house.... They measured the walls with long rods and if the measurements did not tally they pulled down the section that they could not account for. They tapped every wall and floor for hollow spots; and on sounding anything hollow they smashed it in.[2]

After four days of searching, the pursuivants gave up. Fr. Gerard emerged from his hiding place "very wasted and weak with hunger and lack of sleep" after having spent his time "squatting in a very confined space."[3] On this occasion the pursuivants lost, but on many others they prevailed.

From Fr. Gerard's narration, we can begin to understand the tremendous value of St. Nicholas Owen, one of those great craftsmen who built hiding places for priests in Shakespeare's England. Alice Hogge describes Owen's *modus operandi*:

> Under the cover of carrying out legitimate building or repair work Owen would craft a hiding-place, working in secret and as near to silence as he could manage, for any attention drawn to the location of the hide rendered it useless for its purpose. Even loyal servants were kept from learning the whereabouts of a hide, for fear torture might turn them. Owen's genius was to exploit the main structure of a house, burrowing deep into the masonry of its interior, lodging his hide within the very framework of the building, within what, to the practiced eye of the pursuivants, could only be solid wall or ceiling. His hides are three-dimensional puzzles of Max-Escher-like complexity. And, for maximum safety, every one of them was different.[4]

Several qualities stand out in this description of St. Nicholas Owen's work. He needed great skill to design and construct hiding places that would withstand the searches of teams of pursuivants determined to find what they concealed. The saint also needed to maintain secrecy to avoid compromising his projects. And because his work made him an enemy of the state, he needed tremendous courage to carry out his work. More than anything else, though, he needed a strong and unwavering devotion to the Catholic Church. A weak or hesitant faith barely keeps a Catholic in the pews in favorable times, and could not begin to sustain heroic efforts in times of persecution.

We can draw an analogy between the efforts of recusants (the term for Catholics refusing to attend Anglican services) to hide priests and the challenge of portraying themes sympathetic to Catholicism on stage in Shakespeare's England. If, as many argue, Shakespeare was Catholic, it stands to reason that he would have wanted to express Catholic sympathies through his art. Yet he certainly could not do so openly under Queen Elizabeth I or King James I. Like Catholics in England who harbored priests, he would have had to take extraordinary precaution in hiding and disguising his Catholic faith within his plays.

Of course one cannot rely exclusively on such reasoning as a tool to see Catholic themes in *The Winter's Tale*. After all, hidden Catholic themes probably look a lot like nonexistent Catholic themes. However, this notion of hiding priests provides us with a realistic blueprint for how we might spot and understand Catholicism in the plays of Shakespeare's England. We should not expect to find Catholicism in every line any more than we would expect the pursuivants to find priests hidden in every corner of every room. Likewise, if a secret door were even remotely visible, we would expect to find some attempts to disguise it. This section of the book attempts to "sound the walls" of *The Winter's Tale* to discover the allegorical counterparts to the play's most important characters.

Camillo and Paulina

If we had to briefly summarize *The Winter's Tale*, we could do so without mentioning Camillo or Paulina and still convey the basic story:

> Leontes, the king of Sicilia, unjustly suspects his queen, Hermione, of committing adultery with the king of Bohemia, Polixenes. Leontes's mad jealousy leads him to bring charges of adultery and treason against his queen. Seeking confirmation for his judgment, he also sends two of his lords to Delphos to receive the counsel of the oracle. The lords return the judgment of the oracle: Hermione is chaste, and Leontes is a jealous tyrant. Tragically, the Sicilian king does not realize his madness until after rejecting the counsel of his subjects in Sicilia, and even the judgment of Apollo's oracle. By the time he realizes his error, Polixenes has fled to avoid being poisoned, Leontes has sent his newborn daughter (Perdita) to be abandoned in Bohemia, and his young son, Mamillius, has died in grief at his father's injustice. Worst of all, Hermione dies upon hearing that her son has died. Leontes spends the next sixteen years in penance in Sicilia, while in Bohemia his daughter grows in grace and becomes engaged to Florizel, the son

of Polixenes. Florizel and Perdita return to Sicilia, with Polixenes following. Tremendous joy ensues at the happy reunion, including the miraculous resurrection scene, in which a statue of Hermione comes to life to be embraced by Leontes.

Thus we have the play's most important actions and the roles of the six royal characters, without reference to Camillo (a lord of Sicilia) or Paulina (wife to Antigonus, another lord of Sicilia). To omit Camillo and Paulina, however, is to pass over characters that Shakespeare clearly wanted us to appreciate as uniquely important and virtuous: although of relatively low nobility, they drive almost every good action in the play. Camillo is the first to admonish Leontes against false judgment of Hermione. He then rescues Polixenes by taking him to Bohemia, and eventually facilitates his return (with Perdita and Florizel) to Sicilia. Paulina is the next character to forcefully admonish Leontes (Antigonus and a lord having already opposed Leontes peacefully). She then leads Leontes through his sixteen years of penance, persuades him to avoid remarrying, and effects for him the "resurrection" of Hermione's statue in her chapel.

Shakespeare further highlights the central and beneficent roles of Camillo and Paulina through the respect and admiration of other characters. The only character that speaks ill of Paulina or Camillo is Leontes, when he falsely judges each of them during his madness. Once he regains his senses, he sees Camillo and Paulina as even more worthy of his trust and respect.

Northrop Frye compares the two characters to Kent in *King Lear* (high praise indeed), as they "combine outspoken honest criticism with a fierce loyalty."[5] Camillo and Paulina are loyal to Leontes, but above all else they are loyal to truth and willing to make sacrifices to defend and promote it.

Along these lines, Shakespeare identifies these two characters as doctor-like, with unique abilities to diagnose and cure the emotional, spiritual and intellectual maladies of other characters in the play:

Medicinal References	Lines
Camillo (to Leontes): Good my lord, be cured/ Of this diseased opinion, and betimes,/ For 'tis most dangerous.	1.2.295-297
Camillo: There is a sickness/ Which puts some of us in distemper, but/ I cannot name the disease; and it is caught/ Of you that yet are well.	1.2.383-386
Paulina: I/ Do come with words as medicinal as true,/ Honest as either, to purge him of that humor/ That presses him from sleep.	2.3.36-39
Paulina: Good my liege, I come –/ And, I beseech you hear me, who professes/ Myself your loyal servant, your physician,/ Your most obedient counselor, yet that dares/ Less appear so in comforting your evils.	2.3.52-56
Florizel: Camillo,/ Preserver of my father, now of me,/ The medicine of our house.	4.4.588-589

Shakespeare thus portrays Camillo and Paulina as the spiritual doctors of *The Winter's Tale*, which corresponds to their religious significance. These medicinal references also bring to mind the numerous healing miracles of Saints Peter and Paul described in the *Acts of the Apostles*.

Shakespeare further sets them apart in the last speech of the play, wherein Leontes directs Paulina to take Camillo as her husband. The marriage plans do not seem to make much sense in the literal reading of *The Winter's Tale*: the two characters have not exchanged a word in the play and they have not even appeared on stage together until this last scene. Yet the marriage of Camillo and Paulina is the crowning touch on the allegory, as we shall see.

Several scholars have written about the probable connection between Paulina and St. Paul. Among these, Eugene England notes that:

Leontes is opposed, judged, and ultimately healed not by his victim (as Lear is) but by Paulina, a noblewoman of the realm whose name is not only intentionally Christian but may even suggest her role as a healer in the Pauline tradition.[6]

And Roy Battenhouse sees Paulina develop in the play in a way analogous to the "growth of the Biblical Saul into a St. Paul."[7]

Given their similar roles and ultimate union, we have at least some basis for wondering why Shakespeare apparently gave Paulina a name linked to a Christian saint – St. Paul – without giving her counterpart a parallel name, such as Pietro after St. Peter. The Catholic Church links these saints to such an extent that any feast day of one will also celebrate the other. In his chapter on the Feast of Saints Peter and Paul, Dom Guéranger writes:

> The cross of Peter has transferred to her all the rights of the cross of Jesus. . . . Such being the meaning of this day, it is not surprising that eternal Wisdom should enhance it still further, by joining the sacrifice of Paul to that of Peter. More than any other, Paul advanced by his preachings the building up of the body of Christ. If on this day holy Church has attained such full development as to be able to offer herself, in the person of her visible Head, as a sweet smelling Sacrifice, who better than Paul may deservedly perfect the oblation, furnishing from his own veins the sacred libation? The bride having attained fullness of age, his own work is likewise ended. Inseparable from Peter in his labours by faith and love, he will accompany him also in death; both leaving her to the gladness of the divine nuptials sealed in their blood, whilst they ascend together to that eternal abode wherein that union is consummated.[8]

St. Peter thus appears to be the most logical choice if one had to identify a counterpart to St. Paul.

Certainly the skeptical explanation for why Shakespeare did not name Camillo "Pietro" seems at least possible: that Shakespeare did not really have St. Paul in mind for Paulina. However, looking past the skeptical explanation pays dividends in this particular instance, for one of the most notable Camillos in history did indeed have a link to St. Peter. On May 16, 1605, a few years before Shakespeare wrote *The Winter's Tale*, Camillo Borghese took the name Pope Paul V, as successor of St. Peter to the papacy. Thus, by giving Camillo the same name as the reigning pope, Shakespeare left us with ample reason to look further into the connection between Camillo and Paulina on the one hand, and Saints Peter and Paul on the other.

Camillo as Pope

Before looking to the significance of Camillo Borghese (Pope Paul V) we should first inquire whether the play's text suggests that Shakespeare actually intended the coincidental naming. While many links between Camillo and Pope Paul V arise from historical context, the play provides several meaningful connections between Camillo and popes in general, as Shakespeare identifies Camillo as (a) priest and confessor, (b) "more than a man" by performing miracles, (c) having a position of unique authority, (d) possessing the keys to the posterns, (e) pilot, (f) cupbearer, (g) "holy father," and (h) receiving the reverence traditionally rendered to the pope.

Because one cannot be pope without being a Catholic priest, Leontes's words in the second scene fittingly establish the foundation for seeing Camillo as pope:

> I have trusted thee, Camillo,
> With all the nearest things to my heart, as well
> My chamber counsels, wherein, priestlike, thou
> Hast cleansed my bosom. I from thee departed
> Thy penitent reformed.
>
> (1.2.234-238)

Here Camillo is "priestlike," and Leontes's analogy is to the Catholic sacrament of Penance. Early in the play, therefore, we find a link between Camillo and a primary role of a Catholic priest as confessor. As

Clara Longworth de Chambrun suggests, this reference to the Catholic sacrament of Penance stands out in the play:

> The meditations of Leontes, his tribute to the faithful friend who "priest-like had cleansed his bosom," might find their place in any essay on pious devotion, and it cannot be said that Shakespeare put such passages in *The Winter's Tale* as part of a necessary historical background.[9]

Shakespeare might have chosen any number of ways to show the extent to which Leontes trusted and valued Camillo, but he chose specific allusions to the Catholic priesthood.

Florizel adds to the identification of Camillo as a priest, albeit less directly, when Camillo says he will overcome the difficulties facing Florizel's marriage to Perdita:

> How, Camillo,
> May this, almost a miracle, be done,
> That I may call thee something more than a man,
> And after that to trust thee?
>
> (4.4.536-539)

Florizel's suggestion that Camillo would be "more than man" and perform "almost a miracle" if he were to assist Florizel and Perdita indicates extraordinary reverence for Camillo and also reflects the words that the Catechism of the Council of Trent[10] used to describe the Catholic priesthood:

> Bishops and priests being, as they are, God's interpreters and ambassadors, empowered in His name to teach mankind the divine law and the rules of conduct, and holding, as they do, His place on earth, it is evident that no nobler function than theirs can be imagined. Justly, therefore, are they called not only Angels, but even gods, because of the fact that they exercise in our midst the power and prerogatives of the immortal God.[11]

This is the Catholic doctrine regarding the sacrament of Holy Orders. According to Catholicism, a Catholic priest has the power to forgive sins through sacramental Confession, and to offer Mass, whereby bread and wine are changed into the Body and Blood of Christ. How can these miraculous things be done? They can only be done because the priest receives these extraordinary powers upon his ordination to the Catholic priesthood and thereby becomes, in a sense, "more than a man." Florizel's words therefore build upon the priestly identity of Camillo, whom Leontes has already compared to a priest with the ability to forgive sins.

Shakespeare gives us reasonable basis for associating Camillo with the Catholic priesthood, but does the connection extend to the pope? As the Bishop of Rome, the pope has authority over the entire Church. Indeed, if one had to choose a single characteristic that distinguishes the pope from all other priests and bishops, we might say it is this authority. Throughout the play, Camillo acts with an authority that goes well beyond his position as a lord of Sicilia. Almost to emphasize this, of the four times Shakespeare uses the word *authority* in the play, two refer to Camillo and two refer to Autolycus. One character represents legitimate authority, the other its opposite.

The most significant of these references to Camillo's authority alludes to the authority of St. Peter as head of the Church:

> POLIXENES
>   Come, Camillo,
>   I will respect thee as a father if
>   Thou bear'st my life off. Hence! Let us avoid.
> CAMILLO
>   It is in mine authority to command
>   The keys of all the posterns. Please Your Highness
>   To take the urgent hour. Come, sir, away.
>   (1.2.459-464)

Shakespeare identifies Camillo as having authority, being like a father to a man of much higher station.

Camillo Borghese, with the keys of St. Peter

This same apparent contradiction in relative authority no doubt becomes part of a priest's life from the moment of his ordination, from which point even his parents and teachers will call him "father." Such is the great authority of the priestly vocation. But the authority of a priest stops far short of the authority of a pope.

When Camillo asserts he has authority over the keys to the posterns (gates) of Sicilia, we should consider the words of Christ to Peter:

> Thou art Peter, and it is upon this rock that I will build my church; and the gates of hell shall not prevail against it; and I will give to thee the keys of the kingdom of heaven; and whatever thou shalt bind on earth shall be bound in heaven; and whatever thou shalt loose on earth shall be loosed in heaven.
>
> (Matthew 16.18-19)

The Catholic Church looks to these words as a primary Biblical support for the papacy. To signify this, the papal insignia includes two crossed keys, representing the powers of binding and loosing, and most artistic representations of St. Peter include the two keys. Moreover, this claim to authority over the entire Church was the focal point of intense debate in Shakespeare's England, so Camillo's "authority over the keys" provides a striking and timely link to St. Peter.

It is worth noting that Camillo announces his authority to command the keys in the last lines of the scene, *after* he has discussed his plans to help Polixenes escape. So the audience learns that Camillo will help Polixenes escape before it has any notion that Camillo must unlock the posterns. Unless we believe that locked gates are a crucial element to the plot (which they are not) Camillo's words serve the primary purpose of establishing his unique authority over the keys. Of course Shakespeare knew the significance of the Biblical allusion, which makes it difficult to imagine that he did not intend the connection to Camillo, whom he had already identified as priestlike.

Shakespeare again links Camillo to the authority over the keys in the next scene, once Leontes discovers the escape:

LEONTES
                    How came the posterns
    So easily open?
LORD
                    By his great authority,
    Which often hath no less prevailed than so
    On your command.
LEONTES
                    I know't too well.
                    (2.1.52-56)

This exchange is rich with meaning. Here again, the stress is on Camillo's "great authority," which Leontes bemoans. Interestingly, in this exchange neither the lord nor the king suggest that Camillo has overstepped or abused his authority – the attitude is one of resignation to the foregone conclusion that Camillo has "great authority," something regrettable but nonetheless an authority he wields legitimately.

Another symbol of the pope's authority is that he is "pilot" of St. Peter's barque, which represents the Church. In Catholic writings, some authors refer to Christ as the pilot, and others refer to the pope as the pilot. There is no real contradiction in that, though, as the pope is only the pilot insofar as he is the Vicar of Christ. Shakespeare portrays this symbol of the pope's authority when Polixenes says to Camillo, "Give me thy hand. Be pilot to me" (1.2.446-447). In the allegorical meaning, this provides yet another indication of Camillo's papal authority.

The pope exercises his great authority in several different ways, all for the purpose of protecting the Catholic Church. Throughout the over 2,000-year history of the Church, the popes have had to preserve doctrine and sacramental validity in the face of countless threats. An exchange between Christ and St. Peter puts this role of the pope in terms of feeding Christ's lambs and sheep:

> When therefore they had dined, Jesus saith to Simon Peter: Simon son of John, lovest thou me more than these? He saith to him: Yea, Lord, thou knowest that I love thee. He saith to him: feed my lambs. He

saith to him again: Simon, son of John, lovest thou me? He saith to him: Yea, Lord, thou knowest I love thee. He saith to him: feed my lambs. He said to him the third time: Simon, son of John, lovest thou me? Peter was grieved, because he had said to him the third time: Lovest thou me? And he said to him: Lord, thou knowest all things: thou knowest that I love thee. He said to him: Feed my sheep.

(John 21.15-17)

Christ entrusted to Peter and his successors the duty to feed His flock.

Within the allegory, the pope's responsibility to feed Christ's flock corresponds to Camillo's role of "cupbearer" to Polixenes. A cupbearer serves the king by protecting the cup from poisoning, even to the point of tasting it before presenting it to the king. Similarly, the pope has the duty to feed the faithful with untainted sacraments and doctrines.

Regarding protection of the sacraments, the Eucharist occupies the chief place and the cup brings to mind the holy chalice in which the wine becomes the blood of Christ through transubstantiation. We might thus say the pope "bears the cup" by ensuring that the Mass remains valid and the priests properly ordained and authorized to fulfill their duties.

In addition to protecting the sacraments, the pope has ultimate responsibility for protecting Catholic doctrine. In our present day, we might not think of religious doctrine in relation to a cup. However, James I clearly did, as he wrote:

> For the apparent safetie of me and my posterities, forbidding my people to drinke so deeply in the bitter cup of Antichristian fornications.[12]

He viewed the Catholic Church as holding the "bitter cup of Antichristian fornications." Clearly James I saw the *teachings and practices* of the Church in an unfavorable light. The king and pope disagreed about who safeguarded fundamental religious beliefs: the king thought the Church deviated from what Christ taught, while the pope believed that he and the Church faithfully transmitted those teachings. Because James I made it a point to describe the religious differences in terms of a cup's contents, from a Catholic perspective we can see the successor of St. Peter as the cupbearer. Shakespeare would likely have seen this as well, so the description of Camillo as cupbearer further links him to the pope.

When Leontes asks Camillo to poison Polixenes, Shakespeare illustrates one of the chief threats to Catholic doctrine and sacraments: pressure from secular powers to influence Church policies and practices. Camillo's response temporarily appeases his king:

CAMILLO
    My lord,
    Go then, and with a countenance as clear
    As friendship wears at feasts, keep with Bohemia
    And with your queen. I am his cupbearer.
    If from me he have wholesome beverage,
    Account me not your servant.
LEONTES
                   This is all.
    Do't and thou hast the one half of my heart;
    Do't not, thou splitt'st thine own.
                          (1.2.341-348)

Camillo suggests he will poison Polixenes, but like other lines in this scene with Leontes, he equivocates. Camillo implies that he will give Polixenes an unwholesome beverage only if he is Leontes's servant. Therefore, because Camillo does not ultimately poison Polixenes, he is not Leontes's servant. He is, instead, a faithful cupbearer to Polixenes.

Similarly, the pope must not serve secular powers at the expense of the Faith, even though kings and queens have, through the centuries, attempted to persuade popes to do their bidding. The pope must instead serve God by upholding the teachings of the Church. Shakespeare's England knew that tension all too well. After all, Henry VIII broke with the Catholic Church because the king failed to persuade Pope Clement

VII to annul his marriage to his Queen Catherine so that he could marry Anne Boleyn.

The final links between Camillo and St. Peter to consider before looking to Pope Paul V's role in Shakespeare's England relate to two exchanges in which we see almost cryptic comparisons between Camillo and Polixenes, the king of Bohemia. Each exchange occurs upon the arrival of Florizel and Perdita to Sicilia. Camillo sends them from Bohemia to Leontes with precise instructions about what to say to him – including a white lie that they have been sent by Polixenes (4.4.557-560). The first such exchange begins with a puzzling line from Leontes. Addressing Florizel, Leontes says:

> You have a holy father
> A graceful gentleman, against whose person,
> So sacred as it is, I have done sin.
>
> (5.1.170-172)

These lines ostensibly apply to Florizel's natural father, Polixenes, but the context suggests otherwise. Leontes has responded to Florizel's news that his father had sent him to visit Sicilia; but Camillo, not Polixenes, sends Florizel to Sicilia. Florizel is obfuscating per Camillo's instructions, which should alert us to the possibility that Shakespeare might be as well.

Moreover, while the "holy father" accolade fits Camillo, it does not land well on Polixenes. This identification of Camillo, rather than Polixenes, as Florizel's "holy father," a traditional title of the pope,[13] appears even more credible because Leontes identifies Polixenes as Florizel's "royal father" earlier in the scene:

> Your mother was most true to wedlock, Prince;
> For she did print your royal father off,
> Conceiving you.
>
> (5.1.124-126)

Certainly the title of "royal father" fits Polixenes, and the context here lacks the ambiguity of the "holy father" reference because Leontes describes Florizel's physical resemblance to Polixenes.

To see that Polixenes is the "royal father" and Camillo is the "holy father" requires us to imagine that Shakespeare intended the obfuscation, disguising his true meaning by making it look like something else. Conversely, most of the other allegorical elements described herein were simply hidden, though perhaps in plain sight. Recalling the analogy of concealing priests, which involved both hiding and disguising, we should not find it surprising if Shakespeare used several masterful techniques to conceal the allegory. In so doing, discovering his technique for hiding one element of the allegory would not directly compromise any other hiding places concealed by other techniques.[14]

The second subtle comparison between Camillo and Polixenes involves an ambiguous display of reverence to the two characters, which allegorically relates to the reverence paid to popes. The pope's authority over the entire Catholic Church of course engenders a tremendous amount of respect from both Catholics and non-Catholics. We see this even in our own day, as bishops and heads of state kneel to kiss the "Fisherman's Ring" of St. Peter's successor to the papacy. Henry VIII, while still a papist, had this same reverence for the pope, as he expressed in a letter to Pope Leo X: "Most Holy Father: I most humbly commend myself to you, and devoutly kiss your blessed feet."[15]

In similar fashion, a lord describes to Leontes and Florizel the meeting of Perdita's foster father and brother with Camillo:

> Camillo, sir. I spake with him, who now
> Has these poor men in question. Never saw I
> Wretches so quake. They kneel, they kiss the earth,
> Forswear themselves as often as they speak.
> Bohemia stops his ears, and threatens them
> With divers deaths in death.
>
> (5.1.197-202)

These lines seem to leave open the remote possibility that the "poor men" kneel, kiss the earth and forswear themselves in response to Polixenes (Bohemia), but that is the less likely meaning. Camillo has the "poor men in question" and Polixenes has his ears stopped. Within the literal hierarchy of the play, Polixenes is the "poor men's" king, for they have come from Bohemia, and Camillo is a mere lord of Sicilia. As such, we would expect the men to pay primary respect to Polixenes. However, the apparent meaning of these lines fits well within the allegorical reading, showing a degree of reverence for Camillo matching that of Catholics for the pope.

Although these two exchanges present some ambiguity, Shakespeare helps us resolve the uncertainty through the lines of Leontes when he realizes his great error in judgment about Hermione:

> Apollo, pardon
> My great profaneness 'gainst thine oracle!
> I'll reconcile me to Polixenes,
> New woo my queen, recall the good Camillo,
> Whom I proclaim a man of truth, of mercy;
> For, being transported by my jealousies
> To bloody thoughts and to revenge, I chose
> Camillo for the minister to poison
> My friend Polixenes: which had been done
> But that the good mind of Camillo tardied
> My swift command, though I with death and with
> Reward did threaten and encourage him,
> Not doing it and being done. He, most humane
> And filled with honor, to my kingly guest
> Unclasped my practice, quit his fortune here,
> Which you knew great, and to the hazard
> Of all incertainties himself commended,
> No richer than his honor. How he glisters
> Through my rust! And how his piety
> Does my deeds make the blacker!
>
> (3.2.153-172)

Leontes makes this declaration at the most intense moment of the play, so the audience understandably may miss the profound distinction in his references to Polixenes and Camillo. It is also easy to pass over the fact that Leontes devotes so many lines to praising Camillo with little mention of Hermione, and none of Mamillius or Perdita. But reading these lines at leisure we can understand what Shakespeare intended: Polixenes is a friend and kingly; Camillo is good, a man of truth and mercy, who glisters through Leontes's rust, most humane, filled with honor, and a man of piety. If these words from Leontes were all we knew about Camillo and Polixenes, which would be a "royal father" and which a "holy father?" Clearly we would see Camillo as the "holy father."

To summarize these connections between Camillo and the pope, we began with a possible link between Camillo and St. Peter based on his relationship to Paulina and the fact that Camillo was also the first name of the pope who reigned while Shakespeare wrote the play. We found that Shakespeare identifies Camillo as a priest with unique authority, including the authority of St. Peter and his successors. These textual identifications of Camillo with St. Peter's successors to the papacy invite us to look further into whether Pope Paul V's tenure as pope from 1605 to 1621 would have had any significance to members of Shakespeare's audience.

Before turning to Pope Paul V, though, we should pause to evaluate the significance of Camillo's connection with St. Peter's successors. Shakespeare unequivocally portrays Camillo as a noble and almost heroically good character. As we will see, though, James I detested the papacy, so Shakespeare probably could not have staged the play with a pope portrayed in a favorable light, let alone as a clear hero. That being the case, the degree of identification between Camillo and the pope already explored is more daring than we would have thought possible. In the pages that follow, several aspects of the allegory will point to a closer identification between Camillo and the pope, but we already have reason to wonder at Shakespeare's remarkable decision to link them as closely as we have seen above.

However bold Shakespeare was in tying Camillo to St. Peter, the risk of discovery was mitigated somewhat by the nature of the production. Much of the dialogue pointing to the allegory takes place in the midst of the dramatically overwhelming scenes of Hermione's persecution in Acts II and III and "resurrection" in Act V. Surely it is easier to see the connection today, when we can leisurely read the play, rather than assimilate details as we watch it performed. Conversely, Shakespeare's audience generally would not see the play in print until 1623, when the First Folio was published, years after his death.

The last speech of Leontes almost seems like an acknowledgement from Shakespeare that many details of the play, and hence the allegory, require more time to process:

> Good Paulina,
> Lead us from hence, where we may leisurely
> Each one demand and answer to his part
> Performed in this wide gap of time since first
> We were dissevered. Hastily lead away.
>
> (5.3.153-157)

Shakespeare benefitted, in a sense, from the fact that his audience could not leisurely examine the allegory's details. And even if members of the audience had suspected the papal ties, Shakespeare might have pointed to Camillo's nominal role as a lord of Sicilia: how can a lord of Sicilia be pope? Even so, as we explore Camillo's role within the tale in the pages that follow, we may marvel at Shakespeare's ability to hide the allegory from those who would have protested.

Pope Paul V and James I

To see Pope Paul V's importance to Shakespeare's audience, we should first consider the situation in England before King James I ascended the throne. From the moment of Henry VIII's break from the Catholic Church to the death of Queen Elizabeth I (with the exception of Queen Mary's short reign), England had been a difficult country for Catholics.

As one indication of the challenges facing Catholics, priests were subject to imprisonment, and even execution in many instances, for saying the Mass. Even lay Catholics simply supporting priests saying the Mass were in jeopardy as Evelyn Waugh describes:

> Anyone inducing him to offend in this way was fined a hundred marks in the first case, four hundred in the second, and in the third forfeited his entire property and was imprisoned for life.[16]

The penalties for practicing Catholicism varied over the decades leading up to time in which Shakespeare wrote *The Winter's Tale*, but generally speaking one could not actively practice the Catholic faith in England without real fear of persecution.

With the death of Queen Elizabeth I, English Catholics hoped for more favorable treatment from King James. Some Catholics, including Clement VIII (pope from 1592-1605), even believed that James I might convert. Antonia Fraser describes a letter that James I's queen, Anne (who had recently converted to Catholicism), wrote to the pope:

> The Queen's letter to Rome of 1601 was ostensibly an answer to the Pope's communication to her husband. The king could not reply himself, Anne explained, since he had to be circumspect. Not only could the Pope be assured of the Queen's own devotion, and her care to educate her children in the Catholic Faith, but Anne went further and hinted that King James might soon grant liberty of conscience to Catholics. . . . By July 1602, Pope Clement, already happy at the news about Queen Anne, was urging the conversion of her husband. There had in fact been a rumor of this conversion – which must have seemed a miraculous development – on the continent as early as 1599.[17]

Contrary to the hopes of Queen Anne and England's other Catholics, James I did not convert. And on November 5, 1605 (Guy Fawkes Day), life for Catholics in England suffered another devastating setback when authorities discovered the "Gunpowder Plot" by a small group of English Catholics to blow up the House of Lords.[18]

THE WINTER'S TALE AND HIDDEN CATHOLIC ENGLAND | 29

The Gunpowder Plot – November 5, 1605 (Guy Fawkes Day)

By the account of Fr. John Gerard, who knew the plotters, the plot was not generally supported by Catholics:

> The dealers in that tragical device [The Gunpowder Plot] had so little hope of help from other Catholics, either spiritual or temporal, towards their designments in that plot, that they neither did nor durst impart the same even to their nearest and dearest friends, in whom otherwise they had all confidence and trial both for secrecy and fidelity in other matters.[19]

Fr. Gerard would not have helped his cause by saying the opposite, but we can gather from him that there was no universal support of a Catholic plot to injure King James, even though the king might have believed there was.

The discovery of the Gunpowder Plot greatly exacerbated the hardships of Catholics in England. Alice Hogge details the laws that followed soon thereafter:

> The acts that followed were far-reaching. No known Catholic recusant might enter a royal palace. No known Catholic recusant might come within 10 miles of the City of London. No known Catholic recusant might practice law or medicine, or hold a commission in the Army or Navy; neither might a known Catholic recusant, nor anyone with a recusant wife, hold public office.... It was made lawful for any Crown officer, 'if need be', forcibly to enter any house in the country in pursuit of a known Catholic recusant. Recusancy fines were stiffened and new penalties were introduced targeting those Church papists who attended their local church, but refused to receive communion.[20]

Perhaps the most contentious aspect of the reinvigorated persecution of Catholics came in the form of the *Oath of Allegiance*, promulgated in 1606, which required Catholics to swear allegiance to the king, against the pope's authority to depose the king:

> I, A.B., do truly and sincerely acknowledge ... that our sovereign lord, King James, is lawful and rightful King ... and that the pope neither of himself nor by any authority of Church or See of Rome, or by any

> other means with any other, has any power to depose the king . . . or to authorize any foreign prince to invade him . . . or to give licence to any to bear arms, raise tumults. . . . Also I do swear that notwithstanding any sentence of excommunication or deprivation I will bear allegiance and true faith to his Majesty. . . . And I do further swear that I do from my heart abhor, detest, and abjure, as impious and heretical this damnable doctrine and position, that princes which be excommunicated by the pope may be deposed or murdered by their subjects or by any other whatsoever. And I do believe that the pope has no power to absolve me from this oath. I do swear according to the plain and common sense, and understanding of the same words.[21]

The Oath's controversy centered on the requirement to swear that it was "impious and heretical" that the pope could depose princes that had been excommunicated. The debate no longer has significant relevance in our age, but clearly it did in Shakespeare's England. As we will see in the chapters that follow, this Oath resonates with some of the play's most important scenes.

Whether or not Catholics ought to have taken the Oath, many refused to do so as a matter of conscience. For these men and women, the potential consequences were severe. As Fr. James Brodrick, S.J. relates:

> The penalties for refusing the Oath were indeed dreadful, in general life imprisonment and the confiscation of all property for a second refusal by any Catholic man or woman over the age of eighteen.[22]

Given the severe penalties that Catholics faced as a result of the Oath, we should not find it surprising that the conflict prompted the pope to intervene.

Pope Paul V wrote to James I around the time the Oath was issued. As the Catholic Encyclopedia entry for Pope Paul V describes:

> On 9 July, 1606, he wrote a friendly letter to James I of England to congratulate him on his accession to the throne, and referred with grief to the plot recently made against the life of the monarch. But he

prays him not to make the innocent Catholics suffer for the crime of a few. He promises to exhort all the Catholics of the realm to be submissive and loyal to their sovereign in all things not opposed to the honor of God. Unfortunately the oath of allegiance James demanded of his subjects contained clauses to which no Catholic could in conscience subscribe.

Thus, Camillo Borghese (as Pope Paul V) entered England's religious controversy with a conciliatory yet firm defense of Catholicism, and advocacy for the welfare of James I's Catholic subjects. Pope Paul V subsequently wrote to English Catholics, informing them that they could not take the Oath in good conscience.

Donna Hamilton describes the "international paper war" that resulted from Pope Paul V's intervention:

> Although at the start many Catholics were favourably disposed to taking the oath, Pope Paul V challenged those convictions by issuing a breve, dated 22 September 1606, that ordered English Catholics not to take it. When the Archpriest George Blackwell, head of English Catholics, took the oath anyway and then wrote a letter advising others to do the same, the Pope issued yet another breve, dated 23 August 1607, repeating his original command. Cardinal Bellarmine responded by writing to Blackwell to condemn his action, and subsequently, James began his own writing on the oath. This chain of events set in motion the international paper war. [23]

With the scale and implications of this controversy, Shakespeare and everyone in his audience would likely have had strong opinions on whether or not James I should require his Catholic subjects to take the Oath.

Today Catholics around the world learn of St. Thomas More, St. Edmund Campion, St. John Fisher and the many other English Martyrs. In so doing, we learn of a reality in Shakespeare's England that, though foreign to us, would have occupied the thoughts of the play's first audiences on a more or less constant basis.

Timeline of Relevant Events in Shakespeare's England	
December 1581	St. Edmund Campion executed at Tyburn
March 1603	James I becomes King of England
May 1605	Camillo Borghese becomes pope, taking name of Paul V
November 5, 1605	Gunpowder Plot discovered
June 1606	Oath of Allegiance issued
July 1606	Paul V writes letter to James I, requesting that innocent Catholics not be made to suffer for the Gunpowder Plot
September 1606	Paul V issues first letter admonishing Catholics against taking the Oath
August 1607	Paul V issues second letter admonishing Catholics against taking the Oath
1608	James I issues the *Apologie* for the Oath, which responds to the two letters of Paul V against the Oath
1609	James I issues the *Premonition* to all Christian monarchs, defending the Oath
1610-1611	Shakespeare writes *The Winter's Tale*
November 5, 1611	*The Winter's Tale* performed at court on the anniversary of the Gunpowder Plot's discovery

Joseph Pearce summarizes how Catholics in Shakespeare's England (including a few very close to Shakespeare) viewed their circumstances at around the time *The Winter's Tale* was first staged:

> As a result of these ruinous laws, the number of openly defiant Catholics decreased steadily during King James's reign. Many Catholics began reluctantly to attend the Anglican services as the only way of avoiding financial ruin or imprisonment. After more than seventy years of largely unmitigated persecution the resolve of many of England's Catholics was at least beginning to weaken. It is, therefore, interesting to note that members of Shakespeare's own family were still resolutely defiant. In May 1606, Shakespeare's daughter Susanna was on the list of recusants brought before Stratford's church court.[24]

All of which suggests that if Shakespeare's allegorical meaning touched on the Catholic struggles in England, it would speak to the foremost cares of many in his audience, including perhaps his daughter Susanna as Pearce suggests.

Hermione, Leontes, and Their Offspring

As we have seen in the preceding chapters, Shakespeare intended Camillo and Paulina to represent Saints Peter and Paul, respectively. Additionally, Camillo has a special link to Pope Paul V, the successor of St. Peter at the time Shakespeare wrote the play. These connections are intriguing but do not amount to much of an allegory in isolation. In other words, they do not tell a story. For that, we must look further into the possible allegorical roles of the other characters in *The Winter's Tale*, beginning with Hermione and Leontes.

By exploring Pope Paul V's link to Shakespeare's England we can begin to see the roles of Hermione and Leontes in the allegory. The conflict between Pope Paul V and James I resulted in an "international paper war," and as W.B. Patterson observes:

> The flood of published works that came from European presses was sufficient to make James's ideas familiar to any educated person with the slightest interest in ascertaining what they were.[25]

We may thus take it for granted that Shakespeare and many in the play's first audiences would have understood not only the desperate state of affairs facing English Catholics, but also the ways in which James I and his Catholic foes discussed their religious differences. If, then, we want to consider whether Shakespeare really had in mind an allegory about life as a Catholic under James I, we should first look to this international paper war.

As this chapter explores, Leontes uses the same imagery in denouncing Hermione as James I used in denouncing the Catholic Church. James I dedicated a significant portion of his *Premonition* to comparing the Church to the "whore of Babylon" (the Antichrist) from the book of the Apocalypse. Three principal aspects of this attack on the Church are worth considering in connection with the allegory: a claim that the Church is an adulteress, a rejection of calling the Church "Queen," and an attack on the idea of the Church as the "Mystical Body of Christ." Through these themes we can see the relationships between Hermione and the Catholic Church and Leontes and James I.

In his *Premonition,* James I used the imagery of true and false spouses to distinguish between what he considered to be the true and false Christian churches:

> Because as Christ his trew Spouse and Church is represented by a Woman . . . so here is the Head of his adulterous spouse or false Church represented also by a woman, but having a cup full of abominations in her hand: as her selfe is called a Whoore, for her spirituall adulterie, having seduced the Kings of the earth to be partakers of her Spiritual fornication.[26]

The first thing to note about this astonishing passage is that James I believed some actual Christian church represented the spouse of Christ – he would, of course, see his own church as the "trew Spouse." Conversely, Catholics believe (then and now) that their Catholic Church is the "true spouse of Christ" as that imagery is used in the Bible. But James I accused the Catholic Church of spiritual adultery, seducing the kings of the earth to be "partakers of her spiritual fornication."

This charge of adultery resembles Leontes's mistaken belief that Hermione has committed adultery with Polixenes. In the first three acts, while every other character sees Hermione as good and worthy of great respect, Leontes accuses her of infidelity:

> She's an adult'ress; I have said with whom.
> More, she's a traitor, and Camillo is
> A fedarie with her, and one that knows
> What she should shame to know herself.
>   (2.1.89-92)

Leontes sees Hermione as an adulteress and a traitor, though she is clearly neither. Moreover, Leontes believes Hermione has seduced the only other king in the play, Polixenes – this corresponds to James I's assertion that the Catholic Church has "seduced the kings of the earth." And just as Leontes denounces Camillo as being a fedarie (a partner or accomplice) with Hermione, the pope would symbolically be a principal accomplice of any misdeeds of the Catholic Church. Thus we can see that Shakespeare sets up the primary conflict in *The Winter's Tale* to match the conflict between James I and the Catholic Church at the time he wrote the play.

In addition to likening the Church to the "whore of Babylon," King James I attacked the Catholic Church's understanding that it is a Queen:

> For shee glorifieth her selfe living in pleasure, and in her heart saith, shee fitteth as a Queene (outward prosperitie being one of their notes of a trew Church) and is no Widow; for her Spouse Christ is bound to her by an inviolable knot (for he hath sworne never to forsake her) and she shall see no mourning: for she cannot erre, nor the gates of Hell shall prevail against her.[27]

Thus, according to King James I, the Catholic Church considers itself a favored queen. The king believed he knew better, however, seeing it as an adulterous spouse. As James I suggests, the representation of the Church as a queen derives from the image of the Church as the spouse of Christ, bound together "by an inviolable knot." Although these allusions are from the Bible, James I thought the Catholic Church had lost its status as the true church and queen. So while the Church was once entitled to the title of queen, it had become an adulteress according to the king.

Shakespeare adapts this imagery of the true Church as a queen to the relationship between Leontes and Hermione. When Leontes doubts the virtue of his spouse, he refers to her as a traitor and an adulteress, echoing the language James I used to describe the Catholic Church and Catholics. Only in those moments that precede and follow his madness does he call Hermione "queen." As the following table illustrates,

Leontes changes his opinion of Hermione rapidly upon learning that she had persuaded Polixenes to remain in Sicilia after his planned departure, and then changes it again upon realizing that he has falsely judged his queen.

Leontes's References to Hermione	Scene
Tongue tied our queen?	1.2.29
Hermione, my dearest, thou never spok'st/ To better purpose.	1.2.89-90
Leontes: How came't, Camillo,/ That he did stay? *Camillo*: At the good queen's entreaty. *Leontes*: At the queen's be't. Good should be pertinent;/ But so it is, it is not.	1.2.218-221
My wife's a hobbyhorse, deserves a name/ As rank as any flax wench that puts to/ Before her trothplight.	1.2.276-278
My wife is nothing	1.2.294
She's an adulteress	2.1.78
O thou thing!	2.1.82
She, th' adulteress	2.3.4
Paulina: I say, I come/ From your good queen. *Leontes*: Good queen? *Paulina*: Good queen, my lord,/ Good queen, And would by combat make her good.	2.3.57-61
Our most disloyal lady	3.1.202
This sessions, to our great grief we pronounce/ Even pushes 'gainst our heart – the party tried/ The daughter of a king, our wife, and one/ Of us too much beloved.	3.2.1-4
Apollo, pardon/ My great profaneness 'gainst thine oracle!/ I'll reconcile me to Polixenes,/ New woo my queen.	3.2.151-155

Before his madness, Leontes refers to Hermione as queen. While he subsequently doubts her virtue, he dishonors her with the same language that James I used to criticize the Catholic Church. After his madness has passed, Leontes again refers to Hermione as queen. Hermione, of course, does not change. Rather, only the king's perception of the queen changes.

So too, the Catholic Church was the virtuous Queen in the eyes of Catholics worldwide, including English monarchs prior to Henry VIII's break with Rome. After that break, those opposing the Catholic Church would argue that it had somehow lost its way and forfeited its claim to spouse of Christ. At the time Shakespeare wrote *The Winter's Tale*, James I considered the Catholic Church to be an adulteress, but English Catholics retained hope that, like Leontes, James I would one day recognize the Catholic Church as the virtuous Queen.

The final connection between Hermione and the Catholic Church to consider at this point relates to King James I's rejection of the identification of the Church as the Mystical Body of Christ:

> To her selfe shee taketh, in calling her selfe the visible Head of the mysticall Body of Christ, in professing herselfe to bee the dispenser of the mysteries of God, and by her onely must they bee expounded.[28]

We will explore this concept further in later chapters, but the Catholic Church teaches that it is the Mystical Body of Christ, as described in the letters of St. Paul. James I naturally opposed this teaching because it confers on the Church an exclusive claim to being the Church established by Christ.

How does Shakespeare liken Hermione to the Mystical Body of Christ? As we have seen, Leontes uses the same imagery to denounce Hermione as James I uses to attack the Catholic Church. In addition, there are many instances throughout the play in which Hermione represents various aspects of Jesus Christ. Just as we could appreciate the allegory simply by following the way in which Leontes refers to Hermione in terms of an adulteress or good queen, we can see the allegory by comparing Hermione to Christ in her sufferings, trial, death, and ultimate "resurrection." Although Shakespeare never uses the term "Mystical Body of Christ" in the play, he incorporates so many distinct references to Hermione as both the Church and Christ that we can reasonably conclude that he intended the same concept that James I had described in his *Premonition*.

The conflicts between Leontes and Hermione on the one hand, and James I and the Catholic Church on the other, match each other in intensity as well. When we consider that James I addressed his *Premonition* to all Christian monarchs, many of whom were Catholic, we can see how strongly James I felt on this point of the "adultery" of the Catholic Church. W. B. Patterson highlights this point:

> James's *Premonition* was, among other things, his attempt to stake out a broad middle ground of faith and practice on which, he hoped, Christians could agree. Nevertheless much in the treatise had an anti-papal character, making it certain to anger many of James's intended readers.[29]

King James I was in many ways very gifted, and apparently had a deep faith, but this rhetorical device struck many as disconnected from reality. Leontes has a similar disconnect from his subjects in the play, as he alone has what he deems the correct knowledge of Hermione. The religious allegory in *The Winter's Tale* involves many other connections between Hermione and Leontes and their allegorical counterparts, but they all build upon this remarkable similarity in how the respective kings view Hermione and the Church.

The tumultuous relationship between Leontes and Hermione produces two children. As Leontes represents the English monarch and Hermione represents the Catholic Church (the Mystical Body of Christ), it seems reasonable to view the offspring of their union as the Catholic Church within England. We can see the image of the national churches as offspring of the Mother Church from the words of St. Edmund Campion:

> In condemning us you condemn all your own ancestors – all the ancient priests, bishops and kings – all that was once the glory of England, the isle of saints, and the most devoted child of the See of Peter.[30]

According to the saint, England was the most devoted child of the See of Peter prior to Henry VIII breaking from the Church. At first glance, this seems like it might fit with seeing Mamillius and Perdita as Catholic Churches within England. However, we must refine this interpretation based on an odd detail Shakespeare provides about the offspring of Leontes and Hermione: Hermione nurses Perdita but she does not nurse Mamillius.

In Act II, Leontes says to Hermione, "Give me the boy. I am glad you did not nurse him" (2.1.57). Leontes elaborates by saying the Mamillius has too much of Hermione's blood in him, with the suggestion that nursing him would have made Mamillius even more like his mother. Conversely, Hermione does nurse Perdita, as she reveals in Act III:

> My third comfort,
> Starred most unluckily, is from my breast,
> The innocent milk in its most innocent mouth
>
> (3.2.98-100)

This detail about which child nursed from Hermione, and which did not, is especially interesting because Mamillius dies (unexpectedly) and Perdita survives (unexpectedly). Clearly Shakespeare is not trying to make a medical argument about nursing, so the literal reading is generally unsatisfactory on this point.

Consistent with what we have seen throughout this book, the allegorical context provides the best light for interpreting this remarkable detail. In a speech to Parliament from 1604, James I makes four statements that together help form a theological metaphor that matches the nursing imagery Shakespeare employs with Hermione, Mamillius and Perdita:

> At my first comming, although I found but one Religion, and that which by my selfe is professed, publikely allowed, and by the Law maintained: Yet found I another sort of Religion, besides a private Sect, lurking within the bowels of this Nation. The first is the trew Religion, which by me is professed, and by the Law is established: The second is the falsly called Catholikes, but trewly Papists: The third, which I call a sect rather than Religion, is the Puritanes and Nouelists.

James I's thoughts about the two religions in England – the Protestant religion he practiced, and the hidden Catholic faith – correspond to Leontes's thoughts about Mamillius and Perdita respectively. In the allegory, Leontes acknowledges Mamillius as his offspring but does not recognize Perdita (who was "hidden" in Hermione's womb and then in prison with Hermione) as his own.

> I acknowledge the Romane Church to be our Mother Church, although defiled with some infirmities and corruptions, as the Iewes were when they crucified Christ: And as I am none enemie to the life of a sicke man, because I would haue his bodie purged of ill humours; no more am I enemie to their Church, because I would haue them reforme their errors, not wishing the downethrowing of the Temple, but that it might be purged and cleansed from corruption.

James I acknowledges the Catholic Church to be the Mother Church but sees it as corrupt with errors, like a sick man. In the allegory, Hermione is mother both to Mamillius and Perdita. During her trial, Hermione laments that Leontes has barred her from Mamillius, "like one infectious" (3.2.98).

> And againe I must subdivide the same Layickes into two rankes, that is, either quiet and well minded men, peaceable Subiects, who either being old, have retayned their first drunken in liquor upon a certaine shamefastnesse to be thought curious or changeable: Or being young men, through evill education have never bene nursed or brought up, but upon such venim in place of wholesome nutriment.

According to James I, the Catholic Church nurses its followers with venom instead of wholesome milk. Leontes is glad that Hermione did not nurse Mamillius because he did not want the boy poisoned with her influence. In the allegory, Hermione nurses Perdita with what she calls "innocent milk," just as Catholics believe their religion is true and good.

> As I am no stranger to you in blood, no more am I a stranger to you in Faith, or in the matters concerning the house of God. And although this my profession be according to mine education, wherein (I thanke God) I sucked the milke of Gods trewth, with the milke of my Nurse.

Like many of those who shared his religion, James I was not nursed with the milk of Catholicism, but with what he believed to be the milk of God's truth, corresponding to the Anglican religion. Similarly, Leontes is glad that Hermione did not nurse Mamillius. Leontes ultimately bars Hermione from seeing Mamillius in attempt to limit her influence.

James I also used similar nursing imagery in a 1610 speech to Parliament so it seems highly unlikely that Shakespeare's use of the imagery in *The Winter's Tale* is simply coincidental. One may debate the question of whether there is any theological justification for seeing the Anglican Church as an offspring of the Catholic Church, but because James I used that imagery we need not delve into Shakespeare's orthodoxy for mirroring it in the play.

Shakespeare gives us additional reason to see Mamillius as the allegorical representation of James I's religion through a short exchange between father and son:

LEONTES
          How now, boy?
MAMILLIUS
  I am like you, they say.
LEONTES
          Why, that's some comfort.
                (1.2.207-208)

Leontes wants Mamillius to be more like himself and less like Hermione, so he takes comfort in the boy's revelation that people say he is more like his father. Within the allegory, this corresponds with James I's approval of the publicly allowed religion and rejection of what he believed to be Catholic errors. From the perspective of Catholics, this mindset is the root of heresies and schisms because it subjects the religion to the individual believer's ideas rather than subjecting the ideas of the individual believer to the religion that Christ established. The problem is of course significantly worse when the individual believer is a monarch with the power and willingness to suppress religions that conflict with his own.

Seeing Mamillius as the corollary to the publicly allowed religion in England also adds meaning to the boy's eventual fate. From the literal perspective, the audience must believe that Mamillius dies of anxiety at seeing Leontes persecute Hermione. The allegorical significance is oddly more realistic than the literal meaning: if, as James I believed, the Anglican Church was an offspring of the Catholic Church, it would die from having been cut off from the spiritual and doctrinal nourishment from the Mother Church; and a rejection of the Mystical Body of Christ is a rejection of Christ, which also leads to spiritual death.

Interestingly, just as the Catholic Church was the primary opponent of the Protestant churches, we see Hermione as the only character in the play who criticizes Mamillius: "Take the boy to you. He so troubles me,/ 'Tis past enduring" (2.1.1-2). With no textual precursor for this rebuke, the audience must attribute Hermione's anxiety to a combination of her pregnancy and the boy "being a boy," none of which adds meaning to the play. However, the allegorical meaning is so fitting that we would find something amiss of Hermione had not shown any displeasure with Mamillius. In other words, a lack of tension between the two characters would indicate that Shakespeare saw no real conflict between James I's religion and the Mystical Body of Christ.

Now that we have seen the allegorical relationships between Hermione, Leontes and their children, we should explore whether

Shakespeare provided clues to their identities through their names. The first character name to consider is the one with the most evident allegorical meaning, Leontes. The name Leontes has a clear association with lions, as "leo" is the Latin word for lion. Like other British monarchs, James I had many lions on his coat of arms, some versions having as many as fifteen.

The meaning of Hermione's name is more complicated and more interesting. The *New Variorum* version of *The Winter's Tale* connects the name Hermione with the Greek word for "pillar-like."[31] Although we cannot know with any certainty that Shakespeare intended this meaning, there is reason to believe that it is at least possible.[32] This allusion to the Church as pillar-like has Biblical roots in the "First Epistle of St. Paul to Timothy":

> But if I tarry long, that thou mayest know how thou oughtest to behave thyself in the house of God, which is the church of the living God, the pillar and ground of the truth.
> (1 Timothy 3.15)

This meaning of Hermione's name would therefore identify her with the "church of the living God," which Catholics of course identify as the Catholic Church. This connection becomes even more probable when we find her as a statue at the beginning of the play's last scene – she is literally pillar-like.

Hermione's name also includes the word "ermine" within it (that is, hERMIoNE). The ermine is a traditional symbol of innocence and purity based on the belief that it would rather die than dirty its white coat. This resembles Antigonus's dream about Hermione:

> To me comes a creature,
> Sometimes her head on one side, some another;
> I never saw a vessel of like sorrow,
> So filled and so becoming. In pure white robes,
> Like very sanctity, did she approach.
> (3.3.18-22)

THE WINTER'S TALE AND HIDDEN CATHOLIC ENGLAND | 45

King James I (with lions and ermine)

Hermione's "pure white robes" match both her innocence and the coat of the ermine. Antigonus even sees the pure white robes as a symbol of sanctity.

The pure white robes also call to mind the description of the Church from St. John's Apocalypse:

> Let us be glad and rejoice, and give glory to him; for the marriage of the Lamb is come, and his wife has prepared herself. And it is granted to her that she should clothe herself with fine linen, glittering and white. For the fine linen are the justifications of saints.
>
> (Apocalypse 19, 7-8)

St. John connects the glittering, white linen with the justification of the saints. Given the Christian references throughout the play, it seems highly probable that Shakespeare intended the connection between "fine linen, glittering and white" and "pure white robes." And that connection remains even if Shakespeare did not recognize (or care) that the word "ermine" was in Hermione's name.

Thus we can see two possible meanings of Hermione's name that would further link her to the Catholic Church. While it is possible that Shakespeare would not have seen either meaning, it seems likely that he intended one or both. At the very least, we can say that each meaning fits Hermione within both the literal and allegorical meanings of the play.

Turning to the names of the children, Shakespeare actually gives us the meaning of Perdita's name: Hermione directs Antigonus to name her daughter Perdita "for the babe is accounted lost forever" (3.3.31-32). "Perdita" means "lost" in Latin. Within the allegory, it makes sense to see Perdita as lost because she represents the Catholic Church in England, which was effectively lost and in exile at the time the play was first performed.

Finally, as Robert Adams notes in his description of the play's first scene, Mamillius's relationship with Hermione is reflected in his name:

> For no immediate reason, talk turns to Leontes' son, prince Mamillius. Archidamus, though but newly arrived, has seen him and praises him, actually speaking in the process his curious name. It compounds a diminutive –*lillus* with the word for mother, *mama*, or perhaps breast, *mamma*.[33]

As Mamillius's mother represents the Catholic Church (the Mystical Body of Christ), the diminutive form indicates something that resembles the Church but is a smaller or inferior version. Such a meaning is entirely consistent with the Catholic view of James I's church.

Taken in isolation, these naming choices might seem inconsequential – the characters must have names, and, with any name, we might envision connections that Shakespeare never intended. Nonetheless, each of the play's major characters has a name associated with the allegorical meaning. Although we could ignore each such connection through character names and still see the full allegory, the pattern of intentional naming seems evident and worth exploring. We should not hesitate to imagine that Shakespeare had some purpose in mind.

Polixenes, Sicilia, and Bohemia

Looking at the allegory within *The Winter's Tale*, one could see nearly the entire picture without considering the significance of Polixenes, Sicilia, and Bohemia. After all, the two kings must have kingdoms, so we might say that Shakespeare simply chose those already in Robert Greene's *Pandosto*, which provides as least some of the source material for the play. And Leontes must accuse Hermione of seducing someone, so we need not dwell too long on Polixenes's symbolic role beyond that of the seduced king. And yet, when we explore the significance of Polixenes, Sicilia, and Bohemia it becomes apparent that Shakespeare leaves us with an allegory so complete that we may justifiably wonder if he left any detail in the play wholly out of its scope.

As with most allegorical connections throughout the play, we can best appreciate the role of Polixenes by considering how King James I and Leontes viewed the Catholic Church and Hermione, respectively. James I wrote that the Catholic Church had "seduced the kings of the earth,"[34] an accusation that resembles Leontes's belief that Hermione had seduced Polixenes, the Bohemian king. In the first instance, then, Polixenes represents "the kings of the earth," whom James I believed were seduced by the Catholic Church. This allegorical role becomes more interesting when we consider the Greek roots of Polixenes's name: *poly* (meaning "many") and *xenos* (meaning "stranger" or "foreigner"). So King Polixenes, by name, is like *many foreign kings* to Leontes. And thus in a sense Leontes suspects Hermione of seducing many foreign kings (*King Poly-Xenos*); or the "kings of the earth," to use James I's language.

This connection is strengthened when we consider that James I began his *Premonition* to all Christian monarchs in defense of the Oath as follows:

> To the most sacred and invincible prince, Rodolphe the II, by Gods Clemencie Elect emperour of the Romanes; King of Germanie, Hungarie, Boheme, Dalmatie, Croatie, Sclavonie, Etc.[35]

Thus, James I wrote one of the most significant letters of his reign to "many foreign kings" (*King Polixenes* in a sense) addressing the letter principally to Rudolf II, a Catholic, who was Holy Roman Emperor and the king of Bohemia.

Polixenes's allegorical connection has even greater significance when we consider that Leontes's counterpart in Greene's *Pandosto* was the king of Bohemia, and Polixenes's counterpart was king of Sicilia. Shakespeare gave each king a new name and, to the consternation of critics, switched Bohemia and Sicilia. Thus we can assume that Shakespeare deliberately chose to have Polixenes as king of Bohemia and Leontes as king of Sicilia, and this interpretation provides the first part of a plausible explanation: that Polixenes of Bohemia corresponds to the "many foreign monarchs" to whom James I addressed his remarkable letter.

Another support for seeing Sicilia as England (and Bohemia as sympathetic to Catholicism) derives from the events taking place in Shakespeare's England. In Act IV, Polixenes refers to Sicilia as "that fatal country" (4.2.20), a description that fits England of Shakespeare's day: acting on religious convictions had meant death for many Catholics since Henry VIII, as it had for many Protestants under Queen Mary's reign.

In his biography of St. Robert Bellarmine, Fr. James Brodrick, S.J., relates the toll on priests during the reign of James I:

> All eighteen priests who were condemned solely for their priesthood in the reign of James were offered their lives and sometimes even their freedom if they would but take the King's Oath. They chose rather to die a dreadful and degrading death.[36]

These priests knew they risked execution if caught in England. Evelyn Waugh recounts the concept of England that priests in training had for their eventual place of martyrdom:

> One of [St. Edmund Campion's] particular jokes, in which they all shared, was the terror with which they looked towards England and the probability of a painful death.[37]

In these lines about England, we see the same sentiment that Polixenes expresses about Sicilia: it was, indeed, a "fatal country" for Catholics, especially priests. We also see that saints sometimes have an odd sense of humor.

St. Edmund Campion's background provides another connection between the real and fictional Bohemia. The saint spent six years teaching at the Jesuit college in Prague, Bohemia.[38] Thus, in the letter he wrote in anticipation of being captured in England (*Campion's Brag*), Campion began:

> To the right honourable, the lords of Her Majestie's Privy Council: Whereas I have come out of Germanie and Boemeland, being sent by my Superiours, and adventured myself into this noble Realm, my deare Countrie, for the glorie of God and benefit of souls.[39]

For St. Edmund Campion, Bohemia was a place of preparation for his mission to England, the land he would die trying to make Catholic.

Bohemia was also a destination for Catholics fleeing England under the persecutions of Elizabeth I and James I. As Alfred Thomas suggests:

Sixteenth-century and early-seventeenth century Bohemia was one of the most tolerant places in Europe, so tolerant in fact that many English Catholics sought refuge there.[40]

In *The Winter's Tale*, Bohemia is the destination not only of Camillo and Polixenes (its king), but also Perdita, whom were all forced out of Sicilia by Leontes. St. Edmund Campion's letter to his fellow Jesuit, Robert Arden, provides some interesting color on this role of Bohemia:

> For this at least we are indebted to those by whose heresy and persecution we have been driven forth and cast gently on a pleasant and blessed shore.[41]

For St. Edmund Campion and many other English Catholics, Bohemia was a land of refuge, "a pleasant and blessed shore."

Fr. Peter Milward also notes the geographical sense of seeing Sicilia as England:

> Surely Sicilia, being a three-cornered island, or (as it was known in classical times) Trinacria, stands for England, while Bohemia becomes the Catholic continent. Then, if the events recorded by Greene as happening in Bohemia are transposed by Shakespeare to Sicilia, it may well be because the dramatist is thinking of similar events having taken place in his native England.[42]

This geographical aspect of the allegory would even resolve Ben Jonson's amusing critique of the play. As Northrop Frye writes:

> Ben Jonson remarked to his friend Drummond, as an example of Shakespeare's carelessness in detail, that in this play he'd given a seacoast to Bohemia, which was a landlocked country.[43]

Perhaps Shakespeare was not being so careless about details after all; and at the very least he is in good company with St. Edmund Campion, whose letter quoted above spoke of Bohemia's blessed shore.

Neither the fictionalized Bohemia of *The Winter's Tale* nor the actual Bohemia was fully Catholic. However, they were both Catholic *enough* in the same way as it relates to the allegory: the Catholic king of each Bohemia was the designated counterpart to the king of Sicilia/England and it is the land where the Catholic faith of Sicilia/England is preserved.

The Oracle and Rome

Although the play's abundant Catholic imagery forms the basis for a coherent allegory, *The Winter's Tale* follows Greene's *Pandosto* with many important references to "the gods," "sacred Delphos" and Apollo's temple. For some critics, Shakespeare's use of pagan themes effectively bars any Christian interpretation of the play. Many of these readers acknowledge the equally unambiguous Christian references but see them as anachronistic.

If Shakespeare had written *The Winter's Tale* as a history play set in the classical Greek world, the Christian imagery would of course be anachronistic. And if that had been the case, we could ponder whether the playwright was confused or merely adding levity with the Christian allusions. But the play was set in Sicilia and Bohemia, without any essential roots in ancient history: Leontes's appeal to the oracle undoubtedly adds another layer to the madness of his insisting on Hermione's guilt, but that is the most meaningful contribution of the Greek imagery to the plot. In other words, Shakespeare could have omitted the oracle and all we would have lost from the literal reading would be the idea that Leontes rejects what he had previously considered a certain source of truth. So the natural reading of the play suggests that clear Christian imagery is historically proper and the classical Greek allusions are anachronistic, rather than the other way around.

So why would Shakespeare have retained Greene's pagan themes? Shakespeare appears to have carried over the pagan themes from *Pandosto* as the most effective means of fully developing the Catholic ideas that he could not have made an overt part of the play's literal meaning. As S. L. Bethell observes:

> I should myself regard the religious atmosphere as emphatically Christian, while the pagan suggestions give authenticity to the story and serve to 'distance' the Christian attitudes, presenting them in a new setting so as to counteract the deadening influence of familiarity and escape the deadly influence of contemporary controversy over minor theological questions.[44]

By establishing the oracle as a clear truth-teller, and then connecting the oracle to Rome through the allegory, Shakespeare thus invites us to see Rome as a source of truth. So although Shakespeare could not have directly portrayed Rome as a source of truth in the play, he conveys the same message by linking Catholic Rome and the oracle.

The connection between Rome and the oracle was by no means novel. Comparing the oracle to Rome was both logical and common. Indeed, as Fr. Henry Sebastian Bowden remarks:

> The most remarkable instance of Catholic imagery in the play is when the poet goes out of his way to describe the Oracle of Delphi. Now it must be remembered that Rome was the Delphi of medieval Europe.[45]

Moreover, Fr. Peter Milward observes that sixteenth-century Protestant writers referred to Papal decrees in terms of the oracle at Delphos.[46]

The most significant connection between the oracle and Rome derives from the Catholic doctrine that the Church cannot teach error with respect to faith and morals. In a formulation of the doctrine from 468, St. Simplicius (pope from 468 to 483) wrote:

> Those genuine and clear truths which flow from the very pure fountains of the Scriptures cannot be disturbed by any arguments of misty subtlety. For this same norm of apostolic doctrine endures in the successors of him upon whom the Lord imposed the care of the whole sheepfold, whom He promised He would not fail even unto the end of the world, against whom He promised the gates of hell would never prevail, by whose judgment He testified that what was bound on earth could not be loosed in heaven.[47]

So the Catholic Church will not err in matters of faith or morals because Christ entrusted care of the Church to St. Peter and his successors. Thus, from the Catholic perspective, the pope is the Christian equivalent of the oracle with respect to matters of faith and morals.

Leontes initially looks to the oracle to confirm his (false) opinion about Hermione. Having already rejected the counsel of Camillo, Leontes seeks a "better" answer from the oracle. This recalls Henry VIII's initial appeals to Rome for the dissolution of his marriage to Catherine, and perhaps even James I's belief that he could call an ecumenical council to resolve the religious crisis.[48] Leontes implicitly attributes to the oracle the equivalent of the pope's infallibility in matters of faith and morals:

> I have dispatched in post
> To sacred Delphos, to Apollo's temple,
> Cleomenes and Dion, whom you know
> Of stuffed sufficiency. Now from the oracle
> They will bring all, whole spiritual counsel had,
> Shall stop or spur me. Have I done well?
> (2.1.183-188)

At this point, Leontes seems willing to accept even an unfavorable verdict from the oracle. However, when the oracle returns judgment that "Hermione is chaste, Polixenes blameless/ Camillo a true subject, Leontes a jealous tyrant" (3.2.131-132), Leontes declares that "There is no truth at all i' th' oracle" (3.2.138). Only when he hears of Mamillius's death does he accept the truth of the oracle and begin to repent.

Leontes's temporary opinion that there is no truth in the oracle resembles James I's view that there was no truth in Rome. In at least a few instances, James I ridiculed what he believed to be Rome's false claims to infallibility:

> And therefore I would have wished the Pope, before hee had set downe this commandement to all Papists here, That, since in him is the power by the infability [sic] of his spirit, to make new Articles of Faith when ever it shall please him, he had first set it downe for an

Article of Faith, before he commanded all Catholikes to believe and obey it.[49]

But how they are now come to be Christs Vicars, nay, Gods on earth, triple-crowned, Kings of heaven, earth and hell, Judges of all the world, and none to judge them; Heads of the faith, Absolute deciders of all Controversies by the infallibility of their spirit, having all power both Spirituall and Temporall in their hands.[50]

In these attacks on the doctrine of papal infallibility, James I did not refer to Rome as the oracle. Yet he believed the Catholic Church arrogates to itself all that is important about the oracle in *The Winter's Tale*: god on earth, judge of the world, and "absolute decider" of all controversies. This helps us understand why Catholics in Shakespeare's England had for years been fixed in the moment when Leontes declares there is no truth in the oracle. These Catholics adhered to the faith of their ancestors and the decrees from Rome, just as Leontes had intended to adhere to the verdict of the oracle. For English Catholics, their king's refusal to accept the authority of Rome, which English monarchs had accepted for centuries, would seem as troubling as Leontes's refusal to see truth in the oracle whose guidance he had initially sought.

Shakespeare provides another connection between Rome and the oracle when describing the ceremony at Delphos. As Fr. Peter Milward remarks:

The wonder elicited in the minds of Dion and Cleomenes at the sight of "the temple" at Delphos, the solemnity of the "sacrifice" and "the ear-deafening voice of the oracle" (3.1.2-9), seems to correspond not so much to anything the dramatist might have learnt from classical sources concerning [Delphos] as to the sight of the newly built basilica of St. Peter's in Rome and the solemnity of a Papal High Mass celebrated there.[51]

Without much, if any, alteration, Dion's description of the ceremony at Delphos could be taken as a Catholic Solemn High Mass: "Oh, the sacrifice!/ How ceremonious, solemn, and unearthly/ It was i' th' offering!" (3.1.6-8). Fr. Milward suggests that the scene most closely resembles a Papal High Mass at St. Peter's in Rome. Taken together with the idea that Rome represents the oracle as source of truth, the description of Delphos makes it seem almost certain that Shakespeare intended the connection. So, far from suggesting a pagan reading of the play, Shakespeare's use of the oracle provides yet another dimension to the Catholic allegory within *The Winter's Tale*.

Dramatis Personae

We have already seen strong connections between the characters in *The Winter's Tale* and historical figures of the religious drama in Shakespeare's England. The next sections will explore how these connections develop over the course of the play's five acts. Before raising the curtain to Act I, Scene 1, though, we should consider who sat (or stood) in Shakespeare's audience when the play was first performed.

Scholars generally agree that the play was written between 1610 and 1611, with the earliest recorded performance on May 15, 1611. In a speech before Parliament on March 21, 1610, James I discussed his Catholic subjects and the extent to which the government should enforce the Oath of Allegiance:

> Papists are waxed as proud at this time as ever they were, which makes many to think they have some new plot in hand.... As for Recusants, let them bee all duely presented [with the Oath] without exception: for in times past there hath been too great a connivence, and forbearing of them, especially of great mens wives, and their kinne and followers. None ought to be spared from being brought under the danger of Law, and then it is my part to use mercie, as I think convenient.... And that yee all may know the trewth of my heart in this case, I divide all my Subjects that are Papists, into two rankes: either olde Papists, that were so brought up in times of Poperie, like old Queene Mary Priests, and those, that though they bee younger in yeeres, yet have never drunke in other milke, but beene still nursed in that blindnesse: Or else such as doe become Apostats; having once

beene of our Profession, and have forsaken the trewth. . . . For the former sort, I pitie them; but if they bee good and quiet Subjects, I hate not their persons; and if I were a private man, I could well keepe a civill friendship and conversation with some of them: But as for those Apostates, who, I know, must be greatest haters of their owne Sect, I confesse I can never shew any favourable countenance toward them, and they may all of them be sure without exception, that they shall never finde any more favour of mee, further then I must in Justice afford them. And these I would have the Law strike the severliest upon, and you carefullest to discover.[52]

Of the Papists in England, then, we see that there were two classes according to James I: the merely blind to whom the king might show mercy; and those who had once followed in the religion of Henry VIII and James I, to whom the king would give no quarter.

The Catholics in Shakespeare's audience would have been intensely aware of their plight under James I. Indeed, the Catholics in the audience were living the reality presented in the first acts of the play – the allegory is about them in a sense.

But the allegorical interpretation of *The Winter's Tale* speaks to a far larger audience than those who saw the play's first productions. Though this book considers numerous reasons to set the allegory in the years following the Gunpowder Plot, it seems reasonable that Shakespeare had a broader view in mind. As we will see, the most significant conflicts in the play parallel the most significant religious conflicts in Shakespeare's England, which changed dramatically after the Gunpowder Plot was discovered. However, many of these religious conflicts were generally present as soon as Henry VIII broke with Rome.

These conflicts all derived from the question of whether the pope, as successor of St. Peter, has authority over the entire Christian Church. Henry VIII and James I (and the kings and queens before and between them) generally took it for granted that Christ had established a church, to which all must belong to save their souls. But, like Henry VIII, James I believed the Catholic Church was wrong in asserting that Christ had given St. Peter and his successors, as popes, the authority over the entire Church.

Of course, Henry VIII had not always disagreed with the Catholic Church. Although historians debate the actual authorship, Henry VIII nominally wrote *Defense of the Seven Sacraments* in support of the pope and the Catholic Church against Martin Luther's attack on the Catholicism. Pope Leo X responded by bestowing on Henry VIII the title of "Defender of the Faith." Henry VIII later found reason to regret his defense of the Catholic Church and pope, but he kept the title nonetheless, as did his successors.

St. Robert Bellarmine reflected on King James I's use of this title that had originally meant defender of the Catholic Faith:

> Nobody is ignorant that this title was given by Pope Leo X to Henry VIII in recompense for that monarch's book on the Seven Sacraments against Luther and other innovators of the age. Consequently, if it be asked what the word "faith" in the title signifies, there is plainly no other answer but that it signifies the faith held by him who gave the title, professed by him who received it, and defended in the book on account of which it was bestowed. The man who dignified the king of England with that most honourable title was either the Vicar of Christ, as we Catholics believe, or Antichrist, as Protestants and Calvinists maintain. If he be Vicar of Christ, why does not the defender of Christ's faith hear, acknowledge and venerate him? If, on the other hand, he be Antichrist, why does a Christian Prince glory in a title coming from such a source? Why, in a word, does he carry about the mark of the Beast?[53]

For Catholics in England, James I was, in crucial respects, a continuation of Henry VIII as a persecutor of the Church. Thus, we can see Leontes as broadly representing the king of England who opposed the Catholic Church while retaining the title Henry VIII earned defending it.[54]

Similarly, although Camillo specifically represents Pope Paul V in a meaningful way, his character is a champion of the papacy in general. Thus if we find that Camillo's character resonates with St. Thomas

More and St. John Fisher, who opposed King Henry VIII; St. Edmund Campion who opposed Queen Elizabeth I; or St. Robert Bellarmine and Fr. Robert Persons who opposed King James I, there is good reason: each of these men, and many others, opposed Anglicanism on the same grounds. If Shakespeare intended these broader characterizations of Camillo and Leontes, the allegory loses none of its immediacy. It simply portrays the condition of Catholics in England in its more historically full context. Indeed, the allegory within *The Winter's Tale* should give consolation and hope to all Catholics, especially those facing persecution for adhering to their religion.

Despite these broader associations, Shakespeare seems to have clearly intended an allegory set at the time of the play's first performances. Aside from specific connections to the Gunpowder Plot and writings surrounding the Oath, a key reason to believe Shakespeare set the allegory in his day has to do with the structure of the play. The first three acts of the play are tragic while the last two fit the pattern of Shakespeare's comedies. If Shakespeare wrote the first three acts as a reflection of his day, then the last two acts are hopeful, representing something desired but not yet realized.

If, on the other hand, Shakespeare intended the allegory to represent a previous period, what do the last two acts represent? They would not represent a "hope" for improved circumstances because, even with the passage of sixteen years (between Acts III and IV), the audience would clearly not have seen a materialization of that hope under Henry VIII or Elizabeth I. Such an allegory would have had some resonance with the religious and political realities at the time of the play's first performance, but it would lack what this allegory offers at its best: both a profoundly tragic vision of the plight of contemporary English Catholics and a clear and beautiful representation of what Catholics in the audience might have had in their prayers.

To summarize this section, it seems reasonable to say that if we had been devout Catholics in Shakespeare's England, we would have found considerable interest, if not consolation, in seeing within *The Winter's Tale* the following list of allegorical actors:

Dramatis Personae:
Leontes, King of Sicilia (*King James I*)
Camillo, lord of Sicilia (*St. Peter's successor, Pope Paul V*)
Hermione, Queen to Leontes (*Catholic Church/Mystical Body of Christ*)
Mamillius, son to Leontes and Hermione (*Anglican Church*)
Perdita, daughter to Leontes and Hermione (*Catholic Church in England*)
Paulina, wife to Antigonus (*St. Paul figure*)
Polixenes, King of Bohemia (*all Catholic monarchs*)
Oracle at Delphos (Delphi), oracle (*Rome*)

Scene -- Partly in Sicilia (*England*), and partly in Bohemia (*Bohemia*)

In the sections that follow we will be able to add Florizel, Antigonus, and perhaps even the bear to the list and refine the allegorical identities of these already listed.

Notes

[1] S.J. stands for *Societas Jesu* (in Latin) or Society of Jesus, also known as the Jesuits. St. Ignatius Loyola founded this religious order in 1540.

[2] Fr. John Gerard, S.J., *Autobiography of a Hunted Priest*, 59.

[3] Ibid. 62.

[4] Alice Hogge, *God's Secret Agents: Queen Elizabeth's Forbidden Priests and the Hatching of the Gunpowder Plot*, 118-119.

[5] Northrop Frye, *Northrop Frye on Shakespeare*, 165.

[6] Eugene England, "Cordelia and Paulina, Shakespeare's Healing Dramatists." *Literature & Belief 2*, 75.

[7] Roy Battenhouse, "Theme and Structure in *The Winter's Tale*." *Shakespeare Survey 33*, 137.

[8] Abbot Guéranger, O.S.B., *The Liturgical Year: Time After Pentecost, Book III*, 310.

60 | A TALE TOLD SOFTLY

[9] Clara Longworth de Chambrun, *Shakespeare Rediscovered*, 131.

[10] Pope Saint Pius V presided over the Council of Trent in 1545.

[11] *Catechism of the Council of Trent*, 318.

[12] King James VI & I, 276.

[13] In *The Life and Death of King John*, Shakespeare uses the term "holy father" in an unveiled reference to the pope, as Pandulf says to King Philip, "This, in our foresaid Holy Father's name,/ Pope Innocent, I do demand of thee" (3.1.145-146).

[14] As discussed in the Preface, Fr. Gerard praised St. Nicholas Owen for this same ability to vary the types of hiding places he constructed so as to reduce the possibility that the discovery of one would lead to the discovery of others.

[15] Henry VIII, 156.

[16] Evelyn Waugh, *Saint Edmund Campion: Priest and Martyr*, 25.

[17] Antonia Fraser, *Faith and Treason, The Story of the Gunpowder Plot*, 16.

[18] Some scholars have argued that the Gunpowder Plot may have been fabricated, perhaps to impose further sanctions on Catholics. For purposes of this study, I assume that popular history is correct, although I would (as a Catholic) be happy to learn that most historians have it wrong.

[19] Fr. John Gerard, S.J., *The Condition of Catholics under James I*, 8.

[20] Hogge, 380.

[21] King James VI & I, 250-251.

[22] James Brodrick, S.J., *Robert Bellarmine: Saint and Scholar*, 273.

[23] Donna B. Hamilton, *Shakespeare and the Politics of Protestant England*, 132.

[24] Joseph Pearce, *The Quest for Shakespeare: The Bard of Avalon and the Church of Rome*, 152.

[25] W.B. Patterson, *King James VI and I and the Reunion of Christendom*, 100.

[26] King James VI & I, 324.

[27] King James VI & I, 327.

[28] King James VI & I, 325.

[29] Patterson, 95.

[30] Evelyn Waugh, *Saint Edmund Campion: Priest & Martyr*, 205.

[31] *A New Variorum Edition of Shakespeare: The Winter's Tale*, 8.

[32] Julia Gasper and Carolyn Williams write that Shakespeare is known to have used North's *Plutarch* for certain names in the play and that the OED cites the following as one of two explanations of the word *herm* or *herma*: "Three Hermes of stone (which are four

square pillars) upon the tops of which they set up heads of Mercurie." Julia Gasper and Carolyn Williams, "The Meaning of the Name 'Hermione'."

[33] Robert A. Adams, *Shakespeare –The Four Romances*, 94.

[34] King James VI & I, 324.

[35] King James VI & I, 288.

[36] Brodrick, 275.

[37] Evelyn Waugh, *Saint Edmund Campion: Priest and Martyr*, 95. Evelyn Waugh's biography of St. Edmund Campion also recounts the reaction of Campion's fellow clerics to the news of his mission to England: "It was not until March that the Austrian Provincial would allow his departure. In the time of waiting Campion continued without interruption in the normal order of the school, but there was the aura about him of one devoted to another destiny. A Salesian father, James Gall, an ecstatic, came to the door of Campion's cell, on the even of his departure, and inscribed above it *P. Edmundus Campianus Martyr*. Some days before, another father had painted the emblem of martyrdom, a garland of roses and lilies, on the wall at the head of Campion's bed." (Waugh, 83)

[38] Waugh, 74.

[39] Waugh, 217.

[40] Alfred Thomas, *A Blessed Shore: England and Bohemia from Chaucer to Shakespeare*, 168.

[41] Thomas, 175. Thomas goes on to speculate, "Since in *The Winter's Tale* Bohemia becomes a refuge for Perdita as it did for Campion and his fellow exiles from England, it is intriguing to speculate whether Shakespeare knew about Campion's letter, especially since its recipient, Robert Arden, may have been a relative of Shakespeare's mother. In the early-modern period letters were frequently intended as public documents to be read by or to a group of people, often members of the same family; so it is not impossible that Shakespeare had been exposed to Campion's letter in some form or other. If Fr. Peter Milward, Stephen Greenblatt and others are correct that Shakespeare met Campion either in Warwickshire or Lancashire during the latter's fateful mission to England in 1580-81, the young playwright may have heard the Jesuit deliver a sermon in which Bohemia is presented as a 'blessed shore.'"

[42] Milward, 258.

[43] Northrop Frye, *Northrop Frye on Shakespeare*, 160-161.

[44] S. L. Bethell, *The Winter's Tale: A Study*, 38.

[45] Henry Sebastian Bowden, *The Religion of Shakespeare: Chiefly from the Writings of the Late Mr. Richard Simpson*, M.A., 289.

[46] Fr. Peter Milward, *Shakespeare's Other Dimension*, 131-132.

[47] Denzinger, *The Sources of Catholic Dogma*, number 160.

[48] W.B. Patterson, *King James VI and I and the Reunion of Christendom*, 37.

[49] King James VI & I, 256.

[50] King James VI & I, 307.

[51] Peter Milward, S.J., 261.

[52] King James VI & I, 544-545.

[53] Brodrick, 266-267.

[54] Fr. Peter Milward, S.J., one of the foremost experts on Catholic elements in Shakespeare's plays, suggests several reasons to see the play set in Henry VIII's day. *Milward*, 259-260.

SECTION TWO

The Catholic Tragedy: Acts I - III

Having seen the outline of what seems like a plausible reason why we should read *The Winter's Tale* as an allegory for the Catholic vision of religious struggles in Shakespeare's England, we can look more closely at *how* to read it as such, from first scene to last. This section considers the first three acts of the play, which sadly reflect Catholic life under James I at the time of the play's first performance.

Common Beginnings and Hope

Prior to James I ascending the English throne, many Catholics hoped that the king might show more favor to their religion than had Queen Elizabeth. As W.B. Patterson describes:

> While in Scotland, James and Anne of Denmark, his queen, had been in touch with Pope Clement VIII through secret emissaries who sought to win the favor of the pope as well as of several Catholic heads of state. The king's intentions were evidently to prepare for his peaceful accession in England by preventing invasions or civil wars on behalf of rival candidates and plots against his life by zealous Catholics.

The effect of these missions, however, was to raise in the minds of Catholic leaders abroad the possibility of James's conversion.[1]

The first scene of the play portrays these hopes allegorically in two prominent ways: first, Camillo and Archidamus discuss the connections between Sicilia (representing England) and Bohemia (representing pro-Catholic Europe) that form the basis of Catholic hopes; and second, the characters express great hope for Mamillius, the son of Leontes and Hermione.

We should recall that Shakespeare retained the settings of Greene's *Pandosto* for *The Winter's Tale* but switched them: Leontes's counterpart in *Pandosto* was king of Bohemia, and Polixenes's counterpart was king of Sicilia. Undoubtedly the allegory would be more apparent if Shakespeare had chosen Rome instead of Bohemia; but if he had done that we would not know the play because it never would have made it past the censors. Within the allegory, Sicilia represents England and Bohemia represents pro-Catholic Europe, which is as close to "Rome" as we could expect within a Catholic allegory.

The play begins with Camillo and Archidamus discussing the affection between Sicilia and Bohemia:

> Sicilia cannot show himself overkind to Bohemia.
> They were trained together in their childhoods,
> and there rooted betwixt them then such an affection
> which cannot choose but branch now.
> (1.1.21-24)

The key allegorical concept in these lines is that Leontes (and thus James I) had early connections to the Catholic world. In his letter to Christian monarchs, James I addressed his childhood connection to the Catholic Church:

> Neither can my Baptisme in the rites of their Religion make me an Apostate, or Heretike in respect of my present profession, since we all agree in the substance thereof, being all Baptized In the Name of the

Father, the Sonne and the holy Ghost: upon which head there is no variance amongst us.[2]

When James I refers to "their Religion," in which he was baptized, he means Catholicism, the religion of his mother Mary, Queen of Scots. Although James I adamantly denied being raised as a Catholic, his early link to Catholicism was one of the reasons Catholics had hope that he might ultimately tolerate their religion or even convert.

The first scene continues with Camillo telling Archidamus that despite the separation of Sicilia and Bohemia, they have maintained close ties:

> Since their
> more mature dignities and royal necessities made
> separation of their society, their encounters, though
> not personal, hath been royally attorneyed with
> interchange of gifts, letters, loving embassies, that
> they seemed to be together though absent.
> (1.2.24-29)

This revelation that Leontes had previously maintained contact with Polixenes despite their separation is not especially relevant within the literal context of the play – after all, Polixenes had already been visiting Leontes in Sicilia for the previous nine months by the time the play begins. From an allegorical perspective, though, this points to the communications James I had with Catholic leaders prior to ascending the English throne. In his biography of St. Robert Bellarmine, Fr. James Brodrick describes the significance of these communications, particularly a letter from King James I's queen:

> It is dated from Dalkeith, July 31, 1601, and addressed to Cardinal Borghese, then protector of the Scottish nation at Rome, and subsequently Pope Paul V. It is signed by James's Queen, Anne of Denmark, but expressly claims to have been written on the authority of James himself, in answer to letters received by him from Pope Clement VIII. The King, wrote Queen Anne, could not personally

reply to the most welcome letter of his Holiness because of the danger of his answer falling into the hands of Queen Elizabeth, but had given her authority to do so in his name to Cardinal Borghese.[3]

Fr. James Brodrick also relates the story behind the following seemingly innocuous passage from Bellarmine's book:

> On the contrary, they were drafted rather in favour of the King of Scotland [King James I], because they consisted of an exhortation to the Catholics to promote, as far as in them lay, the succession of an upright and orthodox monarch, and the envoys of that King had given good reasons for believing that their master was such a one, and not at all averse from embracing the Catholic Faith. This hope received a striking confirmation when the King himself addressed extremely kind letters to the Pope [Pope Clement VIII], and the Cardinals Aldobrandini and Bellarmine, in which he begged, among other things, that some Scotsman might be raised to the purple, to act as his representative at the Court of Rome.[4]

St. Robert Bellarmine wrote these lines to rebut King James I's assertion that correspondence from Pope Clement VIII to English Catholics was meant to obstruct his succession of Queen Elizabeth I to the throne. That James I had instead maintained amicable correspondence with Pope Clement VIII to further his chances of becoming king was a tremendously unwelcome revelation for the king. In response, James I stopped the publication and distribution of his *Apology for the Oath of Allegiance* (which contained the misleading claim about his correspondence with Clement VIII) and indeed issued orders to have as many copies as possible bought back. He then "renounced the world, the flesh, and the devil, that he might devote all his energies to the composition" of a preface for the revised edition.[5] Thus, Camillo's lines about continued communications between Sicilia and Bohemia have great significance to the allegorical meaning.

Archidamus and Camillo close the scene by discussing Mamillius, the son of Leontes and Hermione. As we have seen, Mamillius and Perdita represent the two religions James I found upon his accession: the religion he professed, which was openly practiced and allowed by law in England (Mamillius); and the hidden Catholic religion (Perdita). Any hopes for the improvement of Catholic life under the new king would depend primarily upon a change in his religious views, ideally through his conversion to Catholicism. Within the allegory, these hopes would be reflected primarily in hopes for Mamillius (rather than Perdita), which is what we see as Camillo and Archidamus conclude the first scene:

> CAMILLO
> I very well agree with you in the hopes of
> him. It is a gallant child, one that indeed physics the
> subject, makes old hearts fresh. They that went on
> crutches ere he was born desire yet their life to see him
> a man.
> ARCHIDAMUS
> Would they else be content to die?
> CAMILLO
> Yes, if there were no other excuse why they
> should desire to live.
> ARCHIDAMUS
> If the King had no son, they would desire
> to live on crutches till he had one.
>
> (1.1.37-47)

These lines play only a limited and somewhat confusing role in the literal drama that follows because *The Winter's Tale* ends happily without the king having a son.[6] However, this dialogue of course reflects the great anticipation that James I might convert and allow for greater toleration of the Catholic Religion.

The first and second parts of the play's opening scene thus converge – Catholics had high hopes that the king might eventually allow the public practice of Catholicism; and they based their hopes on the connections James I had with the Catholic world prior to his arrival in England.

The scenes that follow in the play's first three acts allegorically portray the ways in which the Catholic hopes are tragically ended by James I's persecution of the Catholic Church, particularly in the aftermath of the Gunpowder Plot. Shakespeare could have set the beginning of the religious allegory after the Gunpowder Plot, but by showing the initial hopes of Catholics he solidifies the allegorical connections and leaves us a more reliable history and story of Catholic life under James I.

The Madness of Leontes

From the hopeful beginning, the play soon turns to the irrational jealousy of Leontes. After Leontes fails to convince Polixenes to remain longer in Sicilia, he directs Hermione to try to persuade the Bohemian king to stay. When Hermione succeeds, Leontes immediately becomes suspicious. Shakespeare provides very little matter to fuel Leontes's jealousy, but the Sicilian king feeds on it until he believes that his queen carries a child fathered by Polixenes. The gradual progression of Leontes's madness is gut-wrenching. From the perspective of Catholics in Shakespeare's England, their king's wild assertions that the Catholic Church was an adulteress would have been no less painful.

As discussed above, Pope Paul V (Camillo Borghese) became an important figure in Shakespeare's England by defending the Church against James I's accusations and the Oath. So too, before leaving Sicilia with Polixenes, Camillo defends Hermione more vigorously than any other character. Though he is merely a lord of Sicilia, Camillo sternly rebukes the King of Sicilia for his misguided suspicions about Hermione:

> I would not be a stander-by to hear
> My sovereign mistress clouded so without
> My present vengeance taken.
>   (1.2.278-28)

Camillo's strong words go well beyond indignation at simply hearing an honorable lady falsely accused. Catholicism teaches that blasphemy is a grave sin, and, within the allegory, Leontes has blasphemed by insulting Hermione, who represents the Mystical Body of Christ. Camillo's censure of Leontes emphasizes this religious judgment by putting it in terms of sin: "You never spoke what did become you less/ Than this, which to reiterate were sin" (1.2.281-282).

Camillo's forceful tone with Leontes is also much more authoritative than we would expect considering his role as lord of Sicilia. However, his words undoubtedly fit his allegorical position as pope, both because Camillo's judgment deals with matters of faith and morals and he is addressing the king not as a subject but as a moral authority. Likewise, Leontes's response to Camillo's rebuke is defensive – as he simply presents his trivial reasons for suspicion – which would be surprising in response to a lord of his own country, and yet fitting in response to the pope.

Camillo then entreats Leontes to "be cured of this diseased opinion" about Hermione (1.2.295-296), but the madness has already taken hold. Camillo later diagnoses the king's madness: "The fabric of his folly, whose foundation/ Is piled upon his faith" (1.2.428-429). This observation concerning Leontes's *faith* seems to make significantly more sense in the allegorical meaning of the play. If, in other words, we do not read the allegorical meaning, to what does the mention of "faith" apply in Camillo's critique? Leontes's suspicion that Hermione has committed adultery is factually inaccurate, but we could attribute that to simple misperception, insecurity or a number of other causes without touching upon his faith. From a Catholic perspective, though, James I's treatment of the Catholic Church was founded on his faith, something that the king readily acknowledged.

How did King James I view the differences between his faith and that of the Catholic Church? In a speech before Parliament he described the differences in terms of an illness:

> I acknowledge the Romane Church to be our Mother Church, although defiled with some infirmities and corruptions ... and as I am none enemie to the life of a sicke man, because I would have his bodie

purged of ill humours; no more am I enemy to their Church, because I would have them reforme their errors.[7]

So James I acknowledged the Catholic Church as the "Mother Church" of Christianity. However, he believed that it had somehow lost its status as the "true church" by virtue of certain errors. He saw it as sick, in need of purging.

James I extended the notion of sickness to individual believers of the Catholic Faith. Thus, James I defended his Oath as necessary:

> For the apparent safetie of me and my posterities, forbidding my people to drinke so deeply in the bitter cup of Antichristian fornications.[8]

Of course James I's Catholic subjects would have seen their "cup" of Catholic belief as wholesome rather than full of "anti-Christian fornications," such being the difference in faith between James I and Catholics.

Leontes uses similar imagery in describing his unique (and mistaken) ability to see Hermione's adultery:

> There may be in the cup
> A spider steeped, and one may drink, depart,
> And yet partake no venom, for his knowledge
> Is not infected; but if one present
> Th' abhorred ingredient to his eye, make known
> How he hath drunk, he cracks his gorge, his sides,
> With violent hefts. I have drunk, and seen the spider.
> (2.1.39-45)

Leontes's description of the spider in the cup resembles James I's description of the bitter cup poisoning his Catholic subjects. In each case, the subjects fail to detect what the king believes to be the adulterous nature of the queen in question.

And what did James I think of those in England prior to Henry VIII who had faithfully adhered to Catholicism, the only Christian religion they or their ancestors had known? Could he truly believe that the "bitter cup of antichristian fornications" had poisoned all Christians in England prior to the break with Rome? In his speech to Parliament following the Gunpowder Plot, the king judges his ancestors and subjects:

> And therefore doe we justly confesse, that many Papists, especially our forefathers, laying their onely trust upon Christ and his Merits at their last breath, may be, and often times are saved. . . .I therefore thus doe conclude this point, that upon the one part many honest men, seduced with some errors of Popery, may yet remaine good and faithfull subjects: so upon the other part, none of those that trewly know and beleeve the whole grounds, and schoole conclusions of their doctrine, can ever prove either good Christians, or faithfull subjects.[9]

This reasoning seems to match that of Leontes: so long as Catholics did not "infect their knowledge" with truly knowing their Faith, they might drink without partaking of the venom. In this way, James I believed some of his Catholic ancestors might have saved their souls.

Leontes's madness spreads so rapidly in part because of his almost comical arrogance:

> How blest am I
> In my just censure, in my true opinion!
> Alack, for lesser knowledge! How accurst
> In being so blest!
>
> (2.1.36-39)

To all appearances, Leontes is not especially "blest" at this juncture of the play – and his "true opinion" lacks all truth. These lines are stunning not simply because he is terribly mistaken, but because his high self-regard insulates him from the reasoning of others.

We can see a striking parallel in James I's advice to his son about discerning the "true religion":

> And for keeping your conscience sound from that sicknesse of superstition, yee must neither lay the safetie of your conscience upon the credit of your owne conceits, not yet of other mens humors, how great doctors of Divinitie that ever they be; but yee must onely ground it upon the expresse Scripture: for conscience not grounded upon sure knowledge, is either an ignorant fantasie or an arrogant vanitie. Beware therefore in this case with two extremities: the one, to beleeve with the Papists, the Churches authority, better than your own knowledge; the other, to leane with the Anabaptists, to your owne conceits and dreamed revelations.[10]

James I based his "sure knowledge" on his personal interpretation of the Bible, which he believed to be sounder than that of the "great doctors of Divinity." He, like Leontes, considered himself blessed in his "true opinion." Apparently, James I did not place much weight on the fact that "the great doctors of Divinity" found conclusive support in the Bible for the authority of the pope and the other Catholic teachings that he disputed.

Eamon Duffy writes of Cardinal Reginald Pole's thoughts on this line of thinking:

> At the root of all Pole's thought about the value and place of preaching and of the Bible lay his doctrine of the church as the only house of God, the one location of grace.... He returned repeatedly to a text from Deuteronomy, read in Lauds every Saturday morning: "Ask your father, and he will show you, your elders, and they will tell you." The church provided an unbroken chain of witness, the truth handed on from father to son without interruption. The claim of the protestants to have the ancient fathers of the church on their side was false, for they could not trace the doctrines they preached back through their own fathers and grandfathers to those remote times. The chain of witness was broken. To claim to have discovered new Christian truth, not by receiving it from the church, but by reading the Bible, as the protestants did, was to attempt to invent oneself, to "make their own hedd by reading their master and father, which is a great absurditie."[11]

Thus stands the Catholic argument against the reasoning of both James I and Leontes, who placed so much value on their "certain knowledge" and "true opinions." Protestants broke the "chain of witness" going back to Christ and thus lost the true faith, despite their sense of self-assurance.

King James I's profound sense of confidence may also have played a role in allowing Shakespeare to hide the allegory within *The Winter's Tale*. Joan Hall provides interesting commentary on this:

> If Leontes appears to act out an extreme version of James I's beliefs on the divine rights of kings, we may wonder how daring this presentation of monarch seemed to Shakespeare's contemporaries. Yet *The Winter's Tale* was well-received by James. The fact that it was performed at court on November 5, 1611, the sixth anniversary of the Gunpowder Plot – a date on which to celebrate the apparently miraculous escape of king and Parliament from death by explosion – suggests that it was not perceived as a critique of royal authority. Having a high opinion of the sacredness of his kingship, James may have failed to see much connection between himself and the blustering Leontes.[12]

As we consider other similarities between James I and Leontes, James I's apparent failure to see the connection – as suggested by the fact that the play survived so that we can read it today – may seem one of the most extraordinary and fortuitous circumstances surrounding the allegory.

Naturally, neither James I nor his followers would have considered their views on Catholicism to be madness. Likewise, Leontes does not see his views about Hermione and her supporters as mad either, until after Mamillius and Hermione die. He repents when he finally sees the disastrous results of his madness.

Leontes clashed with Hermione and her supporters in the same ways that James I opposed the Catholic Church and Catholics. By making it clear to the audience that Leontes was blinded by his irrational suspicions about Hermione, Shakespeare invites the audience to reach the same conclusion about Leontes's allegorical counterpart, James I.

The next three chapters attempt to illustrate the legal, theological and rhetorical manifestations of Leontes's madness, and their remarkable parallels to the battlefronts between James I and Catholics.

Plots and Oaths

Part of the religious landscape in Shakespeare's England since Henry VIII's break with Rome involved the related realities of plots and oaths. Those familiar with the life of St. Thomas More will recall that he ultimately lost his freedom and life for refusing to take the Oath of Supremacy. There were also real and imagined plots to dethrone the monarchs who insisted that their subjects take these oaths of loyalty that conflicted with Catholicism. Fittingly, then, *The Winter's Tale* includes both plots and oaths.

As previously discussed, Shakespeare wrote *The Winter's Tale* just a few years after the Gunpowder Plot. Catholics universally denounced the plot, even if they could sympathize with the plotters' dire circumstances that prompted them to undertake desperate actions contrary to their faith. Fr. Oswald Tesimond, who knew the plotters – and indeed was accused of aiding them – wrote:

> I only wish to remind our enemies that the common opinion which they and nearly everybody in the country had of us before this latest happening was the same, namely that in every adversity we showed great patience and humility . . . Finally, let them remember, that out of so many thousands of patient Catholics, they have found a few exceptions in all these years. Nevertheless, these few, out of resentment, have made very clear to the world how heavy and unsupportable is the yoke which we all bear in this most cruel and inhuman persecution. Scarcely affected among those who know anything is the opinion of our innocence and the justice of the cause for which we suffer.[13]

The plot failed and thus served only to increase the hardships of the patient and long-suffering Catholics in England.

The play's allegory does not address the Gunpowder Plot directly but does allude to it with imaginary plots and the resulting hardships for Leontes's subjects. Once Leontes discovers that Camillo and Polixenes have left Sicilia, he begins to suspect a conspiracy against himself: "There is a plot against my life, my crown/ All's true that is mistrusted" (2.1.47-48). Leontes's indictment against Hermione also alleges that she has conspired with Camillo to kill the king (3.2.15-17). At no point in the play is there a conspiracy against Leontes's life or crown. His paranoia is simply another symptom of his madness, one that spurs him to further persecute his innocent subjects.

The intensity of Leontes's madness increases after Polixenes's escape and he begins to pursue the "sessions" to condemn Hermione. Faced with resistance from all whom he encounters, his demands become more forceful, ultimately becoming calls for oaths of allegiance. When Paulina attempts to persuade the king to accept his newborn daughter, Leontes demands that his subjects banish Paulina:

> On your allegiance,
> Out of the chamber with her! Were I a tyrant,
> Where were her life? She durst not call me so
> If she did know me one. Away with her!
> (2.3.121-124)

We should recall that Leontes is the king speaking directly to his subjects, so his command should suffice to have Paulina dismissed, without demands for allegiance. In other words, what is the dramatic purpose of "on your allegiance" in his speech? This line shows us that Leontes has lost control of his subjects, but seems otherwise superfluous. As we will consider in great detail in a subsequent chapter, Leontes also requires Antigonus to take an oath of allegiance that becomes a central part of the play's plot.

Leontes's demands for oaths of allegiance in opposition to Hermione resemble James I's Oath of Allegiance in opposition to the Catholic Church and the pope:

> I, A.B., do truly and sincerely acknowledge . . that our sovereign lord, King James, is lawful and rightful King . . . and that the pope neither of himself nor by any authority of Church or See of Rome, or by any other means with any other, has any power to depose the king &c., or to authorize any foreign prince to invade him &c., or to give licence to any to bear arms, raise tumults. . . . Also I do swear that notwithstanding any sentence of excommunication or deprivation I will bear allegiance and true faith to his Majesty. . . . And I do further swear that I do from my heart abhor, detest, and abjure, as impious and heretical this damnable doctrine and position, that princes which be excommunicated by the pope may be deposed or murdered by their subjects or by any other whatsoever. And I do believe that the pope has no power to absolve me from this oath. I do swear according to the plain and common sense, and understanding of the same words.[14]

The Oath did not simply require Catholics to swear allegiance to the king – it also required them to reject "as impious and heretical" the "damnable doctrine" that princes who had been excommunicated by the pope could be deposed or murdered by their subjects. The nuances of the Oath of course mattered to those asked to take it; and while Catholics could reject the idea of murdering the king, it was far from certain that they could declare that it was *impious* and *heretical* that an excommunicated king could be deposed. To swear that would require a religious determination that they were not in a position to make.

Shakespeare gives his audience a few additional clues that the allegory deals specifically with the controversy surrounding the Oath of James I. When Leontes directs Camillo to kill Polixenes, Camillo initially replies by assuring the Sicilian king that he will "fetch off Bohemia" (1.2.333). Ultimately, though, he rejects the idea of murdering the Bohemian king:

> To do this deed,
> Promotion follows. If I could find example
> Of thousands that had struck anointed kings
> And flourished after, I'd not do't.
> (1.2.355-358)

Has Camillo changed his mind about killing Polixenes or does he intentionally deceive Leontes when he says he will "fetch off" Polixenes? By all appearances, Leontes believes that Camillo would kill Polixenes. Yet Camillo's emphatic philosophical objection to striking "anointed kings" suggests that he never truly assents to Leontes's suggestion. He does not, in other words, grapple with a protracted cost-benefit analysis of whether he would be better off obeying Leontes. Moreover, although Camillo's statement that he would "fetch off Bohemia" could imply he would murder Polixenes, it could instead signal his intention to take the king of Bohemia away from Sicilia, which is precisely what he does.

Camillo's apparent equivocation touches closely a particular concern James I had regarding his Catholic subjects, which we can see in the last words of the Oath of Allegiance: "I do swear according to the plain and common sense, and understanding of the same words." Like the priests who might have equivocated under questioning to avoid disclosing information that would put the lives of their supporters at risk, Camillo's equivocation saves the life of Polixenes. It also spares Leontes from the horror of being responsible for the death of his friend and fellow king.

The Oath also prompted Pope Paul V to address to the question of whether he (or any other pope) would ever direct the murder of a king. The answer from Rome came from St. Robert Bellarmine (under the pseudonym of Matteo Torti), but applies to the Pope: "I abhorre Parricide, I detest all conspiracies."[15] As St. Robert Bellarmine elaborated in his letter to Archpriest Blackwell:

> For it was never heard of from the Churches infancie untill this day, that ever any Pope did command, that any Prince, though an Heretike . . . though a persecutor, should be murdered; or did approve of the fact, when it was done by any other.[16]

Within the allegory, when Camillo (as pope) says he would never strike an anointed king, he echoes the point that Cardinal Bellarmine was making about all popes. This is especially interesting when we consider that Shakespeare develops Camillo as a good man who would presumably never consider killing *any* innocent person. Camillo's consideration of whether he would kill an innocent anointed king thus seems out of place in the literal meaning of the play. And yet this provides another strong connection between Camillo and Pope Paul V. It also makes it more difficult to imagine that Shakespeare did not intend the allegorical parallel to the Oath of Allegiance.

Pope Paul V responded to James I's Oath with a letter to English Catholics exhorting them to remain faithful in the face of persecution:

> Wellbeloved Sonnes, Salutation and Apostolicall Benediction. The tribulations and calamities, which yee have continually sustained for the keeping of the Catholike Faith, have always afflicted us with great griefe of minde. . . . For wee have heard how you are compelled, by most grievous punishments set before you, to go to the Churches of Heretikes, to frequent their assemblies, to be present at their Sermons. Truely wee doe undoubtedly beleeve, that they which with so great constancie and fortitude, have hitherto indured most cruell persecutions and almost infinite miseries, that they may walke without spot in the Law of the Lord; will never suffer themselves to be defiled with the communion of those that have forsaken divine Law. . . . As likewise you cannot, without most evident and grievous wronging of Gods Honour, bind your selves by the Oath, which in like manner we have heard with very great griefe of our heart is administered unto you.[17]

According to Pope Paul V's letter, taking James I's Oath would cause "evident and grievous wrongdoing to God's honor" and incur eternal punishment. This choice between enduring cruel persecution and compromising one's faith thankfully seems foreign to most of us, but it puts *The Winter's Tale* in its proper historical context. Such matters always have eternal consequences but they also had dire temporal consequences in Shakespeare's England. The depictions of plots and oaths in the play thus provide additional timely links between James I and Leontes, and Pope Paul V and Camillo.

Accusations of Treason

James I and Leontes naturally met with opposition from their subjects in response to their demands for allegiance. The two kings responded to such opposition in similar fashion, by accusing those who opposed their wills of treason.

The indictment for treason read against Hermione shows how rapidly and extensively Leontes's madness progresses within a few scenes:

> Hermione, Queen to the worthy Leontes, king of Sicilia, thou art here accused and arraigned of high treason, in committing adultery with Polixenes, King of Bohemia, and conspiring with Camillo to take away the life of our sovereign lord the King, thy royal husband; the pretense whereof being by circumstances partly laid open, thou, Hermione, contrary to the faith and allegiance of a true subject, dids't counsel and aid them, for their better safety, to fly away by night.
>
> (3.2.12-21)

Leontes accuses Hermione of high treason for committing adultery with Polixenes and conspiring with Camillo. Neither basis for the accusation of treason has any merit. Leontes makes similarly baseless accusations against all who support Hermione in opposition to his will: Leontes exclaims "Traitors!" (2.3.73) when Paulina presents Perdita; and he calls those present "a nest of traitors!" (2.3.82) just a few lines later. Shakespeare makes these accusations of treason a distinctive feature of the king's madness.

Just as Leontes condemns support of Hermione as treason, James I saw support of the Catholic Church as treason. The king accused Catholics of treason even before the discovery of the Gunpowder Plot. Fr. Oswald Tesimond related of the plotters that:

> Those gentlemen heard from day to day how the king grew more incensed against the Catholics, and the sort of language he used against them at all times and in all places. In particular, he was used to calling them traitors. This is the name which is hated in England more

than anything else, and more, perhaps, than in other lands. This was for no reason other than the profession of their religion. Indeed, the king would often end his talk by saying that anyone who knew what was due to his native country and still believed in the articles of faith of the Roman Church could not be a loyal subject.[18]

Although English law had an expansive definition of treason, mere belief in Catholicism fell outside the scope of the law. However, acting in accordance with such beliefs too often fell within the scope of the law.

Defending the Oath, James I wrote that he did not intend to force Catholics to abandon their religion but wanted the Oath to separate traitors from good subjects:

> To the end that I might hereby make a separation, not onely betweene all my good Subjects in generall, and unfaithfull Traitors, that intended to withdraw themselves from my obedience; But specially to make a separation betweene so many of my Subjects, who although they were otherwise Popishly affected, yet retained in their hearts the print of their natural dueties to their Soveraigne.[19]

Thus, James might consider a "Popishly affected" Englishman to be a good subject, rather than a traitor, but *only* if he or she took the Oath.

Modern readers likely consider James I's views of "Catholic treason" to be just as spurious as Leontes's accusations of treason. Shakespeare certainly seems to have shared that view, and he offers a much more sophisticated view of what constitutes real treason. Paulina responds to the accusation of treason by turning it against Leontes, saying that none are traitors except the king himself:

> LEONTES
>   A nest of traitors!
> ANTIGONUS
>   I am none, by this good light.
> PAULINA
>   Nor I, nor any
>   But one that's here, and that's himself; for he

> The sacred honor of himself, his queen's,
> His hopeful son's, his babe's, betrays to slander,
> Whose sting is sharper than the sword's; and will not –
> For, as the case now stands, it is a curse
> He cannot be compelled to't – once remove
> The root of his opinion, which is rotten
> As ever oak or stone was sound.
>
> (2.3.82-91)

For Leontes, anyone who disagrees with his opinion is a traitor. Paulina, on the other hand, considers Leontes to be a traitor to the extent that he betrays the "sacred honor" of himself and his royal household. She thus makes "sacred honor" the measure of fidelity. In doing so, she asserts that God, and not the king, has fixed the laws and truths that Leontes (and all others) must follow. More particularly, Paulina tells the king that he has become a traitor by slandering the sacred honor of himself and his royal household. And we can infer that Paulina appeals to Leontes using such language because he too understands the need to uphold the sacred honor.

James I would likely have understood the concept of his "sacred honor." He wrote extensively of the king's duty to follow God's law above all else in his *Basilicon Doron* (written to his son, Henry):

> As he cannot be thought worthy to rule and command others, that cannot rule and dantone his owne proper affections and unreasonable appetites, so can he not be thought worthie to governe a Christian people, knowing and fearing God, that in his owne person and heart, feareth not and loveth not Divine Majestie. Neither can any thing in his government succeed well with him, (devise and labour as he list) as coming from a filthie spring, if his person be unsanctified: for (as the royal Prophet saith) *Except the Lord build the house, they labour in vaine that build it: except the Lord keep the City, the keepers watch it in vaine.*[20]

Given King James I's keen sense that he must act in accordance with God's laws, we can imagine that he might have concurred with Paulina's argument to Leontes that a king is a traitor when he acts against his sacred honor.

While Paulina's appeal to the king's sacred honor seems relatively straightforward, the latter part of her speech is considerably more difficult to understand at first glance. After lecturing Leontes on how he betrays his sacred honor, Paulina adds a parenthetical comment: "For, as the case now stands, it is a curse/ He cannot be compelled to't." What is the "it" to which "he" cannot be compelled? And why does Paulina seemingly interrupt herself to opine on it? The note to the Bevington version of the play explains the lines to mean: "since he is King, he regrettably can't be compelled to change his deeply rooted opinion." This clever explanation is theoretically possible. But it does not account for the apparent randomness of Paulina's comment, so it leads us to believe that Shakespeare was rather clumsy with his language.

The allegorical reading offers a more sensible and satisfying interpretation. The "it" in the allegorical reading corresponds to Leontes's demands that Antigonus take up Perdita to dispose of her. As we will see in a subsequent chapter, Leontes ultimately compels Antigonus to dispose of Perdita by demanding his allegiance. All of this relates allegorically to the Oath. Paulina says Antigonus ("he") cannot be compelled to take the Leontes's oath because it is a curse. Likewise, Catholics could not take the Oath of James I because it was like a curse, as we saw from the words of Pope Paul V in the previous chapter: "As likewise you cannot, without most evident and grievous wronging of Gods Honour, bind your selves by the Oath."

This transition from the discussion of Leontes to a discussion about Antigonus within the middle of Paulina's speech appears random but it follows from her statement that the sting of the king's slander is sharper than the sting of the sword. Later in the scene, Antigonus puts his hands on the hilt of Leontes's sword as he swears to perform the king's bidding. Accordingly, we can read Paulina's lines to mean that Antigonus cannot be compelled to take the Oath (which is a curse) and that the sting of the sword (e.g., the punishment for his disobedience) is not as sharp as the sting caused by the king violating his sacred honor. She thus denounces Leontes while encouraging her husband to resist the king's threats.

Paulina continues by saying that Leontes's opinion is rotten "as ever oak or stone was sound" (2.3.90-91). Paulina contrasts Leontes's rotten opinion with the soundness of oak and stone, but there is something odd about the comparison. Even though we typically imagine stone and oak to be very hard and solid, either can become unsound (the oak by rotting, for instance). If, in other words, we think of oak and stone literally as physical objects, Paulina's reasoning seems fundamentally flawed.

Again, we can find more meaning in the allegorical context. As Clare Asquith notes, oak is a symbol of England in Shakespeare's plays.[21] As one illustration of how "sound" England is, we can consider the praise of Pope Paul V in encouraging English Catholics to resist the Oath. In his first of two letters, the pope writes:

> Truely wee doe undoubtedly beleeve, that they which with so great constancie and fortitude, have hitherto indured most cruell persecutions and almost infinite miseries, that they may walke without spot in the Law of the Lord; will never suffer themselves to be defiled with the communion of those that have forsaken the divine Law.[22]

Here the pope highlights the fortitude of English Catholics in enduring cruel persecutions so as to remain faithful to their religion. In the second letter, the pope emphasizes another aspect of their strength:

> Surely this newes did trouble us and that so much the more, because having had experience of your obedience (most dearely beloved sonnes) who to the end ye might obey this holy Sea, have godlily and valiantly contemned your riches, wealth, honour, libertie, yea and life it selfe.[23]

For the sake of obeying the guidance of the popes, the English Catholics valiantly sacrificed so much. Thus, following the praise of Pope Paul V, we may take Paulina's words allegorically for the notion that although James I's false opinions about the Church may hurt himself and certain people who follow him, the character of the faithful English Catholics will remain sound.

But what does Paulina's reference to the stone mean? In the Gospels, Christ is the "stone which the builders rejected" (Matthew 21.42, Mark 12.10, Luke 20.17). Because Hermione represents the Mystical Body of Christ, she corresponds to the stone. Hermione will also be the "dear stone" in Act V and seeing her contrasted with Leontes makes perfect sense here.

Thus, allegorically, James I's opinion is rotten while both the Mystical Body of Christ (the Catholic Church) and England are sound. From a Catholic perspective, James I had betrayed his sacred honor by ignoring the counsel of the Catholic Church, which had helped guide English monarchs for centuries prior to Henry VIII. So although James I accused Catholics of treason for their beliefs, he was the one who had truly earned the title of traitor.

Would any in Shakespeare's England have found meaning in this interpretation? Judging from the words of St. Edmund Campion, it seems almost certain:

> There shall never want in England men that will have care of their own salvation, nor such as shall advance other men's; neither shall the Church here ever fail so long as priests and pastors shall be found for their sheep, rage man or devil never so much. For what have we taught, however you may qualify it with the odious name of treason, that they did not uniformly teach? . . . God lives; posterity will live; their judgment is not so liable to corruption as that of those who are now going to sentence us to death.[24]

The saint sets the same battle lines as Paulina does: those with care for their salvation in England (oak), and the Church (stone), vie against the rotten opinions of man (Leontes). Ultimately, despite the attacks of those like James I, there will always be faithful Catholics in England so long as there are priests to tend to the flock. Paulina and St. Edmund

Campion measured accusations of treason not against the whims of the king but against the same truth that the king has a sacred honor to protect. Such has been the formula of martyrs throughout the history of Christianity.

Tyranny and Heresy

Before considering the question of tyranny, it is worth acknowledging two factors that might soften our view of King James I's treatment of Catholics. First, his England had long used harsh laws to coerce citizens to conform to the prevailing religion – James I certainly put his own stamp on this practice, but he and others were quick to defend his record by citing Queen Mary's treatment of Protestants during her short reign. Second, although his justifications for his persecution of his Catholic subjects seem complicated at best (and at times completely disingenuous), he does at least consider that they too may act with sincerity in trying to follow their consciences. He does not, in other words, merely assume that all Catholics are knaves bent on destroying the government.

Granting this, Shakespeare and many of his contemporaries seem to judge the question of James I's tyranny the same way we in the modern Western world would view similar restraints on *peaceful* practice of religion. In his speeches before Parliament and in his writings, James I devoted a fair amount of attention to defending himself against these accusations. Although one may argue that the need to repeatedly defend himself against allegations of tyranny speaks volumes against the king, it is worth examining his arguments in some detail. And to appreciate his complex arguments, it helps to first consider how Shakespeare portrays the conflict allegorically.

Leontes's indictment accuses Hermione of "acting contrary to the faith" of a true subject. We may easily pass over the importance of these words, but upon reflection they seem odd: what is "the faith" of a true subject and how does it connect to the accusation of treason? Shakespeare makes it clear that Hermione remains a "true subject" throughout the play, and never wavers in her beliefs. Leontes, on the other hand, loses his faith in Hermione's goodness and then requires that all share his mistaken judgments about her. It seems, then, that a "true subject" must change his or her beliefs (or faith) to match that of the king or else commit treason. When, as in this case, the king's faith is mistaken and he threatens those who disagree with him, he is undeniably a tyrant. Not surprisingly, the judgment of the oracle confirms this (3.2.133).

To what extent did James I require his "true subjects" to adhere to his religion? Perhaps the most remarkable aspect of James I's treatment of Catholics was his insistence on following his own conscience by forcing his Catholic subjects to betray their consciences:

> But of one thing would I have the Papists of this Land to bee admonished, That they presume not so much upon my Lenitie (because I would be loathe to be thought a Persecuter) as thereupon to thinke it lawfull for them to dayly increase their number and strength in this Kingdome, whereby if not in my time, at least in the time of my posteritie, they might be in hope to erect their Religion again. No, let them assure themselves, that as I am a friend to their persons if they be good subjects: so am I a vowed enemie, and doe denounce mortall warre to their errors: and that as I would be sory to be driven by their ill behavior from the protection and conservation of their bodies and lives; So will I never cease as farre as I can, to tread down their errors and wrong opinions. For I could not permit the encrease and growing of their Religion, without first betraying my selfe, and mine owne conscience.[25]

What is the ill behavior of these Catholics? What were their errors that the king needed to "tread down?" Their religion was, of course, the religion of virtually all Christians in England prior to Henry VIII. From the Catholic perspective, James I's persecution of the Church naturally seemed as tyrannous as Leontes's persecution of Hermione and her supporters. England's Catholics had simply maintained the same religious beliefs that their ancestors had held. They became "traitors" when the monarchs, beginning with Henry VIII, adhered to another religion. If one follows the logic of the king's arguments, it seems that Catholics in England were wrong for the same reason Hermione and her supporters were wrong: each made the critical mistake of maintaining their beliefs when their king had changed his.

In defending his "behaviour toward the Papists," the king makes an interesting comparison between his rule and that of his predecessor, Queen Elizabeth I:

> I may trewly affirme, that whatsoever was her just and mercifull governement over the Papists in her time, my governement over them since hath so farre exceeded hers, in mercie and clemencie, as not onely the Papists themselves grewe to that height of pride, in confidence of my mildnesse, as they did directly expect, as assuredly promise themselves libertie of conscience.[26]

James I argues that though his predecessor was merciful, he had been much more so as evidenced by the fact that his Catholic subjects actually began to expect liberty of conscience. He calls it the "height of pride" for Catholics to expect liberty of conscience. So while the king would at times suggest that he had no intention to persecute Catholics because they followed their consciences, he certainly placed rather low value on their consciences.

In 1608, Fr. Robert Persons, S.J., wrote of this in *The Judgment of a Catholic Englishman Living in Banishment for His Religion*:

> Surely, I cannot but wonder, that this Minister was not ashamed to call this the height of pride, which is generally found in all Protestants never so humble: yea the more humble ... the more earnestly are they both in bookes, speaches, and preachings, to prove that liberty of Conscience is most conforme to Gods law, and that wresting, or forcing of Consciences, is the highest Tyranny, that have be exercised upon man.[27]

Fr. Persons (sometimes spelled Parsons) accompanied St. Edmund Campion on the mission to England but escaped martyrdom. When he wrote that forcing of consciences is the highest tyranny, he did so as a man who had risked his life in England under that tyranny.

Clearly James I understood that it might appear that he persecuted Catholics because of their religion. In defense against such accusations, he developed a fairly nuanced justification for his governance:

> I doe constantly maintaine that which I have said in my Apologie: That no man, either in my time, or in the late Queenes, ever died here for his conscience. For let him be never so devout a Papist, nay, though he professe the same never so constantly, his life is in no danger by the Law, if he breake not out into some outward acte expressly against the words of the Law.[28]

James I asserted that he never persecuted Catholics based on their religion; he rather persecuted them because they broke the laws that forbade active practice of their religion. It almost goes without saying, though, that a Catholic cannot in good conscience decide to not act as a Catholic. Acting in accordance with their consciences required them to act in ways "expressly against the words of the law." Their consciences required them to attend Mass and receive the Catholic sacraments when they had an opportunity to do so. But, as we saw above, James I called it the "height of pride" for Catholics to feel entitled to liberty of conscience.

Like James I, Leontes dismisses the accusation of tyranny with the same nod to the fact that he lets the justice system act in the persecution of the innocent:

> Let us be cleared
> Of being tyrannous, since we openly
> Proceed in justice, which shall have due course,
> Even to the guilt or purgation.
>
> (3.2.4-7)

Leontes alone accuses Hermione of adultery and treason and he ultimately rejects the oracle's judgment that Hermione is chaste. Throughout Act III, Leontes attempts to "force consciences," but believes he proceeds in justice because he essentially makes it the law that his subjects must agree with him about Hermione. As he says, he believes this process should clear him of "being tyrannous." Shakespeare makes it evident in several ways, though, that Leontes was being both unjust and tyrannical.

Thus, we can apply to Leontes what St. Robert Bellarmine wrote of King James I:

> In deciding whether a man is a martyr, it matters little whether he was killed because he professed the Catholic faith, or because he broke the Law which commanded him to renounce the same. It was an old trick of the pagan Roman Emperors to make a law against the Christian Religion, and then murder men, not intolerantly on account of religion, of course, but for offending the majesty of the constitution.[29]

St. Robert Bellarmine highlights the hypocrisy of the practice adopted by James I and Leontes. Even more importantly, he focuses on what makes a martyr – dying for profession of the Faith. The cloak of "justice" neither robs the martyr of his or her crown nor absolves the tyrant of his sin. Shakespeare and St. Robert Bellarmine are saying the same thing about Leontes and James I, respectively.

So James I faced accusations he was a tyrant, but he also had to respond to claims from Catholics that he was a heretic. According to St. Thomas Aquinas, a heretic "intends to assent to Christ, yet he fails in his choice of those things wherein he assents to Christ, because he chooses not what Christ really taught, but the suggestions of his own mind."[30] Shakespeare portrays Leontes as one who desperately wants to know and adhere to the truth. And yet the Sicilian king rejects the clear truth about Hermione in favor of the unsound "suggestions of his own mind." He does so while sincerely believing that he is right and that everyone else is wrong.

James I naturally rejected claims that he was a heretic, writing that, "I am sure none will condemn me for an Heretike, save such as make the Pope their God."[31] The king certainly knew that Catholics do not literally consider (or make) the pope to be God. James I also realized that England's Christians prior to Henry VIII were Catholic. Whether or not he cared to admit it, he should have also recognized that his religious beliefs would have been foreign at any time in the history of England prior to Henry VIII. As such, his views would have been deemed heretical by the vast majority of knowledgeable Christians throughout the history of England prior to Henry VIII.

Nonetheless, James I insisted that he professed the true religion, and that Catholics were in error:

> At my first coming, although I found but one Religion, and that which by my selfe is professed, publickely allowed, and by the Law maintained: yet found I another sort of Religion, besides a private sect, lurking within the bowels of this Nation. The first is the trew Religion, which by me is professed, and by the Law is established: the second is the falsely called Catholics, but trewly Papists: the third, which I call a sect rather than religion, is the Puritanes and Novelists.[32]

Thus James I and Catholics considered each other to be heretics. Unfortunately for English Catholics at the time Shakespeare wrote *The Winter's Tale*, James I's religion was the one established by law.

In the play, Leontes also faces the accusation that he is a heretic, a title that he earns by doubting the innocence of Hermione:

> LEONTES
>   I'll ha' thee burnt.
> PAULINA
>   I care not:
>   It is an heretic that makes the fire,
>   Not she which burns in't. I'll not call you tyrant;
>   But this most cruel usage of your queen,
>   Not able to produce more accusation
>   Than your own weak-hinged fancy, something savors
>   Of tyranny and will ignoble make you,
>   Yea, scandalous to the world.
>   (2.3.114-121)

As with the reciprocal accusations of heresy between James I and Catholics, Paulina asserts that she is not a heretic but Leontes is. And, Paulina's response is no mere rhetorical jab, for Camillo has already made it clear that Leontes's madness is grounded on his faith, corresponding to the charge of heresy. Paulina brings the moment back to the religious drama of Shakespeare's England, where Catholics who openly practiced their religion were deemed by James I to be heretics, and put to death in the most gruesome ways.

If we substitute the word "queen" for "Catholic Church" in Paulina's speech – "this most cruel usage of the *Catholic Church*" – we can imagine the same sentiment on the lips of all Catholics who refused to take the Oath. We can also imagine that when Paulina tells Leontes his persecution of Hermione will make him "scandalous to the world" (2.3.121), many in the audience saw an unfortunate resemblance to the international paper war King James I ignited with his Oath of Allegiance. From the perspective of Catholics, James I did unfortunately become scandalous to the world through his vehement attacks on the Catholic Church.

Finally, it is worth reflecting on the strikingly edifying nature of Paulina's response, "I care not:/ It is an heretic that makes the fire/ Not she which burns in it" (2.3.114-116). She does not care if Leontes has her burnt, so long as she is not an heretic.[33] Like all of us, Paulina knows she must die at some point – but she realizes that dying as a saint, rather than as a heretic, matters far more than the sufferings one might endure while dying. We can see in her words an unmistakable echo of Christ's warning to His apostles: "And fear ye not them that kill the body, and are not able to kill the soul: but rather fear him that can destroy both the soul and body in hell" (Matthew 10.28).

Fr. James Brodrick relates the story of a Jesuit priest faced with the oath in 1608, St. Thomas Garnet:

> His is a very explicit case, as among the great throng assembled at Tyburn to see him die was the Earl of Exeter, a member of the Privy Council, "who endeavored to persuade the confessor to save his own

life by taking the Oath, alleging that several priests had taken it, and that many more looked upon it as a disputable matter in which faith was not concerned: why therefore should he be so stiff, and not rather embrace the offer of the King's clemency, by conforming as others had done? Father Thomas replied: "My Lord, if the case be so doubtful and disputable, how can I in conscience swear to what is doubtful as if it were certain? No, I will not take the Oath, though I might have a thousand lives. . . . This new oath is so worded as to contain things quite foreign to allegiance, to which in my opinion no Catholic can with a safe conscience swear."[34]

And so St. Thomas Garnet refused the Oath with safe conscience, choosing instead to die a brutal death. As he rejected the Oath, he exclaimed that he was "the happiest man this day alive."[35] It seems that like Paulina he cared not for the manner of death, for he was dying as a saint.

Antigonus's Decision

In defending Hermione more vigorously than any other characters in the play, Camillo and Paulina represent the two types of English Catholics who would not take King James I's Oath: like Camillo, many had to flee England; like Paulina, others remained and simply accepted the penalties for opposing the Oath. Fr. Brodrick writes that the French ambassador in London, La Boderie, related the following to King Henry IV immediately after the proclamation of the Oath:

> The poor Catholics were still incredibly numerous, and resolved for the greater part in a way almost past belief, to suffer everything rather than give up their religion. . . . Many Catholics are making ready to go into exile, and among them some so old that I think they are seeking foreign shores merely to find there a peaceful grave. It is an admirable thing to see large numbers who are in no wise frightened by all the penalties. I could not have believed that so much fervour and zeal were still to be found in our religion.[36]

La Boderie marvels at how well so many English Catholics maintained their faith in the face of persecution. In a real sense, though, they were simply doing what they should to do as Catholics.

Act II, Scene 3 – Antigonus takes the Oath

Not all Catholics in England, however, resisted the Oath. The most glaring example was Archpriest George Blackwell, who had been appointed head of England's secular clergy (i.e., those who were not members of religious orders such as the Jesuits). Although he initially opposed the Oath, he later changed his mind. Indeed, he had such a prominent role in defending the Oath against the attacks of St. Robert Bellarmine and Pope Paul V that one might reasonably question how these men could believe in the same religion.

The pages that follow set forth the numerous ways in which Shakespeare connects Archpriest Blackwell to Antigonus in the allegory. We shall also see that Shakespeare gives us ample reason to associate Antigonus (and thus Blackwell) with Judas, the model of all clerics who betray Christ and the Church. The table below illustrates Blackwell's central role in the controversy surrounding the Oath.

Date	Event
June 1606	The Oath of Allegiance is issued.
September 22, 1606	Pope Paul V writes to English Catholics condemning the Oath: it "contains many issues that are openly contrary to faith and salvation."
1607	Archpriest Blackwell is imprisoned for his Catholic Faith.
July 7, 1607	Despite initially opposing the Oath, Archpriest Blackwell writes letter from prison to the Catholic priests of England encouraging them to take the Oath.
August 23, 1607	Pope Paul V sends a second letter to English Catholics telling them they cannot take the Oath and expressing his displeasure with Blackwell's support of the Oath and suppression of the pope's first letter.
September 28, 1607	St. Robert Bellarmine writes to Blackwell encouraging him to resist the Oath, even if it leads to martyrdom.
November 13, 1607	Blackwell writes to St. Robert Bellarmine, entreating the Cardinal to be less severe.
January 20, 1608	Blackwell writes another letter to Catholics in England, defending the Oath and criticizing St. Robert Bellarmine.
1608	James I writes *Triplici Nodo, Triplex Cuneus* in defense of the Oath against the letters of Pope Paul V and St. Robert Bellarmine.
January 12, 1613	George Blackwell dies in prison, maintaining his defense of the Oath.

In the eyes of the pope and St. Robert Bellarmine, Archpriest Blackwell was throwing out the Faith by taking and defending the Oath. He thereby jeopardized his own soul and the souls of his followers. In a letter that Blackwell refused to promulgate to English Catholics, Pope Paul V wrote:

> Such an Oath cannot be taken without hurting of the Catholike Faith and the salvation of your soules; seeing it conteines many things which are flat contrary to Faith and Salvation.[37]

St. Robert Bellarmine's letter to Blackwell also made it clear that Catholics could not take the Oath:

> For if you will diligently weigh the whole matter with your selfe, trewly you shall see, it is no small matter that is called in question by this Oath, but one of the principall heads of our faith, and foundations of Catholicke Religion.[38]

Even if one thought the Oath did not contain matters that opposed the Catholic Faith, the fact that the pope and Cardinal Bellarmine had written in such strong terms would have made it difficult for a Catholic to take the Oath with safe conscience. By encouraging Catholics to take the Oath, Blackwell created a distinct crisis for those who saw it as their duty to adhere to the guidance of the Catholic hierarchy, especially the pope.

Fascinatingly, Blackwell's initial opposition to the Oath matches Antigonus's history in the play. Antigonus was among the first who opposed Leontes:

> Be certain what you do, sir, lest your justice
> Prove violence, in which three great ones suffer:
> Yourself, your queen, your son.
> (2.1.128-130)

Antigonus defends the honor of Hermione against her husband's unjust allegations of infidelity. While Antigonus's subsequent change of heart makes him a more tragic character in the play, Shakespeare could have omitted this initial opposition without much, if any, detriment to the literal meaning. By building this into Antigonus's character, though, he strengthens the connection to Blackwell, who initially opposed the Oath.

Similarly, Antigonus initially has good intentions with respect to Perdita, saying he would "pawn the little blood" he has left "to save the innocent" (2.3.166-167). Within a few lines of this heroic sentiment, though, he agrees to follow Leontes's awful command:

> We enjoin thee,
> As thou art liegeman to us, that thou carry
> This female bastard hence, and that thou bear it
> To some remote desert place quite out
> Of our dominions, and that there thou leave it,
> Without more mercy.
> (2.3.173-178)

Leontes does not demand that Antigonus kill Perdita, yet he does command him to leave her for dead.

Antigonus immediately understands the awful result of his allegiance to Leontes:

> I swear to do this, though a present death
> Had been more merciful. – Come on, poor babe.
> Some powerful spirit instruct the kites and ravens
> To be thy nurses! Wolves and bears, they say,
> Casting their savageness aside, have done
> Like offices of pity. – Sir, be prosperous
> In more than this deed does require! – And blessing
> Against this cruelty fight on thy side,
> Poor thing, condemned to loss!
> (2.3.184-192)

Shepherd and Clown later rescue Perdita, but when Antigonus swears allegiance to Leontes he believes the infant is "condemned to loss" and that he is the instrument of the king's cruelty. These lines come just a few lines after Antigonus has said he would do anything, including give his own blood, to save Perdita.

What causes Antigonus to abandon his resolve to help Perdita? Within the context of the play, the only plausible explanation is that Leontes tells Antigonus that he and his wife will die if he breaks his oath (2.3.170-172). Thus, the reality of the possible punishment made him waver in his resolve.

What caused Blackwell to change his mind about the Oath? In his July 7, 1607 letter from prison to Catholic priests, he writes:

> But the urging supereminent point was, to knowe, whether I had altered, or reteined still the continuance of my former opinion about the lawfulnesse of taking the Oath of Allegiance: For answere; finding what hatred, and iealoufnesse wee haue incurred, in the opinion of his Maiesty and the State, for the refusall of the Oath; and thereupon making a review of the reasons, drawing mee into the former publike approbation thereof.[39]

So Blackwell reconsidered his reasoning after discovering how much hatred Catholics had incurred from the king and government for their refusal to take the Oath. Later in this letter, he encourages the priests to instruct the faithful to take the Oath so that they will not lose their estates. Of this path of taking the Oath he says, "surely this will bring us gaine, and increase of many comforts."

What did Blackwell think of the other path, the one taken by St. Thomas Garnet who chose a gruesome death rather than the Oath, saying, "I will not take the Oath, though I might have a thousand lives"? In his letter to the Catholics of England, Blackwell wrote: "Deceive not therefore your selves (brethren) such sufferings are not the way to Martyrdome, nor approved of God." He initially opposed the Oath. Under examination from those who hated Catholicism, however, he was "enlightened" to reject the unambiguous guidance of the pope and the highly respected Cardinal Bellarmine, as well as the examples of the saints who chose death over compromise with the Catholic Faith.

It is important to note that in his letters to Bellarmine and English Catholics Blackwell does not address the most contentious lines of the Oath: "I do from my heart abhor, detest, and abjure, as impious and heretical this damnable doctrine and position, that princes which be excommunicated by the pope may be deposed . . ." As Stefania Tutino observes:

> Blackwell obviously chose his words with extreme care. Not only was there no trace of the adjectives "impious and hereticall", but he left out even the adjective "unlawfull". . . . The fact that the archpriest passed over such grave theoretical questions posed by the oath becomes more comprehensible by the end of the letter.[40]

Tutino goes on to note that Blackwell's letter ends with appeals to the temporal hardships to be avoided by taking the Oath. It is hard to imagine that Blackwell's letters would have been especially helpful for those Catholics who wanted actual guidance on the legitimacy of taking an Oath that declared the deposing power to be impious, heretical and damnable. Catholics in England would have understood the temporal cost of not taking the Oath, so to speak; what they needed to know was the *eternal* cost of taking the Oath. Opposing the pope and Cardinal Bellarmine, Blackwell completely dismissed these eternal costs. Indeed, his encouragement seems rather like the arguments non-Catholics would make to the martyrs on the scaffold to get them to abandon just a portion of their religion to save their lives.

As Antigonus arrives in Bohemia at the end of Act III, he recounts the words Hermione had told him in his dream the previous evening:

> Good Antigonus,
> Since fate, against thy better disposition,
> Hath made thy person for the thrower-out
> Of my poor babe, according to thine oath,
> Places remote enough are in Bohemia;

> There weep and leave it crying. And, for the babe
> Is counted lost forever, Perdita,
> I prithee, call't. For this ungentle business,
> Put on thee by my lord, thou ne'er shalt see
> Thy wife Paulina more.
>
> (3.3.26-35)

Antigonus "throws out" Hermione's poor babe, Perdita, against his better disposition, because he adheres to his oath to Leontes. Although Leontes imposes the "ungentle business" on Antigonus, Antigonus is still responsible for his actions.

The appearance from Hermione does nothing to change Antigonus's course. After he lays the baby on the ground, his speech shows the perplexing state of his conscience:

> The storm begins. Poor wretch,
> That for thy mother's fault art thus exposed
> To loss and what may follow! Weep I cannot,
> But my heart bleeds; and most accurst am I
> To be by oath enjoined to this.
>
> (3.3.48-52)

He sees himself as accursed to be following his oath and yet he blames the innocent Hermione for Perdita's fate. He does not merely choose to do the wrong thing through fear of the consequences that follow doing the right thing. Rather, he allows his fear of disobeying Leontes to change his practical conception of right and wrong. Of course nothing about Hermione's innocence has changed since the scene in which Antigonus vigorously defended her honor.

Blackwell's letter to Cardinal Bellarmine shows a similar interplay of blame, adherence to oaths, and lamentable fates:

> Besides, if your Amplitudes most mild disposition could but in the least part conceive the ruines of Catholicke families, which the refusall of this othe would bring upon us; assuredly you would not dissent from us, who by most wofull examples doe finde, that from thence

were like to proceede, not onely the losse and hazard of soules, but the lamentable extirpation of the whole Catholicke state amongst us.[41]

Antigonus faced the king's wrath if he broke his oath, so he disposed of Perdita. Blackwell feared the king's wrath if he did not take the Oath, so he went against his initial judgment of the Oath and the clear guidance from the pope and Cardinal Bellarmine. And just as Antigonus blames Hermione for the fate of Perdita, Blackwell essentially blamed the Catholic Church for the fate of Catholics in England.

The play provides a quick judgment of Antigonus's actions, as he says "I am gone forever," and with one of the more remarkable stage directions in Shakespeare's plays, he exits "pursued by a bear" (3.3.57). Thus, the harshest condemnation of a character in the play is not of Leontes, who in his madness causes so much destruction, but of Antigonus who *knowingly* commits an evil act that conflicts with his "better disposition."

Shakespeare mitigates Antigonus's guilt by allowing him to be both enjoined by an oath and confused about the actual merits of the king's judgment. One could argue that Archpriest Blackwell's guilt for taking the Oath was mitigated in the same way. Yet, within the allegory, Shakespeare makes the argument that being confused and bound by an oath will not be enough at the time of judgment. St. Robert Bellarmine was trying to make the same point to poor Blackwell.

As Antigonus dies on land, his crew perishes at sea:

FIRST GENTLEMAN
    What became of his bark and his followers?
THIRD GENTLEMAN
    Wrecked the same instant of their
    master's death and in view of the shepherd; so that
    all the instruments which aided to expose the child
    were even then lost when it was found.
                        (5.2.68-73)

Antigonus is the "master" of his "bark" and those travelling with him are his "followers," rather than simply his crew or companions. The idea that Antigonus led his followers to their demise strongly suggests that his allegorical counterpart must have led or encouraged others to take the Oath. This points to Archpriest Blackwell, who arguably did more than any other person in England to encourage Catholics to take the Oath.

St. Thomas More's *The Sadness of Christ*, which he wrote while awaiting his execution in 1535, includes a similar image. Commenting on Judas, and warning against keeping bad company, the saint wrote:

> It rarely happens that a person who is foolish enough to cast his lot with those who are headed for shipwreck in an unseaworthy vessel get back to land alive after the others have drowned in the sea.[42]

St. Thomas More invokes the imagery of the unseaworthy vessel in implicit contrast to the bark of St. Peter. St. Peter, as head of the apostles, steers a seaworthy bark; Judas, the unworthy apostle, does not. While we may doubt whether Shakespeare knew this precise quote from St. Thomas More, the imagery of Judas leading his followers to destruction in his "bark" flows naturally from the notion of St. Peter guiding the followers in his bark to heaven.

Shakespeare indirectly invites the audience to see the comparison between Antigonus and Judas by having Polixenes declare that if he had betrayed Hermione his name would have been yoked with his who did "betray the Best" (1.2.418). Because Polixenes suggests that betraying Hermione would be similar to Judas betraying Christ (the Best), it follows that Antigonus becomes a Judas figure when he betrays Hermione.

Shakespeare also provides more direct indications that he intended the connection between Antigonus and Judas. As we saw above, Antigonus's despair is evident:

> Weep I cannot,
> But my heart bleeds; and most accurst am I

> To be by oath enjoined to this. Farewell!
> (3.3.50-52)

Like Judas, who in anguish sought to return the thirty pieces of silver and then hanged himself, Antigonus sees the need for sorrow but has by this point completely lost hope and given up on repentance. He dies an accursed death.

Comparisons to Judas are especially meaningful (and damning) because the Catholic Church has traditionally taught that Judas is in hell. This conclusion follows naturally from the words of Christ:

> The Son of man indeed goeth, as it is written of him: but woe to that man by whom the Son of man shall be betrayed: it were better for him, if that man had not been born.
> (Matthew 26.24)

Any man who ends up in Heaven is better off than if he had not been born, so Judas cannot be in Heaven. Christ also says that He has kept all those whom the Father had given Him except "the son of perdition" (John 17.12).

An early line from Paulina foresees the unholy death that, like Judas, her husband will ultimately experience:

> Forever
> Unvenerable be thy hands if thou
> Tak'st up the Princess by that forced baseness
> Which he has put upon't!
> (2.3.77-80)

In Catholic theology, the relics of saints are "venerable," worthy of veneration because the saints have won salvation and are in heaven. The Council of Trent thus commanded bishops to instruct the faithful that:

> The holy bodies of the saints and also of the martyrs and of others living with Christ, who were the living "members of Christ and the images of the Holy Spirit," which are to be awakened with Him to

eternal life and to be glorified, are to be venerated by the faithful, through which many benefits are bestowed by God on men."[43]

When Paulina warns Antigonus that his hands will be "forever unvenerable" if he follows through on his oath to Leontes to dispose of Perdita, she effectively says that he will not make it to heaven if he makes the wrong decision. This warning correlates with Hermione's pronouncement in Antigonus's dream that he shall never see his wife again (3.3.34-35). Paulina, who allegorically represents St. Paul, will make it to heaven, and will not find her husband there.

In the context of abundant Christian imagery throughout the play, this fatal despair of Antigonus, Paulina's warning, and Hermione's judgment stand apart as uniquely terrifying precisely because they match the unrepentant despair and accompanying judgment of Judas. Shakespeare clearly wanted the audience to understand the wickedness of Antigonus's actions by showing the horror of his death.

Hermione's greeting to Antigonus in his dream – "good Antigonus" – provides another parallel to Judas. There is something paradoxical about Hermione beginning her speech with the sign of friendship and then describing the evil consequences of "throwing out" Perdita. We see a similar paradox in Christ's words after Judas has betrayed Him in the Garden of Gethsemane:

> And he that betrayed him, gave them a sign, saying: Whomsoever I shall kiss, that is he, hold him fast. And Jesus said to him: Friend, whereto art thou come? Then they came up, and laid hands on Jesus, and held him.
>
> (Matthew 26.48-49)

Christ refers to Judas as "friend" even though He knows that Judas has betrayed Him.

Shakespeare provides additional support for Judas comparison in the naming of "Antigonus," which means "against his ancestors." Although we do not know Antigonus's literal ancestry, we know from Hermione that he has acted against his better disposition. In contrast, Camillo and

Paulina act in accordance with their "better dispositions." Likewise, Judas shared the "spiritual ancestry" of the Apostles, those chosen by Christ. He acted against his ancestors, in that sense, by betraying Christ. From the perspective of Catholics in England, their ancestors had for centuries adhered to the spiritual direction of the pope, and those who abandoned their Faith acted against their ancestors. Blackwell in particular would fit this description because he acted in the name of the Church through his position as archpriest.

We can recognize this concept of acting against one's Catholic ancestors in the words of St. Edmund Campion upon learning of his death sentence:

> In condemning us you condemn all your own ancestors – all the ancient priests, bishops and kings – all that was once the glory of England, the isle of saints, and the most devoted child of the See of Peter.[44]

Catholics in England faced Antigonus's decision every time they expressed their faith openly. Without a doubt they were tempted to decide, as Antigonus did, to go against their better dispositions to preserve their freedom, if not their lives. But, following the counsel of Pope Paul V and St. Robert Bellarmine, and the example of the English Martyrs, many chose to follow the faith of their ancestors. Unfortunately, Blackwell abandoned the faith of his ancestors and encouraged his followers to do the same.

The Judas imagery further supports the connection between Antigonus and Archpriest Blackwell because Judas was the first priest to betray Christ and thus a sad model for those who follow him in betrayal. Indeed, if Shakespeare truly intended the comparison between Judas and Antigonus, the allegorical implication becomes less harsh when we see Antigonus as Blackwell rather than as simply any Catholic taking the Oath. After all, Blackwell occupied a position of responsibility and "unto whomsoever much is given, of him much shall be required" (Luke 12.48).

St. Robert Bellarmine provides more insight into this connection between Judas and clerics who betray the Church:

> For Judas was an apostle of Christ and, thus, named a bishop.... When Judas, the most unhappy of all men, had fallen from the high state of perfection, he lost even the small gain he had so wickedly acquired by giving it back. Having become his own executioner and having been condemned to everlasting punishment, he can serve as an example for all clerics and religious so that they see how they should walk and what dangers threaten them if they do not measure up to the perfection of their state by living a holy life.[45]

We can see this in the allegory, as Blackwell receives the far harsher punishment than his followers because he is their "master."

The details of Antigonus's death add to this idea that clerics have greater responsibility and face more dire consequences for betraying their religion. Clown describes Antigonus's encounter with the bear:

> And then for the land service, to see how
> the bear tore out his shoulder bone; how he cried to
> me for help and said his name was Antigonus, a no-
> bleman. But to make an end of the ship: to see how
> the ship flapdragoned it! But first, how the poor souls
> roared and the sea mocked them, and how the poor
> gentleman roared and the bear mocked him, both
> roaring louder than sea or weather.
> (3.3.92-99)

The bear tore out Antigonus's shoulder bone, which is a fascinating detail that is easy to ignore in the literal reading of the play. The detail becomes more relevant when we read St. Robert Bellarmine's description of one aspect of the Mystical Body of Christ:

> We are accustomed to placing burdens on our shoulders, and so also Christ has done, by placing the burden of the Church's government on the shoulders of the Apostles and their priestly successors.[46]

So the Apostles and their priestly successors, such as Archpriest Blackwell, need sturdy shoulders to support the burdens of the Church's government. It would make sense, then, that Shakespeare would have the bear tear out Antigonus's shoulder if he represented a priest who no longer worthily supported the burdens of the Church. Certainly some faithful English Catholics would have considered Archpriest Blackwell unworthy of his responsibility over the secular priests in England because he had encouraged Catholics to take the Oath while the pope had forbidden it. Indeed, he placed his personal judgment (in favor of the king) above that of the pope's clear guidance.

Unlike Judas who takes his own life, Antigonus loses his life "pursued by a bear." Shakespeare provides abundant context to show that this death represents divine judgment. The bear is therefore important in the play, but it should be evident that the allegory would not be lacking in absence of a historical counterpart for the bear. Shakespeare might have chosen any number of ways for Antigonus to meet his end and the audience likely would have understood that he died an accursed death.

That said, an allegorical counterpart for the bear is worth exploring because the possible candidate fits the pattern of how Shakespeare links the dramatic and historic figures throughout the allegory. Of all the figures in the religious events of Shakespeare's England, one has lacked a role in the allegory thus far: St. Robert Bellarmine. As he was neither a bear nor known to have resembled or acted like one, the connection initially seems fairly remote. Nonetheless, there are a few similarities between the saint and the bear that suggest that Shakespeare may have intended the association.

First, the bear has a role in "judging" Antigonus that resembles Bellarmine's role in admonishing Blackwell. The pope designated Cardinal Bellarmine as the one to respond to both James I and Blackwell. In his letter to Blackwell, the saint delivers the judgment of the Church:

> You have fought a good fight a long time, you have wel neare finished your course; so many yeeres have you kept the faith; do not therefore lose the reward of such labors; do not deprive your selfe of that

crowne of righteousnes, which for so long agone is prepared for you;
Do not make the faces of so many yours both brethren and children ashamed.[47]

More than anyone else, St. Robert Bellarmine tried to persuade Archpriest Blackwell that God would judge him unfavorably if he persisted in defending the Oath. Likewise, although Hermione and Paulina strongly suggest that God will not judge Antigonus favorably if he abandons Perdita, it is the bear that confirms their admonitions and removes all doubt. The bear is the most evident adversary for Antigonus in the play just as Bellarmine is the most evident adversary for Blackwell in the religious drama. It follows that if the allegory is a complete reflection of the religious drama in Shakespeare's day, St. Robert Bellarmine ought to be represented as a forceful opponent to Antigonus. The bear fits that description.

Second, Blackwell's letters to and about St. Robert Bellarmine oddly portray him as severe and bloodthirsty. In his letter to Catholics in England defending his position on the Oath against St. Robert Bellarmine, Blackwell writes:

> The voice that bade *Peter, Kill and eate,* neuer meant that hee should deale so with Princes, cast them out of their seates, and bestow their kingdomes vpon others, or procure them to be killed, that Christians and Catholicke religion might flourish and bee comforted. Meats and drinks may establish our strength; but such proceedings with kings ought to be no foode for our soules . . .
>
> Beware therefore of them in whose mouthes and actions *sanguis nihil est,* bloud is nothing.[48]

The first part of this letter strangely insinuates that the pope thinks he should kill and eat princes. As the Cardinal was the principal advocate for the claims of the papacy and target of Blackwell's letter, we can easily extend this imaginary savagery to Bellarmine. The second part of this quote is apparently meant to suggest that Bellarmine has little regard for the blood of Catholics. It seems likely that the saint simply had more regard for the eternal state of souls than for their blood, so to speak. In any case, Blackwell's description would arguably be more fitting for a bear than for the saint.

Additionally, in his earlier letter to St. Robert Bellarmine, Archpriest Blackwell complains about how the Cardinal has treated him by encouraging him to resist the Oath:

> These things have I read with attention; bewailing my case, that such a heape of censorious animadversions is by you compacted against mee, who cannot comprehende or conceive, how any the least detriment may redound unto the Primacie of the supreme Bishop, by that sense which I, with the acceptance of the Magistrate, did propose before the taking of mine Oath.
>
> I doe therefore very humbly intreate your Amplitude, that these so grievous imputations against me, wrought with threedes of an unsuting colour, may be cut asunder, and vanish into smoke.... Bury therefore in silence (I beseech you) all those loude clamors, sounding euery where against me.
>
> I may seeme somewhat too lavish in ripping up these matters before your Amplitude, who (as I trust) will now reduce your severer censure of me and of my fact, to a better temper of equitie and commiseration.[49]

Blackwell accuses St. Robert Bellarmine of engaging in several aggressive behaviors against him: Bellarmine has heaped censorious animadversions, made grievous imputations (wrought with threads of an insulting color), and censured severely. This severity, coupled with the blood-thirst described in the letter to priests, paints a picture of the Cardinal as a being that almost resembles an angry bear. Archpriest Blackwell's complaints about the "loude clamors, sounding everywhere against" him even resemble Antigonus's exclamation when he first notices the bear, "A savage clamor!" (3.3.55).

St. Robert Bellarmine

The third connection derives from the one biographical note we have about the bear: "They are never curst but when they are hungry"

(3.3.126-127). Within Catholicism, there is a common image of holy persons being "hungry for the salvation of souls." We can see one expression of this from St. Robert Bellarmine's *The Seven Last Words Spoken from the Cross*:

> And what was the source of that comfort which He could find none to offer Him, but cooperating with Him for the salvation of souls after which He so ardently longed? This was the one comfort He sought after, this He desired, this He hungered for, this He thirsted for; but they gave Him gall for His food, and vinegar for His drink.[50]

The Cardinal says that Christ hungered for the salvation of souls and we can easily extend the metaphor to Bellarmine. We get a sense of how the Cardinal was curst (fierce) not only from the complaints of Blackwell but also from the praise of the saint's biographer, Fr. Brodrick: "St. Robert Bellarmine, by nature so peaceable and friendly, seemed destined never to be out of the battle-line."[51] He was fiercely engaged in battle because he, like Christ, hungered for the salvation of souls. Hence the observation about the bear's disposition while hungry fits the saint rather well.

The fourth connection is from James I. In his *Premonition* (much of which is dedicated to denouncing Bellarmine), the king described what he believed to be fictitious depictions of Jesuit martyrdoms found in their monasteries and colleges:

> But as well the walles of divers Monasteries and Jesuites Colledges abroad, are filled with the painting of such lying Histories, as also the books of our said fugitives are faced with such sort of shamelesse stuffe such are the innumerable sorts of torments and cruell deathes, that they record their Martyrs to have suffred here, some torne at foure Horses; some sowed in Beares skinnes, and then killed with Dogges.[52]

The king thought it preposterous that Jesuits should be adorned with bearskins and set upon by dogs. As horrible as the image is, the bearskins provide a link between the persecuted Jesuits and the martyrdoms that resulted in their eternal glory. Surely the Jesuits took some inspiration from this if they depicted the scene on walls of their monasteries and colleges. By labeling the images as "lying histories," James I added to the injury committed by the persecutors who adorned the Jesuits in bearskins. But all such injuries redound to the glory of the saints who suffer them. Seen in this light, there is powerful symbolism in portraying a Jesuit, such as St. Robert Bellarmine, as a bear.

Finally, Clown reports that the bear mocked Antigonus's cries for help: "the poor/ gentleman roared and the bear mocked him" (3.3.97-98). There is a sense in which St. Robert Bellarmine's letter to Blackwell would mock the archpriest if he died while maintaining support of the Oath:

> So many yeeres you haue kept the faith: doe not therefore loose the reward of such labours: do not depriue your selfe of that Crowne of righteousnesse which so long agone is prepared for you. Doe not make the faces of so many your both brethren and children ashamed. Upon you at this time are fixed the eyes of all the Church: yea also, you are made a spectacle to the world, to Angels, to men: Doe not so carie your selfe in this your last Act, that you leaue nothing but laments to your friends, and ioy to your enemies, but rather the contrarie: which we assuredly hope, and for which wee continually powre forth prayers to God. Display gloriously the banner of Faith, and make to reioyce the Church, which you have made heavie.

The saint presents two paths that Blackwell could take. The one path would lead to glory but would require the type of sacrifice that Catholic martyrs have embraced (with God's grace) from the beginning of the Church. The other path is the one Blackwell seemed resolved to take when the play was first performed, when he had supported the Oath in opposition to Pope Paul V's clear guidance. From a Catholic perspective, it led not to glory but to what St. Robert Bellarmine indicated: loss of eternal reward, joy to enemies, lament to friends, and a shame to brethren. Upon facing God's judgment, the poor gentleman would roar and the Cardinal's letter – which was intended to win him back to the path of salvation – would mock him.

Taken together, do these connections prove that Shakespeare intended the bear to represent St. Robert Bellarmine? Certainly there is not that level of absolute proof; and one can see the allegory as complete while dismissing the suggestion that the bear had any allegorical counterpart. Still, it would be odd that one of the greatest masters of the English language would unwittingly create the link that would make so much sense in the allegory.

And if Shakespeare did indeed intend the bear to represent St. Robert Bellarmine, we can see a connection in the names: Shakespeare could have picked from among many animals to pursue Blackwell but he chose the animal in the saint's name, BEllARmine.

Of course, Shakespeare did not end the play in Act III, just as many Catholics would not have entirely abandoned hope for an eventual change of fortune in England. A Catholic Comedy follows a swift passage of Time.

Time

Around 1600, a recusant from Lancashire, William Blundell, wrote a few ditties about life as a Catholic in England. One of them, entitled *Past and Present*, is worth citing in part:

> The time hath been we had one faith,
> And strode aright one ancient path;
> The time is now that each man may
> See new Religions coin'd each day.
>> Sweet Jesu, with mother mild,
>> Sweet Virgin mother, with thy child,
>> Angels and Saints of each degree,
>> Redress our country's misery . . .
> The time hath been men did believe
> God's sacraments his grace did give;
> The time is now men say they are
> Uncertain signs and tokens bare . . .
> The time hath been, within this land,
> One's word as good as was his bond;

> The time is now, all men may see
> New faiths have killed old honesty.[53]

William Blundell gives voice to many of the laments we have seen throughout this section on the play's Catholic Tragedy. The "time hath been" when England was Catholic, while "the time is now" that of new faiths that have upended and undone past religious belief and custom.

Shakespeare has the character "Time" open Act IV of *The Winter's Tale*:

> I, that please some, try all, both joy and terror
> Of good and bad, that makes and unfolds error,
> Now take upon me, in the name of Time,
> To use my wings. Impute it not a crime
> To me or my swift passage that I slide
> O'er sixteen years and leave the growth untried
> Of that wide gap, since it is in my power
> To o'erthrow law and in one self-born hour
> To plant and o'erwhelm custom. Let me pass
> The same I am ere ancient'st order was
> Or what is now received. I witness to
> The times that brought them in; so shall I do
> To th' freshest things now reigning, and make stale
> The glistering of this present as my tale
> Now seems to it.
>   (4.1.1-15)

In these lines from Time we find much that could be applied generally to any passage of time. Read in light of the allegory, though, this passage has even more meaning. Law is overthrown, new custom is planted and old custom is overwhelmed, error is unfolded (or spread), the ancient order is gone and fresh things reign. Whether or not Shakespeare knew it, he and Blundell appear to have been of the same mind about the passing of time in their England. Blundell placed his hope in petitions to Jesus, Mary, the angels, and the saints, that they may "redress our country's misery." In the Catholic Comedy that follows we shall see how Shakespeare portrays the realization of that hope.

Notes

[1] W.B. Patterson, *King James VI and I and the Reunion of Christendom*, 39.

[2] *King James VI & I*, 301.

[3] James Brodrick, S.J., *Robert Bellarmine: Saint and Scholar*, 290.

[4] James Brodrick, S.J., *Robert Bellarmine: Saint and Scholar*, 283.

[5] Id.

[6] Perdita marries Florizel, giving the king a son-in-law.

[7] *King James VI and I*, 139.

[8] *King James VI & I*, 276.

[9] Johann P. Sommervile, ed., *King James VI and I: Political Writings*, 152.

[10] *King James VI & I*, 153.

[11] Eamon Duffy, *Fires of Faith: Catholic England under Mary Tudor*.

[12] Joan Lord Hall, *The Winter's Tale: A Guide to the Play*, 13-14.

[13] Francis Edwards, *The Gunpowder Plot: The Narrative of Oswald Tesimond alias Greenway*, 51. In his *Condition of Catholics under James I*, Fr. John Gerard supports this assertion that James I called Catholics traitors even before the discovery of the Gunpowder Plot.

[14] *King James VI & I*, 250-251.

[15] *King James VI & I*, 340.

[16] *King James VI & I*, 260.

[17] *King James VI & I*, 250.

[18] Edwards, 48.

[19] *King James VI & I*, 248.

[20] *King James VI & I*, 148.

[21] Clare Asquith, *Shadowplay: The Hidden Beliefs and Coded Politics of William Shakespeare*, 143.

[22] *King James VI & I*, 148.

[23] *King James VI & I*, 152.

[24] Waugh, 214.

[25] King James VI & I, 492.

[26] King James VI & I, 253.

[27] Robert Persons, *The Judgment of a Catholicke Englishman Living in Banishment for His Religion*, 38.

[28] King James VI & I, 336.

[29] Brodrick, 293.

[30] Question 11, Article 1 of the *Summa Theologica*.

[31] King James VI & I, 307.

[32] From a 1604 speech to Parliament, Sommervile, 138.

[33] One may object here that whereas Queen Mary was known for burning heretics (Protestants in her judgment), James I almost exclusively executed heretics (Catholics in his judgment) by drawing and quartering. As such, might one wonder if Shakespeare is actually condemning Queen Mary? The overwhelming majority of the allegory's context suggests otherwise, and Shakespeare could have chosen the reference to burning over drawing and quartering for poetic reasons or to disguise the allegory.

[34] Brodrick, 274-275.

[35] Catholic Encyclopedia, *St. Thomas Garnet*.

[36] Brodrick, 274.

[37] King James VI & I, 250.

[38] King James VI & I, 262.

[39] *Blackwels Letter to the Priests, in Mr. George Blackwel, (made by Pope Clement 8 Arch-priest of England) his answeres upon sundry examinations.*

[40] Stefania Tutino, *Law and Conscience: Catholicism in Early Modern England, 1570-1625 (Catholic Christendom, 1300-1700)*.

[41] M. Blakwels answere to Card. Bellarmines Letter.

[42] Thomas More, *The Sadness of Christ*, 78.

[43] Denzinger, number 984.

[44] Waugh, 205.

[45] St. Robert Bellarmine, *Spiritual Writings*, 381-382.

[46] John A. Hardon, S.J., "Communion of Saints: Saint Robert Bellarmine on the Mystical Body of Christ."

[47] King James VI & I, 262.

[48] Master Blakwels Letter to the Romish Catholikes in England.

[49] George Blackwell, *A large examination taken at Lambeth.*

[50] St. Robert Bellarmine, *The Seven Last Words Spoken on the Cross.*

[51] Brodrick, 264.

[52] King James VI & I, 335.

[53] Henry Sebastian Bowden, *Mementoes of the English Martyrs and Confessors for Every Day in the Year,* 13-14.

SECTION THREE

The Catholic Comedy: Acts IV & V

Before proceeding, it is worth considering what Catholics in Shakespeare's England would have hoped for as they found themselves mired in their version of Act III, Scene 2. For those Catholics who retained hope for a happier life in England, what would feasible means for improvement look like? Possibly, James I could have an epiphany, like Leontes did upon the death of Mamillius, and convert to Catholicism. Alternatively, the situation might improve through conversion of the king's children, or at least their Catholic marriages (such as the subsequent marriage of James I's son, Charles I, to Henrietta Maria of France, a Catholic, in 1625). Both paths to conversion are reflected in the last two acts of *The Winter's Tale*.

From Act III, Scene 3 to the beginning of Act V, life in Bohemia and Sicilia runs its course for sixteen years. With the help of Paulina, Leontes performs penance after realizing his error. Perdita grows in grace in Bohemia and, with the help of Camillo, returns to Sicilia with her eventual husband, Florizel. All of this sets the stage for the miraculous last scene of the play.

Preserving Sicilia's Hope

Without needing to set a precise allegorical counterpart for the play's Bohemia, it is reasonable to see the comparisons to the actual Bohemia at the time Shakespeare wrote *The Winter's Tale*. As St. Edmund Campion described it:

> Do you want to know about Bohemia? . . . A mixen and hotch-pot of heresies. But all the chief people are Catholics. The lower orders promiscuous.[1]

In contrast to England, in Bohemia Catholics could profess their religion without fear of persecution. Clown indicates that, like Emperor Rudolf II's Bohemia, varied Christian denominations coexist in Polixenes's Bohemia, as he refers to the singers for the festival and the "one Puritan amongst them" who "sings psalms to hornpipes" (4.2.44-45).

Bohemia is, moreover, a land in which St. Edmund Campion was formed for his eventual martyrdom in England and a place of refuge for some Catholics forced to leave England. Although other parts of Europe – particularly the seminaries that formed missionary priests – played a more important role in supporting England's Catholics, we can count Bohemia among the lands that preserved England's Catholic Faith.

As discussed more fully later, Perdita allegorically represents England's Catholic Church in exile. Hermione greets her daughter after sixteen years of separation by asking where she has been preserved:

> Tell me, my own,
> Where hast thou been preserved? Where lived? How found
> Thy father's court?
>
> (5.3.124-126)

Perdita could answer that she had been preserved in Bohemia. The Catholics in England who jeopardized their freedom to harbor the Jesuit missionaries could just as well answer that their hopes were being preserved in Bohemia, among other places.

Shepherd and Clown find Perdita

In the Bohemia of *The Winter's Tale*, we also find outward professions of the Catholic faith. From the beginning of Act IV, we can sense the simple Catholic outlook (the so-called *Sensus Catholicus*) of Shepherd and his son, Clown, who are the first inhabitants of Bohemia we meet other than Polixenes, Archidamus, and the bear that eats Antigonus. Velma Richmond provides us with a sense of this Catholic portrayal of Bohemia:

> Antigonus chooses the values of this world and holds to an oath that is rooted in sin; and the bear eats him. In contrast, the Old Shepherd instantly responds to the bairn with admiration for the beauty of the newly born creature and mercy at its plight.... Clown, like his father, is compassionate; thus he describes the shipwreck in the tempest, "O, the most piteous cry of the poor souls!" – a phrase that evokes the Catholic concern with the cries of the poor souls in Purgatory – and he undertakes to gather the remains of Antigonus, an act his father calls a "good deed."[2]

Shakespeare gives Clown and Shepherd other lines throughout Act IV and V that likely have Catholic (or at least Christian) associations:

Sensus Catholicus of Shepherd and Clown	
Shepherd: I'll take it up for pity. (3.3.74)	*Showing concept of charity*
Shepherd: Heavy matters, heavy matters! But look thee/ here boy. Now bless thyself! (3.3.109-110)	*To bless oneself is to make the sign of the cross*
Clown: If the sins of your youth/ are forgiven you, you're well to live. (3.3.116-117)	*Showing the concept of Baptism and sacramental Confession*
Clown: Marry, will I. (3.3.131)	*An expression based on the Blessed Virgin Mary's name*
Shepherd: Some hangman must put on my shroud and lay me/ Where no priest shovels in dust. (4.4.459-460)	*Resembling the Catholic burial ceremony*

Shepherd and Clown are among the least sophisticated characters in *The Winter's Tale*, but they play important roles as Perdita's foster father and brother, respectively. Allegorically, their *Sensus Catholicus* is the most important reason Perdita has "grown in grace" as Time describes at the beginning of Act IV.

Perdita shows the depth of her Catholic thinking in an exchange with Polixenes about the flowers in her garden. Although the dialogue (quoted below) does not appear at first glance to have much to add to the allegory, Claire Asquith astutely notes a connection to the religious debate in Shakespeare's England:

> In a charming pastoral debate at the centre of the play, the chaste heroine Perdita pointedly prefers the pure stock of country flowers to the "grafted" varieties proposed by her more sophisticated visitors. The language of the debate comes straight from the theological argument of the day, in which the grafted, hybrid, spotted state religion was denounced by both Catholics and Puritans.[3]

For a specific example of this theological argument, Asquith points to Thomas Stapleton, who wrote that the faith of Protestants was a "bastard slip proceeding of another stock."[4]

Stapleton addresses Queen Elizabeth I in the preface of *The History of the Church of England* (his translation of Venerable Bede's work):

> For faith being one (as the Apostle expressly saith) that one faith being proved to be the same which was first grafted in the hearts of Englishmen, and the many faiths of Protestants being found different from the same in more than forty clear differences gathered out of this present history ... it must remain undoubted, the pretended faith of Protestants to be but a bastard slip proceeding of another stock (as partly of old renewed heresies, partly of new forged interpretations upon the written text of God's word) and therefore not to be rooted in your Grace's dominions, lest in time, as heresies have done in Greece and Africa, it overgrow the true branches of the natural tree, consume the spring of true Christianity, and suck out the joys of all right

religion: leaving to the realm the bark and rind only, to be called Christians.[5]

Stapleton does not hide his theological views: there is one faith, which is the faith first grafted in the hearts of Englishmen, and that is Catholicism. The many Protestant variations are "bastard slips" consisting in part of heresies.

In a wonderful exchange about the flowers and plants in Perdita's garden, Shakespeare uses remarkably similar imagery to show us that the Catholic Faith that Perdita preserves in Bohemia is pure.

> PERDITA
>   Sir, the year growing ancient,
> Not yet on summer's death nor on the birth
> Of trembling winter, the fairest flow'rs o' th' season
> Are our carnations and streaked gillyvors,
> Which some call nature's bastards. Of that kind
> Our rustic garden's barren, and I care not
> To get slips of them.
> POLIXENES
>   Wherefore, gentle maiden,
> Do you neglect them?
> PERDITA
>   For I have heard it said
> There is an art which in their piedness shares
> With great creating nature.
> POLIXENES
>   Say there be;
> Yet nature is made better by no mean
> But nature makes that mean. So, over that art
> Which you say adds to nature is an art
> That nature makes. You see, sweet maid, we marry
> A gentler scion to the wildest stock,
> And make conceive a bark of baser kind
> But a bud of nobler race. This is an art
> Which doth mend nature – change it rather – but
> The art itself is nature.

PERDITA
                    So it is.
POLIXENES
    Then make your garden rich in gillyvors,
    And do not call them bastards.
PERDITA
                    I'll not put
    The dibble in earth to set one slip of them.
                        (4.4.79-100)

Perdita calls flowers produced by grafting "bastards," and though they may be the fairest of the season she does not accept slips of them in her garden. Perdita's argument, both in the literal and allegorical meanings of the play, is that man should not attempt to change the essential nature of what God has given us, even when by appearances the change improves nature. Within the allegory, the argument extends to the notion that God established the Catholic Church, whose essential nature man should not change, however flawed it might seem at times.

Perdita's rejection of the "bastard slip" echoes Thomas Stapleton's language to such an extent that we can scarcely imagine that Shakespeare did not know of Stapleton's imagery and how it was used in the religious debates of his day. Setting aside the numerous other connections in this tale, this alone could establish a presumption that Shakespeare had in mind a defense of Catholicism.

When Perdita returns to Sicilia in Act V, she allegorically brings this preference for Catholicism, which Stapleton called the "first and true Christian faith planted" in England.[6] Catholics in England would have seen even a hybrid state religion as a godsend in comparison with the purely anti-Catholic circumstances in which they found themselves. Yet Shakespeare's allegory presents the grandest hopes of England's Catholics, so Perdita represents the desire for a purely Catholic state religion, as it was prior to Henry VIII's break with Rome.

The act set in Bohemia is truly beautiful and especially welcome after the tragedy of Act III. In terms of Bohemia's place in the play, though, its foremost importance is as the land in which the pure Perdita is preserved for an eventual return to Sicilia. As the character Time announces at the beginning of Act IV, Bohemia is where Perdita has "grown in grace" (4.1.24) during the sixteen years since Leontes banished her. Catholics in England would have had a similar view of Bohemia's role: its "pleasant and blessed shore" provided refuge for English Catholics who preserved the "first and true Christian faith" for a day when it would again be welcome in England.

Penance

While Perdita grows in grace in Bohemia, her father performs penance in Sicilia. Indeed, penance is so intertwined with Leontes's character that it seems as though Shakespeare develops the Sicilian king to give us a lesson on this Christian virtue and the accompanying sacrament.

Although Leontes becomes "the penitent" of the play after he learns of Hermione's death, Shakespeare identifies the king with penance much earlier:

> I have trusted thee, Camillo,
> With all the nearest things to my heart, as well
> My chamber counsels, wherein, priestlike, thou
> Hast cleansed my bosom. I from thee departed
> Thy penitent reformed.
>
> (1.2.234-238)

In this we see that the king believes that when he transgresses, he needs to have his "bosom cleansed" and that for this he turns to Camillo, whom he calls "priestlike." Leontes departs from Camillo as a "penitent reformed." All of this brings to mind the Catholic sacrament of Penance, through which those Catholics who have sinned since Baptism may be forgiven through the ministry of an ordained priest.

The Catechism of the Council of Trent describes the great comfort this sacrament provides:

Each one has good reason to distrust the accuracy of his own judgment on his own actions, and hence could not but be very much in doubt regarding the truth of our internal penance. It was to destroy this, our uneasiness, that our Lord instituted the Sacrament of Penance, by means of which we are assured that our sins are pardoned by the absolution of the priest; and also to tranquilize our conscience by means of the trust we rightly repose in the virtue of the Sacraments.[7]

We can sense that Camillo has previously "destroyed the uneasiness" Leontes had felt regarding his conscience. The Anglican reforms rejected sacramental absolution, so this exchange points to a time in England before James I. Within the allegory, therefore, we should see this as an instance in which Shakespeare has Leontes represent the monarchs of England during Catholic times.[8]

The audience does not learn what sins Leontes may have confessed to Camillo in the past, but it does witness the king's many sins that cause Act III to end in tragedy: he falsely judges his queen, attempts to have Camillo poison Polixenes, and banishes his daughter to what seems like certain death. From the allegorical perspective, these sins all correspond to James I's attacks on the Catholic Church and his Catholic subjects.

As previously discussed, Leontes sins so greatly because he relies too much on his own flawed suspicions and judgments. Camillo, Paulina, Antigonus, and others try to persuade him that his accusations against Hermione are baseless, but he persists. Before and during her trial, Hermione entreats the king to think clearly and see her innocence. Ultimately, though, she must rely on the judgment of the oracle for vindication. The oracle does indeed vindicate Hermione, but Leontes rejects its infallible decree.

Only after Leontes learns that Mamillius has died does he come to his senses. At that point, he immediately grasps the root of his madness: "I have too much believed mine own suspicion" (3.2.151). Leontes then begs pardon of Apollo, declares his intentions to remedy the harms he has caused (insofar as possible), and recites the sins he has committed against Hermione, Camillo and Polixenes.

The scene then takes another stunning turn when Paulina declares that Hermione has died and that Leontes cannot effectively repent of his sins – he can never repay the debt:

> Do not repent these things, for they are heavier
> Than all thy woes can stir. Therefore betake thee
> To nothing but despair. A thousand knees
> Ten thousand years together, naked, fasting
> Upon a barren mountain, and still winter
> In storm perpetual, could not move the gods
> To look that way thou wert.
>
> (3.2.208-214)

Paulina's condemnation is harsh but seems justified on a natural level considering Leontes's tremendous sins against all that was dear to him and Sicilia. Fr. Henry Sebastian Bowden relates that Blessed Thomas Cottam issued a similar condemnation before he was martyred at Tyburn in 1582: "the sins of this realm have deserved infinite punishment and God's just indignation."[9] When he speaks of the sins of the realm, he means those against the Catholic Church under Queen Elizabeth I in particular. Nevertheless, he continued his speech from the scaffold by asking God for mercy in calling His people to repentance.

Paulina's speech focuses exclusively on the notion of "infinite punishment" for Leontes's sins. Her initial judgment lacks the Christian sense of God's mercy that Blessed Cottam displayed. Indeed, Paulina essentially advocates for the despair that led Judas to kill himself.[10] Although Leontes admits to deserving such harshness, a lord rebukes Paulina for her hardheartedness.

Paulina responds with a complete rejection of her earlier judgment:

> I am sorry for't
> All faults I make, when I shall come to know them,
> I do repent. Alas, I have showed too much
> The rashness of a woman! He is touched
> To th' noble heart. What's gone and what's past help
> Should be past grief. Do not receive affliction

> At my petition. I beseech you, rather
> Let me be punished, that have minded you
> Of what you should forget.
>
> (3.2.218-226)

She apologizes, repents, and even asks to be punished instead of Leontes. Shakespeare could have had Paulina deliver a merciful response to Leontes immediately after his expression of remorse, without her initial harshness. Why did he have her change heart?

The lord clearly reminds Paulina of something she understands very well – God may mercifully call sinners to repentance, and we should want that. The parable of the lost sheep provides a good example of this lesson that Christ taught throughout His public ministry:

> What man of you that hath an hundred sheep: and if he shall love one of them, doth he not leave the ninety-nine in the desert, and go after that which was lost, until he find it? And when he hath found it, lay it on his shoulders rejoicing: And coming home, call together his friends and neighbors, saying to them: rejoice with me, because I have found my sheep that was lost? I say to you, that even so there shall be joy in heaven upon one sinner that doth penance, more than upon ninety-nine just who need not penance.
>
> (Luke 15.4-7)

If God wants sinners to repent, who is Paulina (or anyone else) to say that there is no point in such repentance? Of course this lesson is extraordinarily difficult and impossible without God's grace. By having Paulina initially react with condemnation, Shakespeare allows us to see more clearly that her subsequent mercy is especially virtuous rather than the fruit of a mild disposition.

Paulina's admission of being too rash also demonstrates the universal need for God's mercy: "All faults I make, when I shall come to know them,/ I do repent" (3.2.218-219). Her speech suggests that she has acquired the habit of repenting when she sins, which of course indicates that she has sinned in the past. Her repentance, combined with her mercy towards Leontes after he repents, matches the pattern the Jesus taught His disciples:

> If thy brother sin against thee, reprove him: and if he do penance, forgive him. And if he sin against thee seven times in a day, and seven times in a day be converted unto thee, saying, I repent; forgive him.
>
> (Luke 17.3-4)

By allowing the virtuous Paulina to fall and repent, Shakespeare illustrates for us the often difficult to implement lines from the *Our Father*: "forgive us our trespasses as we forgive those who trespass against us."[11]

Even though Paulina wishes she could take back her harsh words, Leontes recognizes his need to do penance. With his restored sanity, he embraces his penance, saying it shall be his recreation to weep over the sorrow he has caused:

> Prithee, bring me
> To the dead bodies of my queen and son.
> One grave shall be for both. Upon them shall
> The causes of their death appear, unto
> Our shame perpetual. Once a day I'll visit
> The chapel where they lie, and tears shed there
> Shall be my recreation. So long as nature
> Will bear up this exercise,[12] so long
> I daily vow to use it. Come and lead me
> To these sorrows.
>
> (3.2.234-243)

It seems unlikely that Shakespeare intended the exchange between Leontes and Paulina to represent the sacrament of Penance, in which a priest absolves the penitent from his or her sins. Instead, in this speech and his subsequent actions, Leontes exhibits the *virtue* of penance. The Catechism of the Council of Trent sets forth three ends of the virtue of penance:

> The first is to destroy the sin and efface from the soul its every spot and stain. The second is to make satisfaction to God for the sins which he has committed, which is clearly an act of justice. . . . The third (end of the penitent) is to reinstate himself in the favor and friendship of God whom he has offended and whose hatred he has earned by the turpitude of sin.[13]

Leontes has sinned greatly and caused tremendous harm, so he deeply senses his need to atone for his sins.

As Act V begins sixteen years later, Cleomenes declares to Leontes, "Sir, you have done enough, and have performed/ A saintlike sorrow" (5.1.1-2). Cleomenes describes Leontes's penance as the performance of a "saintlike sorrow." Leontes has not performed penance solely for the sake of suffering, but rather with an aim of making reparation and growing in holiness. The Church teaches that penance practiced with the right intention is always a means of growing closer to God. As the Catechism of the Council of Trent describes:

> Interior penance consists in turning to God sincerely and from the heart, and in hating and detesting our past transgressions, with a firm resolution of amendment of life, hoping to obtain pardon through the mercy of God. Accompanying this penance, like an inseparable companion of detestation for sin, is a sorrow and sadness, which is a certain agitation and disturbance of the soul, and is called by many a passion. Hence many of the Fathers define penance as an anguish of the soul.[14]

This virtue of penance turns the penitent toward God with the hope of obtaining pardon through God's mercy.

We see one of the clearest fruits of Leontes's penance early in Act IV, as Camillo announces that Leontes wants him to return to Sicilia: "the penitent King, my master, hath sent for me, to whose feeling/ sorrows I might be some allay" (4.2.6-8). Leontes traverses a fascinating array of spiritual milestones in the play: going in the wrong direction, so to speak, in the first three acts, and in the right direction as soon as he learns of Mamillius's death. This request for Camillo's return is clearly an important step. Within the allegory, we can imagine that a king wishing to reconcile himself with the Catholic Church would look not to the parish priest or even bishop of the country, but to the pope.[15]

In his attacks on the Catholic Church, James I referred disapprovingly to a few instances in which kings had performed penance before being reconciled with the pope. One such instance involved the controversy between Pope Gregory VII and Henry IV, the Holy Roman Emperor from 1056 to 1105. Although the conflict came to a head over the question of who could appoint bishops or abbots, the power struggle between Gregory VII and Henry IV shared much of the underlying tension present in the disputes between Rome and England in Shakespeare's day.

The story is well worth knowing, but for present purposes it suffices to consider the penance and reconciliation of Henry IV after Gregory VII had excommunicated him. Warren Carroll describes the scene:

> Henry IV took off his shoes and put on a coarse wool shirt. For three days he knelt in the snow outside the castle of Canossa, imploring Pope Gregory's forgiveness for him, a sinner. . . . On the evening of the third day, Gregory VII agreed to hear Henry's confession, if he would swear to abide by the Pope's final decision on the question of his right to rule and to give the Pope and his legates permanent safe passage conduct guarantees for travel in Germany. The next day Henry made his confession and took the oath; Gregory said Mass and gave Henry communion.[16]

Henry IV's harsh penance brings to mind parts of Paulina's initial condemnation as well as Leontes's recalling of Camillo.

Does Shakespeare give us any indication that Camillo absolves Leontes just as Pope Gregory VII absolved Emperor Henry IV? Certainly the allegorical context suggests that the absolution must occur before Leontes participates in the happy ending (which represents the Mass as we shall see). Their first meeting after sixteen years – and thus the probable occasion for Leontes's confession – takes place off stage and is described to Autolycus by First Gentleman:

> I make a broken delivery of the business,
> but the changes I perceived in the king and
> Camillo were very notes of admiration. They seemed
> almost, with staring on one another, to tear the cases of
> their eyes. There was speech in their dumbness, language
> in their very gesture. They looked as they had
> heard of a world ransomed, or one destroyed. A notable
> passion of wonder appeared in them, but the wisest
> beholder, that knew no more but seeing, could not say
> if the importance were joy or sorrow; but in the extremity
> of the one it must needs be.
> (5.2.10-20)

Within the literal context of their meeting, Leontes and Camillo are expressing great joy at the discovery of Perdita and the fulfillment of the oracle's prophecy. Interestingly, the description of their communication matches what bystanders would observe at the moment of absolution in an open confessional: "There was speech in their dumbness, language/ in their very gesture." With the words of absolution, both the priest and the penitent make the sign of the cross – and the words of both would normally be unintelligible to observers. The rest of the description fits equally well with the finding of Perdita and the reconciliation of an excommunicated sinner with the Church.

Shakespeare provides further clues to his meaning by playing off of Protestant objections to the Catholic sacraments. As Sarah Beckwith describes:

> In describing Catholic ceremonial as dumb, Protestant polemic attempted to deprive it of voice, of the ability to say anything at all. The ritual gestures and words of the priest cannot say anything; they are dumb – silent and stupid. . . . The ascription of dumbness to Catholic ceremonial is repeated in the short introduction to the Book of Common Prayer, "Of Ceremonies, Why Some be Abolished and

Some Retained." The ceremonies of the Book of Common Prayer are "neither dark nor dumb ceremonies, but are set forth that every man may understand what they do mean and to what use they serve."[17]

By having First Gentleman say, "There was speech in their dumbness, language/ in their very gesture," Shakespeare counters this Protestant critique. Although "the wisest beholder, that knew/ no more but seeing, could not" understand the true meaning, Catholics of course knew more than what they simply saw in the priest's gestures.

Thus it appears that Leontes comes full circle, beginning and ending with the sacrament of Penance. Hermione foreshadows Leontes's penance as he sends her to jail to await her trial:

> Adieu, my lord.
> I never wished to see you sorry; now
> I trust I shall.
>
> (2.1.123-125)

Even if Catholics in England did not wish King James I to undergo penance, they surely hoped for his conversion. They would have known, as Hermione does, that such conversion would have inspired James I to embrace the need for reparation just as Leontes does. And many might have prayed to "live on crutches" to see the day when their king or queen sought reconciliation with the pope.

Leontes's Decision

Leontes's many years of penance prepare him to face the moral dilemma foreshadowed by the play's first scene, when Archidamus says: "If the King had no son, they would desire/ to live on crutches till he had one" (1.1.46-47). At issue is whether the king should remarry in pursuit of an heir. Paulina and Dion (a lord of Sicilia) frame the decision that Leontes must make:

> PAULINA
>   You are one of those

>   Would have him wed again.
> DION
>   If you would not so,
>   You pity not the state, nor the remembrance
>   Of his most sovereign name, consider little
>   What dangers, by His Highness' fail of issue
>   May drop upon his kingdom and devour
>   Incertain lookers-on.
>
>   (5.1.23-29)

Dion presents a reasonable case for Leontes to remarry and the only real surprise is that the king faces it sixteen years after Hermione's death. In the ordinary course of events, we would expect the king to have confronted the question of remarriage already.

Given the rather ordinary nature of the question of whether the king should remarry, we might wonder why Shakespeare makes Leontes's decision the primary moral quandary of *The Winter's Tale*. After all, we are accustomed to finding profound and universally applicable lessons in the weighty debates of Shakespeare's plays. In the literal meaning of the play, however, arguing in favor of Leontes's ultimate decision to not remarry depends almost exclusively on the idea that his deceased queen is not actually dead or will come back to life. If Paulina did not subsequently bring Hermione back to life, Leontes still would have found Perdita, but he would have no wife. From this we can scarcely derive a universally applicable lesson that Shakespeare would plausibly approve. The allegorical meaning offers something more profound.

To appreciate the allegorical significance of Leontes's decision, we should first consider Paulina that represents St. Paul, who wrote on the topic of marriage, divorce, and remarriage:

> But to them that are married, not I but the Lord commandeth, that the wife depart not from the husband. And if she depart, that she remain unmarried, or be reconciled to her husband. And let not the husband put away his wife.
>
>   (1 Corinthians 7.10-11)

Those who are married may not separate from each other; but if they do separate, they must reconcile or at least not remarry another person. These words echo those of Christ and are the timeless teaching of the Catholic Church. And although they do not apply to a situation in which one of the spouses dies, we can see the same ideas in the exchange between Leontes and Paulina:

PAULINA
>Yet if my lord will marry – if you will, sir,
>No remedy, but you will – give me the office
>To choose you a queen. She shall not be so young
>As was your former, but she shall be such
>As, walked your first queen's ghost, it should take joy
>To see her in your arms.

LEONTES
>>My true Paulina,
>We shall not marry till thou bidd'st us.

PAULINA
>>That
>Shall be when your first queen's again in breath;
>Never till then.
>>>(5.1.76-84)

Paulina knows that Hermione will live again, so her guidance to Leontes is that he must remain unmarried or else marry the lady Paulina chooses. And she will only choose Hermione when she is "again in breath." Therefore her guidance matches that of St. Paul exactly.

Seeing this match between the marital guidance of St. Paul and Paulina is the first step to understanding the allegorical significance of Leontes's decision. With this foundation, we can consider the decision in three ways: in comparison to the decision of Henry VIII, in the light of Hermione's allegorical role as the Mystical Body of Christ, and as the fulfillment of the oracle's decree.

Although Shakespeare sets certain aspects of the allegory precisely in the time in which he wrote, others cover the condition of Catholics since Henry VIII broke with the Catholic Church. Henry VIII broke with the Church when the pope upheld the teachings of St. Paul and refused to approve of the king's divorce and remarriage. Within the scope of the broader allegory, we can see Leontes's decision as a definitive rejection of Henry VIII's decision to remarry in pursuit of a male heir. Whereas Henry VIII argued about the letter of the law, Leontes ultimately embraces something closer to the spirit of the law (coupled with a trust of Paulina's counsel) as he rejects the suggestion that he would marry in pursuit of an heir, except by Paulina's leave (5.1.69-71). Thus Leontes's decision allegorically mends Henry VIII's break with the Church's teachings regarding the indissolubility of marriage.

We can see another aspect of the allegorical role of Leontes's decision when we consider that Hermione represents the Mystical Body of Christ, the Catholic Church. In this light, Paulina effectively tells the king that he cannot choose a church other than the Catholic Church. Henry VIII broke with the Catholic Church because he could not obtain Rome's consent to his divorce. Leontes's decision allegorically expresses hope for a king who will not look for another church simply to fulfill his personal or political desires, even if those desires appear to be justified on some level.

The final allegorical signification of Leontes's decision relates to the decree of the oracle. Paulina relies on the oracle to support her argument against Leontes remarrying:

> There is none worthy,
> Respecting her that's gone. Besides, the gods
> Will have fulfilled their sacred purposes;
> For has not the divine Apollo said,
> Is't not the tenor of his oracle,
> That King Leontes shall not have an heir
> Till his lost child be found?
>
> (5.1.34-40)

Paulina argues that Apollo has spoken through the oracle and there is no point in trying to remarry in search of an heir: the king will have no heir until Perdita is found. Within the allegory, the oracle represents Rome, the seat of papal authority. Thus, when the pope provides a definitive answer to a question of faith or morals, there is no point in looking for God's will elsewhere.

Paulina ultimately persuades Leontes not to remarry except with her approval. When Leontes passes this test, so to speak, the servant announces the arrival of Florizel and a princess (Perdita), and thus begins the joyful ending of *The Winter's Tale* (5.1.85). Although the literal significance of Leontes's decision would not necessarily justify such a wondrous change of fortune, the allegorical meaning certainly would for Catholics. Leontes's decision mends Henry VIII's breach of divine law in remarrying, reasserts the determination to remain faithful to the Catholic Church, and confirms a resolution to adhere to the definitive pronouncements of the pope. This indeed would be cause for a joyful ending in the eyes of England's Catholics.

The Mass

As we have seen, Leontes has performed his penance and rejected the idea of marrying again. And he has been reunited with Perdita, fulfilling the decree of the oracle. In the final scene, though, Paulina informs Leontes that something more is required before he can approach the statue of Hermione:

PAULINA
                    It is required
    You do awake your faith. Then all stand still.
    On; those that think it is unlawful business
    I am about, let them depart.
LEONTES
                    Proceed.
    No foot shall stir.
                            (5.3.94-98)

Paulina's words recall Camillo's assertion that Leontes's madness in the first part of the play was founded on his faith. He has now rejected the madness that led him to doubt Hermione and reached the doorstep of conversion, which is significant progress. But he must cross the threshold by awakening his faith, as Paulina informs him.

We should consider that Leontes has not simply acceded to Paulina's instruction to awaken his faith but has acted for all present by saying that "no foot shall stir," regaining the moral authority he had lost while unjustly accusing Hermione. Within the allegory, this would resemble the hope that James I would convert to Catholicism, which would result not only in the toleration of Catholicism in England but its promotion.[18]

What follows in the scene resembles the Mass, which of course takes place in church, just as the final scene takes place in Paulina's chapel.[19] Central to the Mass is the Eucharist, which is:

> A sacrament and a sacrifice in which Our Savior Jesus Christ, body and blood, soul and divinity, is contained, offered, and received under the appearances of bread and wine.... It is called the Sacrament of the Altar because it is consecrated and reserved upon an altar. It is offered up on the altar in the Holy Sacrifice of the Mass.[20]

Because the Eucharist *is* Christ according to Catholic theology, we can see Hermione's connection to the Eucharist, as she represents the Mystical Body of Christ.

After Leontes awakens his faith, Paulina proceeds with one of the more cryptic speeches in the play:

>   Music, awake her; strike!
> [*Music.*][21]
> 'Tis time. Descend. Be stone no more. Approach.
> Strike all that look upon with marvel. Come,
> I'll fill your grave up. Stir, nay, come away,
> Bequeath to death your numbness, for from him
> Dear life redeems you. – You perceive she stirs.
>   (5.3.98-103)

We notice first of all that Paulina is using almost formulaic directions, as though she were reciting a ceremony rubric, as a priest does during Mass. We can follow the meaning, it seems, but this is no ordinary speech from Paulina. And because the minister of the Mass must be a priest, we should recall that Paulina's allegorical counterpart, St. Paul, was among the first priests.

The phrase immediately before Hermione "stirs" is arguably one of the most important in the play: "for from him/ Dear life redeems you." In the First Folio edition of the play, these seven words are in parenthesis,[22] set apart from Paulina's words before and after this phrase. Immediately after this phrase, Paulina announces that Hermione stirs. Thus, before Paulina utters the phrase Hermione is stone, and afterwards she is flesh and blood. Setting aside for a moment the substantive interpretation of the phrase, the form and effect resembles the words the priest says at Mass to consecrate the bread into the Body of Christ, and the wine into the Blood of Christ:

FOR THIS IS MY BODY

FOR THIS IS THE CHALICE OF MY BLOOD, OF THE NEW AND ETERNAL TESTAMENT: THE MYSTERY OF FAITH: WHICH SHALL BE SHED FOR YOU AND FOR MANY UNTO THE REMISSION OF SINS.

Of course the priests of Shakespeare's day would say the Mass in Latin, but the English translation of each of these formulas begins with the word "for" and proceeds to describe the transformative action of the sacrament. Clearly Shakespeare was not trying to create a new sacrament but we can see an unmistakable parallel between structure and effect of the consecration at Mass and the formula that animates Hermione's statue.

Turning to the substance of the crucial phrase – FOR FROM HIM DEAR LIFE REDEEMS YOU – it should be clear that the "dear life" that redeems Hermione must refer to someone other than Leontes. Although Leontes has undergone his penance, by no means can we understand that *he* has redeemed the blameless Hermione. Within the context of the play, she has no need of redemption, and certainly not through the actions of Leontes. However, if we reflect on the words a priest says to consecrate the Blood of Christ, we can see that *Christ's* "dear life" – the blood He shed for the remission of our sins – redeems us.

What connection could there be between the Redemption and the animation of Hermione's statue? In his letter to the Ephesians, St. Paul writes: "But God (who is rich in mercy) for his exceeding charity wherewith he loved us, even when we were dead in sins, hath quickened us together in Christ (by whose grace we are saved)" (Ephesians 2.4-5). The members of the Mystical Body of Christ were dead in sin until they were brought to life by the Redemption. As Pope Pius XII expresses in *Mediator Dei*, the life-giving effect of the Redemption continues, especially through the Mass:

> It is an unquestionable fact that the work of our redemption is continued, and that its fruits are imparted to us, during the celebration of the liturgy, notable in the august sacrifice of the altar. Christ acts each day to save us, in the sacraments and in His holy sacrifice. By means of them He is constantly atoning for the sins of mankind, constantly consecrating it to God.[23]

Thus, Paulina's words and their effect on Hermione provide a fitting representation of what takes place at Mass.

The Eucharistic significance of this scene continues with Leontes's declaration about the "resurrected" Hermione:

> O, she's warm!
> If this be magic, let it be an art
> Lawful as eating.
>
> (5.3.109-111)

Leontes's astonishment that the statue of Hermione lives – "O, she's warm!" – again resembles the consecration at Mass, when the bread and wine are turned into the actual body and blood of Christ. The cold bread and wine, so to speak, become the warm body and blood of the Redeemer.

And as Leontes exclaims, the last scene involves a ceremony in which through something like "magic" an inanimate object, the statue, becomes a living being. Because Hermione represents the Mystical Body of Christ, the symbolic parallel to the Catholic doctrine of transubstantiation seems clear. As the Council of Trent stated:

> It has always been a matter of conviction in the Church of God . . . that by the consecration of the bread and wine a conversion takes place of the whole substance of bread into the substance of the body of Christ our Lord, and of the whole substance of the wine into the substance of his blood. This conversion is appropriately and properly called transubstantiation by the Catholic Church.[24]

This conversion of the bread and wine into the substance of the body and blood of Christ surely seems something like "magic" in a secular sense, so we can see the allegorical significance of Leontes's reasoning. And whereas Hermione's sixteen-year transition from living queen, to deceased queen, to inanimate statue, to living queen is preposterous in the literal meaning, the allegorical meaning is quite reasonable.

Leontes's reference to "eating" alludes to communion, which is common to both Catholic and Anglican worship. However, Anglican and Catholic theologies diverge with respect to *what* is eaten. James I vehemently rejected the Catholic belief in transubstantiation. Indeed, Paulina's observation that an explanation of how Hermione lives "should be hooted at/ Like an old tale" (5.3.117-118) fits well with James I's beliefs regarding the Eucharist: he believed that the bread and wine did not become Christ – they were not "warm" or living – for such would be a magic forbidden by his theology. And yet Hermione most certainly comes to life, which corresponds to the Catholic conception of transubstantiation.

It seems likely that Shakespeare has Paulina direct Leontes to "awaken his faith" to specifically address the faith needed to believe in transubstantiation. St. Thomas Aquinas's hymn on the Blessed Sacrament, *Pange Lingua*, has the following beautiful lines:

> Verbum caro panem verum
> Verbo carnem eficit;
> Fitque sanguis Christi merum;
> Et si sensus deficit,
> Ad firmandem cor sincerum
> Sola fides sufficit.

The Catholic Encyclopedia offers the literal translation of these lines as:

> The Word-(made)-Flesh makes by (His) word true bread into flesh; and wine becomes Christ's blood; and if the (unassisted) intellect fails (to recognize all this), faith alone suffices to assure the pure heart.

"Faith alone suffices to assure the pure heart" if the intellect cannot grasp the nature of transubstantiation. Leontes must awaken his faith because he represents James I, who rejected transubstantiation. Paradoxically, the literal action of the play would not require Leontes to "awaken his faith" because Hermione's statue comes to life in a way that is clear to the senses – there is no need for faith when one can simply observe the reality. The faith is thus far more necessary to accept the theological reality presented by the allegorical reading of Paulina's words.

Leontes's reference to eating also points back to Shakespeare's subtle foreshadowing of the Mass. In the previous scene, Paulina's steward reports that the royal characters have gone to Paulina's chapel, where they "intend to sup" (5.2.104). In the literal meaning of the play, this statement makes no sense because the characters do not appear to eat in Paulina's chapel. Within the allegory, though, the reference bolsters the idea that the characters are attending a Mass, in which they would "sup" on the Eucharist.

Another connection to the Mass arises through a Protestant criticism of the Catholic practice of adoring the Eucharist, also called the Blessed

Sacrament. Clare Asquith notes that the term "gazers" was a "nickname for superstitious Catholics who 'gazed' upon the host":

> The "Real Presence" of God was the object of profound devotion: the bread, or host, consecrated by the priest, hung richly ornamented above the altar in every church, representing the spiritual core of England before the Reformation. Merely to set eyes on the host at the moment of consecration was a channel of grace, the reason Catholics were often dubbed as "gazers" by Protestants.[25]

Indeed, James I included "Elevation for Adoration" of the Blessed Sacrament along with transubstantiation in his catalog of "tricks" of Catholicism he denounced in his *Premonition*.[26]

Both Leontes and Perdita are "gazers" in the final scene. As Leontes first appreciates the beauty of Hermione's statue, Paulina begins to draw the curtain, eliciting Leontes's protest. Paulina responds, "No longer shall you gaze on't" (5.3.60). Leontes and Perdita then assert that they would be content to "look on" Hermione's statue (5.3.84-91). Their gazing upon Hermione thus provides yet another connection to the Eucharist, and by extension the Mystical Body of Christ.

With so much to dazzle in this final scene, we may miss certain aspects that would stand out in a softer light. For instance, there are three references to the lawfulness of Paulina's actions within the span of fifteen lines: "those that think this is unlawful business/ I am about, let them depart" (5.3.96-97); "Start not. Her actions shall be holy as/ You hear my spell is lawful" (5.3.104-105); and "If this be magic, let it be an art/ Lawful as eating" (5.3.110-111). What about the last scene might someone consider unlawful? Within the allegorical context, the answer is evident: the Catholic Mass, with its doctrine of transubstantiation, was unlawful in Shakespeare's England.

We can see why the characters would have made a point of the ceremony's lawfulness – for decades, it had been unlawful to even attend a Catholic Mass. And just as it would remain unlawful in Shakespeare's England unless James I changed his faith, Paulina insists that Leontes awaken his faith for the ceremony to proceed. The reappearance of publicly allowed Mass would, for Catholics, be a certain indication that their hopes had been at least partially fulfilled . . . and that they would no longer need to find hiding places for priests.

Perdita's reverence for Hermione also resonates with the sense of Catholic worship:

> And give me leave,
> And do not say 'tis superstition, that
> I kneel and implore her blessing. Lady,
> Dear Queen, that ended when I but began,
> Give me that hand of yours to kiss.
> (5.3.42-46)

Perdita's request for Hermione's blessing certainly has religious significance, and so does the reference to superstition. King James I expressed his view of Catholic superstition in his speech to Parliament a few days after the discovery of the Gunpowder Plot:

> It cannot be denied, That it was onely blinde superstition of their errors in Religion, that led them to this desperate device; yet it doth not follow, That all professing that Romish religion were guiltie of the same.[27]

Whereas most of the allegorical meanings described herein are relatively hidden, here is an instance in which both the allegorical meaning and Shakespeare's judgment of it would likely have seemed evident to the audience. Perdita is an unambiguously good character, and she refers to the view that Catholics were deluded by "blinde superstition," as James I called it. It is almost as if Perdita is saying, "the day is won, we no longer need to hide our faith."

Clare Asquith's insights are particularly relevant here:

> All those present are aware that the ceremony could be seen as "superstition," "magic," "unlawful business," "assisted/ by wicked powers" (5.3.43-96) – precisely the objections leveled at the Mass.[28]

Those present remain because Leontes has said "no foot shall stir," which is a clear signal that the happy ending may proceed even if all that unfolds would have been considered unlawful moments before.

Perdita's Anointing

Within the allegory, Leontes has converted to Catholicism and Paulina has reanimated Hermione, who represents the Mystical Body of Christ, through a ceremony that resembles the Mass. But the play cannot end without a special role for Perdita, which naturally entails a reunion with Hermione. Shakespeare provides such a reunion, but almost everything about it makes sense only to the extent that we appreciate the allegory. Fittingly, Paulina directs the meeting of mother and daughter:

PAULINA
    Please you to interpose, fair madam. Kneel,
    And pray your mother's blessing. – Turn, good lady;
    Our Perdita is found.
HERMIONE
                    You gods, look down,
    And from your sacred vials pour your graces
    Upon my daughter's head! – Tell me, mine own,
    Where hast thou been preserved? Where lived?
                          (5.3.120-125)

This exchange features a few statements that make relatively little sense in the literal meaning but have great significance within the allegory. Why does Paulina ask Perdita to interpose? Why does Paulina direct Perdita to kneel and ask for Hermione's blessing? Why does Hermione ask her daughter where she has been preserved and then where she has lived?

To understand the allegorical implications of these questions, we need to appreciate the state of the Catholic hierarchy in Shakespeare's England. Our Lord gave His Apostles a mission:

> Going therefore, teach ye all nations; baptizing them in the name of the Father, and of the Son, and of the Holy Ghost. Teaching them to observe all things whatsoever I have commanded you: and behold I am with you all days, even to the consummation of the world.
>
> (Matthew 28.19-20)

Shakespeare's England had banished the successors of Christ's Apostles (the Catholic bishops) and had closed the Catholic churches. Even so, Catholicism can still exist through preservation of the religion amongst practicing Catholics. And yet the Catholic priests who administered the sacraments in Shakespeare's England had to do so without the benefit of English bishops. As Msgr. Philip Hughes describes, this disruption has profound implications:

> The episcopal hierarchy, so the Catholic Church teaches as part of the Catholic faith, is not just a good means of ruling the Church, nor even the best means. It is the means divinely provided. It is of the very nature of the Catholic religion that it is a society ruled by bishops. To be ruled by bishops, to be a bishop-ruled institution is an essential part of what God did in calling the Church into existence. Deprived of its hierarchy the Church would cease to exist. The bishops are to it as a vital, natural organ. To suppress the episcopate would be as though we deprived a man of lungs or heart and just as, if the whole Church could be deprived of bishops it would perish, so if in any part of it the local hierarchy is suppressed, Catholic life will inevitably wither away.[29]

In Shakespeare's England, the Catholic clerical hierarchy had affirmatively broken their link to Rome, so it would take a new connection before the Catholic Church could officially transmit the faith to England. Such a connection would be in the form of a recognized hierarchy and churches in England. Prior to the Gunpowder Plot, Catholics had some hopes that James I might convert, which likely would have resulted in the reestablishment of some Catholic episcopal hierarchy. That hope – represented by Mamillius in the allegory – died as James I increased his opposition to the "Mother Church" in the aftermath of the Gunpowder Plot. With Mamillius's death, the hope of Catholic restoration within the allegory passed to Perdita, who was left to die in Bohemia.

Because Hermione represents the Catholic Church within the allegory, she cannot speak to Sicilia (England) *directly* without reestablishing a formal connection. This explains why Paulina must instruct Perdita to "interpose" herself between Hermione and Sicilia. In this way Shakespeare emphasizes the role of the Catholic hierarchy and the need to restore what had been lost when Henry VIII broke with the Church.

But something else must occur before Hermione can communicate to Perdita. Paulina directs Perdita to kneel before her mother and then Hermione prays that the "gods" may bless Perdita. Despite the invocation of the "gods," Hermione's prayer for her daughter resembles the coronation ceremony for a Catholic monarch and the consecration of a bishop.[30] More generally, this prayer is like other prayers and ceremonies in Catholicism that are meant to impart graces to a person or thing (such as a church) that will then have a more holy and noble purpose. Any reestablishment of the Catholic Church in England would have entailed this type of ceremony in one form or another.[31]

Only after Hermione imparts this blessing on Perdita does she address her in a more tender manner: "Tell me, mine own,/ Where hast thou been preserved? Where lived?" While the overall sentiment makes sense, it seems odd that Hermione asks where Perdita has been preserved and then asks her where she has lived. If the answers to the two questions are different, why would they be different? And the passive construction of the first question suggests another question that Hermione does not ask: who has preserved Perdita?

To better understand the meaning, it helps to know that Shakespeare generally uses "preserve" in a religious sense. Indeed, of the sixteen other plays in which Shakespeare uses "preserve," over half include at least one unambiguously religious use, with God (or gods) frequently being the preserver:

Play (line)	Language
Anthony and Cleopatra (5.1.60)	So the gods preserve thee!
Henry IV, Part II (2.4.290)	O, the Lord preserve thy Grace!
Henry V (4.7.107)	God ples it and preserve it
Henry VI, Part II (1.2.70)	Jesus preserve your royal majesty!
Macbeth (4.2.73)	Heaven preserve you!
Pericles (4.6.109)	The good gods preserve you!
Richard II (5.2.17)	Jesu preserve thee!
Richard III (1.3.59)	Whom God preserve better than you would wish!
Tempest (2.1.309)	Now, good angels preserve the king!
Timon of Athens (1.1.171)	The gods preserve ye!

Given the reasonable likelihood that Hermione's use of "preserve" has a religious meaning, we can think about what it would mean for Perdita, representing the Catholic Church in England, to be preserved. The idea of preservation had special meaning to Catholics in England because government policy since Henry VIII (with the exception of Queen Mary's reign) was to effectively eliminate the Catholic Faith from the country. Richard Simpson's biography of St. Edmund Campion cites the mission statement for Fr. Persons and Fr. Campion in England as follows:

> The object intended by this mission is, first, if God be propitious, to preserve and to advance in the faith and in our Catholic religion all who are found to be Catholics in England.[32]

The Catholic Church in England had been effectively lost but Catholics both in England and throughout Europe preserved what they could. They often did so through heroic and saintly efforts, so that the Catholic Church could eventually return to the land that St. Edmund Campion had described as the most devoted child of the See of Peter. Faithful Catholics today eagerly listen to the stories of how Catholics preserved the Faith in England during Shakespeare's time. Surely Catholics living through the persecution would have yearned even more to hear such tales. Fittingly, then, Hermione's first words to Perdita ask her to relate the details of her preservation.

It is worth noting two other moments in the play when Shakespeare suggests this role of Perdita as the lost Catholic Church in England. In Act V, a servant describes Perdita to Paulina with perhaps the highest praise applied to any character in the play:

SERVANT
                        This is a creature,
    Would she begin a sect, might quench the zeal
    Of all professors else, make proselytes
    Of who she but bid follow.
PAULINA
                        How? Not women!
SERVANT
    Women will love her that she is a woman
    More worth than any man; men, that she is
    The rarest of all women.
                            (5.1.106-112)

The servant's praise of Perdita reflects her virtue, even if there is hyperbole in the notion that she could convert all to her sect. Allegorically, this reflects a pious Catholic belief that men and women would flock to the Church were they to see her in her true beauty.

In Act IV, Camillo articulates a similar sentiment when he tells Perdita, "I should leave grazing, were I of your flock,/ And only live by gazing" (4.4.109-110). Again, Camillo's great reverence for Perdita extends to hyperbole in the literal sense of the play yet corresponds more exactly to the allegorical meaning. And the reference to Perdita's "flock" of course has religious connotations and suggests that she is the shepherd of a religious group. It is even possible, though not essential, that Camillo's idea that he could live by gazing connects to the idea discussed earlier regarding "gazing" on the Eucharist. Camillo does not say that he would "live by gazing" on *Perdita*, so we may take these words in the allegorical meaning as: if I were a member of your church, I could live by adoring the Eucharist.

Significantly, these early references by the servant and Camillo envision Perdita as a Church *in potential*: "*were* I of your flock" and "*would she begin a sect.*" This makes sense if we understand what Perdita represents, the "lost" Catholic Church in England.

Hermione's invocation of the gods to pour graces from their sacred vials represents the glorious realization of Perdita's potential. The words of invocation are the first words that Hermione speaks after being brought back to life. Although this has no meaningful purpose in the literal meaning of the play, allegorically it represents one of loftiest hopes of English Catholics. Such a scene would be the clearest indication of the formal reestablishment of the Catholic Church in England.

Saints Peter and Paul

Shakespeare ends *The Winter's Tale* with another strong indication of a Catholic restoration when Leontes directs the marriage of Camillo and Paulina in the last speech of the play:

> Oh, peace, Paulina!
> Thou shouldst a husband take by my consent,
> As I by thine a wife. This is a match,
> And made between's by vows. Thou hast found mine,
> But how is to be questioned, for I saw her,
> As I thought, dead, and have in vain said many
> A prayer upon her grave. I'll not seek far –
> For him, I partly know his mind – to find thee
> An honourable husband. Come Camillo,
> And take her by the hand, whose worth and honesty
> Is richly noted and here justified
> By us, a pair of kings.
>
> (5.3.137-148)

Leontes dedicates most of his last words not to the wonder of Hermione's "resurrection," or to the joy of finding Perdita, but to directing Camillo and Paulina to marry. When we consider that Camillo and Paulina have not appeared on stage together until this scene, let alone exchanged words, surely we can see that Shakespeare has either lost his sense of the play's context or has something rather profound in mind.

As previously discussed, Shakespeare does indeed have something profound in mind with Camillo and Paulina: they represent Saints Peter and Paul. Camillo shares the first name of the successor of St. Peter at the time Shakespeare wrote the play, Camillo Borghese (Pope Paul V). And we have seen the many ways in which Camillo resembles popes in general and Pope Paul V in particular. Paulina's name has an obvious connection to St. Paul and she guides Leontes on the question of remarriage in much the same way that St. Paul discusses the question of remarriage in his first epistle to the Corinthians. Camillo and Paulina are also the two characters who exercise priestly functions in the allegory: Leontes alludes to Camillo administering the sacrament of Penance, and Paulina celebrates the Mass that brings Hermione back to life.

It makes sense that Shakespeare links Camillo and Paulina as allegorical figures of Saints Peter and Paul. Within the Catholic Church, Saints Peter and Paul share a special place of honor. They are together celebrated on June 29, the Feast of Saints Peter and Paul, and also on November 18, the Dedication of the Basilicas of Saints Peter and Paul. In his *Liturgical Year*, Dom Guéranger includes the following liturgical sequence in his description of the latter feast:

> The Church is founded on Peter's faith, and strengthened by Paul's teaching; one holds the key of authority, the other that of knowledge, both for the same work. With Peter for their shepherd and guide, the faithful people rejoice amid the billows of this world; while they grow strong and receive life-giving medicine from Paul's doctrine.[33]

Shakespeare's development of Camillo and Paulina echoes this to a remarkable extent. They are revered together and act "for the same work," but they have different roles. Notably, St. Peter is the shepherd and guide, holding the key of authority.

This is how English Christians would have viewed the two saints prior to Henry VIII's break with Rome.[34] St. Thomas More opposed Henry VIII's break with Rome and ultimately paid the price with his life. At the trial that sent him to his martyrdom, he argued against the right of Parliament to make a law contrary to the laws of God and the Catholic Church:

> Forasmuch as, my Lord, this indictment is grounded upon an act of Parliament directly repugnant to the laws of God and His Holy Church, the supreme government of which, or of any part whereof, may no temporal prince presume by any law to take upon him, as rightfully belonging to the See of Rome – a spiritual pre-eminence by the mouth of Our Saviour himself personally present upon the earth, only to St. Peter and his successors, Bishops of the same See by special prerogative granted.[35]

Thus, St. Thomas More argues that Jesus Christ entrusted to St. Peter and his successors the supreme governance of the Church. When Henry VIII rejected the pope's authority and broke from the Church, there is a sense in which he symbolically banished St. Peter from England. This symbolic rejection of St. Peter continued to James I (excepting the years of Queen Mary's reign).

To elaborate, although King James I would give the Bishop of Rome the first seat amongst bishops, he denied that the Bishop of Rome could be "monarch" of the Church:

> Christ is his Churches Monarch, and the holy Ghost his Deputies: *Reges gentium dominantur eorum, vos autem non sic.* Christ did not promise before his ascension, to leave Peter with them to direct and instruct them in all things; but he promised to send the holy Ghost unto them for that end.[36]

Denying St. Peter the role of pope deprives him and his successors of a position that, as Catholics believe, Christ established when entrusting St. Peter with the keys. Because you cannot reject a person's principal attribute without in a sense rejecting the person, James I (following Henry VIII) symbolically banished St. Peter. We see this symbolic rejection of Peter in the play when Leontes forces Camillo from Sicilia.

In addition to explicitly rejecting St. Peter's role as pope, James I effectively transferred to St. Paul at least part of the respect due to St. Peter. We can get a sense of this from James I's rebuttal of St. Robert Bellarmine's claims that St. Paul acknowledged St. Peter as head of the Church:

> And it is a wonder, why Paul rebuketh the Church of Corinth for making exception of persons, because some followed Paul, some Apollos, some Cephas, if Peter was their visible head: for then those that followed not Peter or Cephas, renounced the Catholike faith. But it appeareth well that Paul knew little of our new doctrine, since he handleth Peter so rudely, as he not onely compareth but preferreth himself unto him. But our Cardinall proves Peter's superioritie, by Paul's going to visite him. Indeed Paul saith, hee went to Jerusalem to visite Peter, and conferre with him; but he should have added, and to kisse his feet.[37]

James I is referring to an episode that St. Paul describes in his letter to the Galatians. Opponents of St. Peter's primacy, and the papacy, often cite this passage, arguing that if St. Paul rebuked St. Peter, Peter could not have had primacy.[38] James I goes even further, adding an emotional dimension as though he were taking sides with St. Paul against St. Peter, his papal successors, and Catholics in general. In the play we see this in Camillo's sixteen-year absence from Sicilia while Paulina remained to guide Leontes.

The marriage of Camillo and Paulina symbolically reunites the saints. Shakespeare could have portrayed this reunion simply by having Camillo return to his previous position, but he evidently intended to emphasize their complementary roles in the Church. In marriage two become one; and similarly Saints Peter and Paul are of one mind in their Faith. As such, one cannot legitimately play one against the other and hope to remain faithful to either.

We can also see that Shakespeare emphasizes the proper roles of the two saints. Although we do not necessarily need to interpret the husband and wife roles of Camillo and Paulina as signifying this distinction in roles between the apostles, it seems likely that Shakespeare would have seen some parallels. We can have more certainty in another manner in which Shakespeare distinguishes the characters: the first character Shakespeare names in the play is Camillo, and the last is Paulina, reflecting the primacy of St. Peter. This takes on more significance when we consider one of James I's arguments against the primacy of Peter:

> As for me, Paul and Peter I know, but these men I know not: And yet to doubt of this, is to deny the Catholique faith; Nay, the world it selfe must be turned upside downe, and the order of nature inverted (making the left hand to have the place before the Right, and the last named to bee the first in honour) that this primacie may bee maintained.[39]

In James I's estimation, placing St. Peter and his successors as heads of the Church was an inversion of nature, such as making the last named to be the first in honor. Shakespeare, however, seems to have sided with his ancestors in making Camillo both the first in honor and the first named within the play.

We can get a sense of how important this "reunion" was to English Catholics from the words of Cardinal Reginald Pole during Queen Mary's short reign:

> "The cause of all the deformation of the church in this kingdom" was, very simply, "that we, withdrawing from the unity and teaching of faith of the Catholic Church, deserted the authority and obedience of the Roman Pontiff, the Vicar of Christ and the successor of St. Peter, for whose faith, lest it might fail, Christ Himself prayed."[40]

If breaking with the successor of St. Peter caused the deformation in the English Church, then this mending of the union would be the cause of immense joy.

Catholics in Shakespeare's England who struggled daily to practice their faith amidst persecution certainly wished life would improve under James I, or at least under his immediate successors, whoever they might be. If they were to articulate what they wanted, we can imagine that it would amount to free practice of the religion of their Catholic ancestors. If we were to *show* what they wanted, we could scarcely do better than Shakespeare did with the last scene in its allegorical meaning: the king awakens his faith, not only personally but for all of England; the Mass, which had been unlawful to even attend, is said publicly; the Catholic Church is officially recognized; and Saints Peter and Paul are symbolically reunited, with the king granting primacy to St. Peter and the popes. If this had been enacted in reality rather than on stage, England's Catholics would have emerged from Act III, Scene II to find a joy that most would not imagine finding until Heaven.

English Heirs in Heaven

As we have seen, the allegory in *The Winter's Tale* extends from first scene to last and offers a complete and devout picture of Catholic life in Shakespeare's England. Each of the key characters and actions in the play has at least some connection to the allegory. Indeed, many aspects of the play make significantly more sense when read in light of the allegory. Yet there is one aspect of the play's joyful ending that lacks a clear connection to the allegory: the oracle's prophecy that Leontes will live without an heir unless Perdita is found. In other words, what is the significance of "heir" to the allegory?

Within the allegory, the oracle represents Rome, so we should expect any allegorical meaning of the oracle's declaration to match statements that would come from the Catholic Church. The full decree of the oracle includes both judgments about how certain characters have acted as well as the prophetic pronouncement about Leontes's heir:

> Hermione is chaste, Polixenes blameless,
> Camillo a true subject, Leontes a jealous tyrant,
> his innocent babe truly begotten; and the king shall
> live without an heir if that which is lost be not found.
>
> (3.2.132-135)

The first five of the six statements could plausibly fit within the allegorical meaning as statements from Rome, even though it might require some creative interpretations to see the pope (Camillo) as a "true subject" and the Catholic Church in England (Perdita) as an "innocent babe truly begotten." Finding an allegorical meaning for the forward-looking statement about the heir is more challenging for two reasons. First, if we take "heir" to mean a successor to James I (Leontes), the statement lacks content relating to faith and morals, so it is not a statement that we would expect to hear from Rome. Second, while the Catholic Church can speak with authority about the consequences of persisting in a life of virtue or a life of sin, it generally does not engage in "crystal-ball" predictions about future contingencies.

So either the pivotal decree of the oracle is irrelevant to the allegory or the word "heir" has another meaning. A probable solution is to see "heir" in the Biblical context. St. Paul's Epistle to the Romans provides a clear example[41]:

> For the Spirit himself giveth testimony to our spirit, that we are the sons of God. And if sons, heirs also; heirs indeed of God, and joint heirs with Christ; yet so, if we suffer with him, that we may also be glorified with him.
>
> (Romans 8.16-17)

If "heirs" means faithful Christians who will save their souls, then the decree of the oracle would certainly appear to have a meaning that fits with the allegory. And yet what would it mean for James I to have heirs in heaven?

St. Thomas Aquinas writes of the duty of kings in connection with both the temporal and spiritual welfare of citizens:

> And because the end of our living well at this present time is the blessedness of heaven, the king's duty is therefore to secure the good life for the community in such a way as to ensure that it is led to the blessedness of heaven: that is, by commanding those things which conduce to the blessedness of heaven and forbidding, as far as it is possible to do so, those which are contrary to it.[42]

If the king has a role in ensuring that the community is led to the blessedness of heaven, then we can see the logic of saying the king can have heirs in heaven.

If the king can have heirs in heaven by fostering the Catholic Faith, then it follows that he can also cause his subjects to lose their souls by preventing them from practicing that Faith. From a Catholic perspective, Henry VIII had profoundly impacted the ability of his citizens to reach heaven. In an extensive letter to his friend, Henry VIII, Cardinal Reginald Pole writes of the damage the king had done in breaking with the Catholic Church:

> Just as the dragon carried with him a third of the stars when he fell from the heavens, so you, when you abandoned obedience, dragged down with you to destruction more than a third of the noblest souls of your kingdom, souls that were citizens of the heavens.[43]

Souls meant for heaven were lost because Henry VIII cast off the yoke of the Catholic Church and effectively forced his subjects to do the same. Cardinal Pole could have replaced the last clause with "souls that were heirs of God and co-heirs with Christ" without changing the meaning.

Cardinal Pole's damning indictment of Henry VIII was accompanied with an appeal for the king to repent, perform penance and return to the Catholic Faith:

> For, my Prince, although I am writing these things to you concerning obedience and penitence, especially on your behalf, nevertheless I am

also writing them on behalf of all who fell with you. The same path stands open for their salvation as well as for yours. Truly, I especially desire the salvation of all.[44]

If the king were to return to the Church, then he would lead many of his citizens to heaven.

Cardinal Pole's message for his friend Henry VIII would have applied to James I as well. James I could have heirs in heaven, but that would require a return of the Catholic Church to England. As the oracle decreed, the king shall live without an heir if that which is lost be not found.

Shakespeare gives us a few additional confirmations that Leontes's personal religious decisions impact all of his subjects. In his madness, Leontes effectively banishes both Camillo and Perdita, who represent the pope and the Catholic Church in England, respectively. In the allegory, this deprives his subjects of the usual means of sustaining the Catholic Faith. After he regains his senses and undergoes sixteen years of penance, Leontes has the opportunity to restore the Faith for himself and his subjects. His exchange with Paulina makes it abundantly clear that he intends that his decision will bind his subjects:

PAULINA
                It is required
You do awake your faith. Then all stand still.
On; those that think it is unlawful business
I am about, let them depart.
LEONTES
                Proceed.
No foot shall stir.

(5.3.94-98)

When Leontes says, "no foot shall stir," he is making a decision on behalf of his subjects. Because Paulina tells Leontes that the decision hinges on his awakening his faith, we know this is a religious decision. As those in

Shakespeare's England would have understood, such decisions had eternal consequences. From a Catholic perspective, such a decision would smooth the way for the king's subjects to become heirs in heaven.

Naturally, Shakespeare could not have been more direct in expressing that James I (Leontes) would be blocking his loyal subjects from heaven by persecuting them for practicing the Catholic Faith. He could not, for instance, replace "heirs" with "citizens of heaven," "saints," or "souls who die in the state of sanctifying grace." And yet by using "heirs" he communicates the same thing in a hidden way that becomes clear once we suspect what he would have been trying to conceal.

Seeing the decree of the oracle in this way also makes it clear that Shakespeare's allegory really is about the same thing that motivated the saints mentioned throughout this small book – the salvation of souls. For one of the most profound explications of this guiding principle, we can turn to St. Edmund Campion's *Brag*:

> When you shall have heard these questions of religion opened faithfully, which many times by our adversaries are huddled up and confounded, [you] will see upon what grounds our Catholike Faith is builded, how feeble that side is which by sway of the time prevaileth against us, and so at last for your own souls, and for many thousand souls that depend on your government, will discountenance error when it is bewrayed [revealed], and hearken to those who would spend the best blood in their bodies for your salvation.[45]

Ultimately, those who risked their lives to promote the Catholic Faith in England were concerned with leading souls to Heaven. St. Edmund Campion indeed spent his best blood for that cause. From what we have seen, Shakespeare was willing to do the same if the hidden tale with *The Winter's Tale* had been discovered. Thanks be to God that he was as good at hiding his allegory as St. Nicholas Owen was at building hiding places for priests.

Notes

[1] Alfred Thomas, *A Blessed Shore: England and Bohemia from Chaucer to Shakespeare*, 174.

[2] Velma Bourgeois Richmond, *Shakespeare, Catholicism, and Romance*, 95.

[3] Clare Asquith, *Shadowplay: The Hidden Beliefs and Coded Politics of William Shakespeare*, 257.

[4] Asquith, 292.

[5] Thomas Stapleton, *The history of the Church of Englande. Compiled by Venerable Bede, Englishman. Translated out of Latin in to English by Thomas Stapleton student in divinite*, 2-3.

[6] Ibid., 2.

[7] *Catechism of the Council of Trent*, 266.

[8] As discussed previously, the allegory generally relates to three time frames: descriptions of past events represent a happy Catholic England before Henry VIII's break with Rome; current actions in Acts I through III correspond with the turmoil under James I at the time Shakespeare wrote the play; and Acts IV and V represent the hoped for restoration of the Catholic Church in England at some future date.

[9] Henry Sebastian Bowden, *Mementoes of the English Martyrs and Confessors for Every Day in the Year*, 141.

[10] Paulina's husband, Antigonus, falls prey to this type of despair after he abandons Perdita.

[11] St. Paul's letters to the Corinthians provide a useful illustration of this forgiveness. In his first letter to the Corinthians, St. Paul excommunicates a man guilty of fornication. In his second letter to the Corinthians, St. Paul pardons the man after he has performed penance, writing: "And if any one have caused grief, he have not grieved me; but in part, that I may not burden you all. To him who is such a one, this rebuke is sufficient, which is given by many: So that on the contrary, you should rather forgive him and comfort him, lest perhaps such a one be swallowed up with overmuch sorrow. Wherefore I beseech you that you would conform your charity towards him" (2 Cor. 2.5-8).

[12] In *Shakespeare's Romances and the Politics of Counter-Reformation*, Thomas Rist suggests that Leontes's intention to "bear up this exercise" may have a connection to the Ignatian Spiritual Exercises (after St. Ignatius Loyola, founder of the Jesuits). Fr. John Gerard used the exercises extensively in England at the time the play was written.

[13] *Catechism of the Council of Trent*, 264.

[14] Id., 263.

[15] We can see this, for instance, in a painting entitled *The Baptism of Constantine*, attributed by some to Giulio Romano, the "rare Italian master" identified as sculptor of Hermione's statue (5.2.98). The painting depicts the Baptism of Constantine by Pope Sylvester, an event that modern historians have questioned (believing Bishop Eusebius of Nicomedia baptized Constantine). However, if the scene of the first Christian Roman Emperor's Baptism must be portrayed in painting, it seems more significant to depict the pope officiating the ceremony, even if historically inaccurate. The same concept would apply to James I, if only symbolically: if he had wished to reconcile with the Catholic Church, it would be fitting for him to communicate this desire to the pope, just as Leontes recalls Camillo.

[16] Warren H. Carroll, *The Building of Christendom*, 508.

[17] Sarah Beckwith, *Shakespeare and the Grammar of Forgiveness*, 26.

[18] This exchange between Paulina and Leontes also calls to mind the distinction within the Catholic Mass between the "Mass of the Catechumens" and the "Mass of the Faithful." Fr. Adrian Fortescque describes the practice of dismissing catechumens and penitents before the Mass of the Faithful, including an insightful story: "The creed in the Roman Mass now hides the transition from the Mass of the Catechumens to that of the Faithful. Before there was a creed the catechumens and penitents were dismissed after the lessons (and sermon, if there was one). This practice continued to the time of St. Gregory I. He tells the story of two excommunicate nuns who were buried in the church. 'When in this church Mass was celebrated and as usual the deacon cried: If any one does not communicate, let him go away, their nurse, who was accustomed to make an offering to the Lord for them, saw them come out of their tombs and leave the church.'" The practice no longer exists in the Church, though the missal for the Tridentine Mass, which Shakespeare would have known, retains the description of first part of the Mass (before the Credo) as the Mass of the Catechumens, and the second part as the Mass of the Faithful.

[19] Although I do not cite Marion Parker's excellent study – *The Slave of Life: A Study of Shakespeare and the Idea of Justice* – I should note that she also see connections between this final scene and the Catholic Mass.

[20] Louis LaRavoire Morrow, *My Catholic Faith*, 260.

[21] Although the connection is more beautiful than necessarily intended, there is a remarkable story of heavenly music at a Mass during the reign of Henry VIII. When the commissioners arrived at London Charterhouse to direct the monks therein to take the oath in favor of Henry VIII (against papal claims), the monks determined that they would rather be martyred, God willing. During the Mass prior to their martyrdom, a miracle occurred. When the Sacred Host was raised, "there came as it were a soft whisper of air, faint indeed to the outward senses, but of mighty power within the soul. Some perceived it with their bodily hearing; all felt it as it thrilled into their hearts. And there came a sound of melody most sweet, whereat the venerable prior was so moved that he melted into a flood of tears, and could not for a long space continue the offering of the Mass.... Thus, my venerable brethren, did the all holy and merciful God deign to strengthen His servants for their last conflict, which was indeed nigh at hand." Dom Bede Camm O.S.B., *Witness to the Holy Mass and Other Sermons*, 23.

[22] The First Folio edition of the play features several instances of parenthesis. While the significance, if any, of the parenthesis is unclear, the fact that these words are in parenthesis supports the idea that the formula is set apart for a reason, just as the words of consecration are in the Mass.

[23] Pope Pius XII, *Mediator Dei*.

[24] Denzinger, *The Sources of Catholic Dogma*, number 877.

[25] Asquith, 7.

[26] King James VI & I, 303.

[27] King James VI & I, 503.

[28] Asquith, 42.

[29] Philip Hughes, *Rome and the Counter-Reformation in England*, 286.

[30] Although Hermione's invocation of the "gods" naturally suggests a polytheistic vision (which might warn against a Catholic interpretation), we should recall that the connection to Catholicism is allegorical and that Shakespeare truly could not have presented the allegory without camouflage. The confines of his art and the censors militated against, for instance, invoking the Holy Trinity rather than "gods." As the Catholic Encyclopedia chapter on coronation describes, the English coronation ceremony dating to the eighth century is set within the Mass. After the reading of the Gospel, the coronation ceremony begins. During the coronation the bishop pours oil upon the monarch's head from a horn. After several other prayers, the Mass resumes.

[31] This would be the case with installing a bishop or consecrating churches.

[32] Richard Simpson, *Edmund Campion: A Definitive Biography*, 156.

[33] Abbot Guéranger, O.S.B., *The Liturgical Year: Time After Pentecost, Book VI*, 292.

[34] Indeed, Dom Guéranger cites the sequence as follows: "In honour of the holy apostles we gladly borrow from the libraries of our Anglican brethren the following Sequence, sung four centuries ago by the venerable church of York." Ibid. Dom Guéranger completed *The Liturgical Year* by 1900, so that the sequence would have pre-dated the play.

[35] William Roper, *The Life of St. Thomas More*, 86.

[36] King James VI & I, 306.

[37] King James VI & I, 307.

[38] Unsurprisingly, Catholics take the opposite view. St. Robert Bellarmine responds to the Protestant argument in his work on the Roman Pontiff: "The example of Paul actually argues for our side; accordingly, he runs to Peter, and confers the Gospel with him, because he recognizes Peter is greater than himself, and he would give example to posterity that they should run to the See of Peter in matters of this sort." St. Robert Bellarmine, *De Romano Pontifice*.

[39] Ibid.

[40] Philip Hughes, *Rome and the Counter-Reformation in England*, 65.

[41] Other examples include the Epistle of St. Paul to Titus 3:7, the Epistle of St. James 2:5, and the First Epistle of St. Peter 3:22.

[42] R.W. Dyson, *St. Thomas Aquinas Political Writings*, 73.

[43] Reginald Pole, *Pole's Defense of the Unity of the Church*, 333.

[44] Ibid.

[45] Waugh, 220.

SECTION FOUR

Hiding Spots and Disguises

The preceding chapters have attempted to describe Shakespeare's plan for the allegory from first scene to last. Some aspects will convince readers more than others, and readers may well disagree on which correlations between the play and religious circumstances of Shakespeare's England seem most certain. Taken altogether, though, it seems that Shakespeare surely intended the allegory these pages have explored. Indeed, Shakespeare has left us an allegory so rich in detail that we may discount even probable points and still have enough to see the full picture.

Although this section bolsters many of the arguments already introduced in this study, its purpose is to explore certain nuances of the allegory that, while fascinating, extend beyond the narration based on the play's chronology. In addition to the simple narrative of Catholic hardships and hopes, Shakespeare built in broader religious themes that flow throughout the play and allow us to appreciate more deeply the convictions shared by English Catholics. Having discovered the Catholic allegory in the previous sections, we can here spend some time admiring these hiding spots and disguises Shakespeare chose for it.

Hermione as the Mystical Body of Christ

To fully appreciate the religious allegory within *The Winter's Tale*, we must accept the idea that Hermione represents both the Catholic Church and Christ. Fortunately, we know that Shakespeare would have been familiar with the doctrine that reconciled the apparent contradiction: in Catholic theology, the Catholic Church is the Mystical Body of Christ. Earlier chapters have introduced this concept, but it warrants a closer look here because Shakespeare appears to have intended his development of the Mystical Body of Christ as a critical defense of the Catholic Church.

This image of the Mystical Body of Christ derives from the Epistles of St. Paul: "He is the head of his body, the Church" (Col. 1.18). Catholics form the Church and are thus part of the Mystical Body of Christ: "You are the body of Christ, member of member" (1 Cor. 12.27) and "So we being many, are one body in Christ, and every one members of one another" (Rom. 12.5). Thus is established the direct connection between Christ and His Church that we see throughout the play in the person of Hermione.

James I rejected the notion that the Catholic Church is the Mystical Body of Christ, but his manner of doing so helps us understand the importance of the imagery in Shakespeare's England:

> To her selfe shee taketh, in calling her selfe the visible Head of the mysticall Body of Christ, in professing herselfe to bee the dispenser of the mysteries of God, and by her onely must they bee expounded.[1]

James I naturally objected to the idea of the Catholic Church as the Mystical Body of Christ because it represented another argument against the Anglican Church. The king's objection also suggests that the concept of the Mystical Body of Christ would have been familiar to many in Shakespeare's audience – if not, James I would have little reason to argue against the idea.

Additionally, in his encyclical on the Mystical Body of Christ (*Mystici Corporis Christi*), Pope Pius XII cites St. Robert Bellarmine, who wrote extensively on the topic:

> As Bellarmine notes with acumen and accuracy, this appellation of the Body of Christ is not to be explained solely by the fact that Christ must be called the Head of His Mystical Body, but also by the fact that He so sustains the Church, and so in a sense lives in the Church, that she is, as it were, another Christ.[2]

As we have seen, St. Robert Bellarmine played a crucial role in the lives of English Catholics at the time Shakespeare wrote the play. Thus two of the principal opponents in the debate over the Oath of Allegiance – St. Robert Bellarmine and King James I – were also opposing each other on the idea of the Church as the Mystical Body of Christ.

The allegorical sense of Hermione as the Mystical Body of Christ develops in the first three acts as Leontes uses the same imagery in judging his queen as James I used in condemning the Catholic Church. As we saw earlier, Leontes denounced Hermione as an adulteress, seducing Polixenes. Similarly, James I denounced the Catholic Church as an adulterous, seducing "the kings of the earth." Moreover, Leontes's careful refusal to call Hermione "queen" while he mistakes her fidelity aligns with James I's rejection of the Catholic Church's claim to being the spouse of Christ, the queen. Leontes's demands of oaths of allegiance against Hermione also resemble King James I's Oath against what he considered to be the overreaching of the Catholic Church.

Shakespeare provides a subtler identification of Hermione as the Church in two seemingly insignificant lines at different points in the play. These lines point to St. Paul's description of the Church as "without spot or wrinkle" (which we will consider below). First we see a lord arguing to Leontes that Hermione is without spot in the eyes of heaven:

> For her, my lord,
> I dare my life lay down and will do't, sir,

> Please you t'accept it, that the Queen is spotless
> I'th'eyes of heaven and to you – I mean
> In this which you accuse her.
>
> (2.1.130-134)

The lord's clarification that he only means that Hermione is spotless regarding the matter of Leontes's accusation is oddly legalistic in nature. The implication is that while Hermione is innocent of adultery, there may be some sense in which she is not altogether spotless.

Then in the last scene we see Paulina and Leontes discussing Hermione's wrinkles:

> LEONTES
> >   But yet, Paulina,
> > Hermione was not as much wrinkled, nothing
> >   So aged as this seems.
> PAULINA
> >   Oh, not by much.
> >
> > (5.3.27-29)

So Hermione definitely wrinkled over the years, but not by much.

The descriptions of Hermione's spots and wrinkles tie to St. Paul's description of the Church:

> Husbands, love your wives, as Christ also loved the church, and delivered himself up for it: that he might sanctify it, cleansing it by the laver of water in the word of life: That he might present it to himself a glorious church not having spot or wrinkle, or any such thing: but that it should be holy, and without blemish.
>
> (Ephesians 5.25-27)

Christ sanctifies the Church so that He might present it to Himself without spot or wrinkle. Significantly, though, this sanctification takes place during the life of the Church, and so the Mystical Body of Christ will only be without entirely "spot or wrinkle" in every respect at the end of time. Until that time, the members of the Church are very much in need of sanctification.

St. Augustine made this argument against those who took St. Paul's words to mean that the Church was without spot or wrinkle during this lifetime:

> But far be it from us that any one of our number should call himself in such wise just, that he should either go about to establish his own righteousness, as though it were conferred on him by himself, whereas it is said to him, "For what have you that you did not receive?" (1 Corinthians 4.7) or venture to boast himself as being without sin in this world, as the Donatists themselves declared in our conference that they were members of a Church which has already neither spot nor wrinkle, nor any such thing (Ephesians 5.27) – not knowing that this is only fulfilled in those individuals who depart out of this body immediately after baptism, or after the forgiveness of sins, for which we make petition in our prayers; but that for the Church, as a whole, the time will not come when it shall be altogether without spot or wrinkle, or any such thing, till the day when we shall hear the words, "O death, where is your sting? O grave, where is your victory? The sting of death is sin." (1 Corinthians 15.55-56).[3]

As St. Augustine suggests, the Church, as a whole, will only be completely free of spots and wrinkles at the end of time.

Why would Shakespeare have incorporated this concept in *The Winter's Tale?* James I attacked the idea of the Church as the Mystical Body of Christ because of what he perceived as the Church's spots and wrinkles, so to speak. In a remarkable speech before Parliament, James I said:

> I acknowledge the Romane Church to be our Mother Church, although defiled with some infirmities and corruptions ... and as I am none enemie to the life of a sicke man, because I would have his bodie purged of ill humours; no more am I enemie to their Church, because I would have them reforme their errors.[4]

The king recognized the Catholic Church as the Mother Church, but rejected it (as we have seen) because of apparent imperfections of its members. However, the Catholic Church does not lose its status as the Mystical Body of Christ because of the imperfections of its members any more than a mother would stop being a mother because of her child's illness. Shakespeare illustrated the same point more openly with the way in which Leontes stops calling Hermione queen when he irrationally suspects her of adultery. So too, Hermione is still the queen even if she has spots and wrinkles. Thus, the concept of spots and wrinkles adds another theological dimension to the defense of the Church as the Mystical Body of Christ.

In addition, the very nature of the Mystical Body of Christ helps explain the concept of spots and wrinkles. As Pope Pius XII writes:

> And if at times there appears in the Church something that indicates the weakness of our human nature, it should not be attributed to her juridical constitution, but rather to that regrettable inclination to evil found in each individual, which its Divine Founder permits even at times in the most exalted members of His Mystical Body, for the purpose of testing the virtue of the Shepherds no less than of the flocks, and that all may increase the merit of their Christian faith. . . . Certainly the loving Mother is spotless in the Sacraments by which she gives birth to and nourishes her children; in the faith which she has always preserved inviolate; in her sacred laws imposed on all; in the evangelical counsels which she recommends; in those heavenly gifts and extraordinary grace through which with inexhaustible fecundity, she generates hosts of martyrs, virgins and confessors. But it cannot be laid to her charge if some members fall, weak or wounded. In their name she prays to God daily: "Forgive us our trespasses;" and with the brave heart of a mother she applies herself at once to nursing them back to spiritual health.[5]

Thus the Church is spotless in many essential respects, all having to do with faithfully transmitting the sacraments and doctrines necessary for the salvation of souls. But even the "most exalted members" of the Mystical Body of Christ may fall through weakness.

In one of the most beautiful speeches in the play, Camillo expresses to Leontes that every man is subject to such weakness:

> My gracious lord,
> I may be negligent, foolish, and fearful;
> In every one of these no man is free
> But that his negligence, his folly, his fear,
> Among the infinite doings of the world
> Sometimes puts forth. In your affairs, my lord,
> If ever I were willful negligent,
> It was my folly; if industriously
> I played the fool, it was my negligence,
> Not weighing well the end; if ever fearful
> To do a thing where I the issue doubted,
> Whereof the execution did cry out
> Against the nonperformance, 'twas a fear
> Which oft infects the wisest. These, my lord,
> Are such allowed infirmities that honesty
> Is never free of. But, beseech Your Grace,
> Be plainer with me. Let me know my trespass
> By its own visage. If I then deny it,
> 'Tis none of mine.
>
> (1.2.248-266)

Camillo represents the successor of St. Peter, so he speaks of the various failings to which *even the popes* may be subject. James I certainly saw real failings in Catholics that called into question the "spotless" nature of the Church. But such trespasses (as Camillo and Pope Pius XII refer to them as) in no way impugn the Church's claims to being spotless with respect to its essential nature within God's plan.

Despite the failings of its members from time to time, Catholicism teaches that the Church is "indefectible."[6] By this the Church means:

> In saying that the Church is indefectible we assert both her imperishableness, that is, her constant duration to the end of the world, and the essential immutability of her teaching, her constitution

and her liturgy. This does not exclude the decay of individual "churches" (i.e., parts of the Church) and accidental changes.[7]

We can see this in the allegorical meaning of Camillo's speech above: he makes no claim to being free from trespasses; he only insists on his honesty, or truthfulness. So too, while even the popes and bishops may be quite flawed in their individual capacities, the Church will faithfully transmit all that Christ has asked her to transmit until the end of time.

So Shakespeare develops Hermione as the Catholic Church not only through parallels to King James I's attacks on the Church, but also through imagery that relates to the theological defenses against such attacks. As we saw earlier, it also seems likely that Hermione's name connects her to the Church. And, significantly, the role of Hermione as the Church is further confirmed by the way in which she fits within the allegory as a whole: although innocent, she is persecuted by the king and defended by only a few faithful souls.

In parallel to the development of Hermione as the Mystical Body of Christ through references to the Church, Shakespeare likens her to Christ. The association between the Church and Christ extends beyond the idea of the Mystical Body of Christ. As St. Robert Bellarmine noted, Christ "so sustains the Church, and so in a sense lives in the Church, that she is, as it were, another Christ."[8] Fittingly, the first three acts feature similarities between Hermione and Christ's Passion and death, while the last act features similarities to His resurrection.

The connection to Christ's Passion begins with a reference to Judas, who betrayed Christ for thirty pieces of silver. Camillo is describing why Leontes has appointed him to murder Polixenes:

> CAMILLO
>   He thinks, nay, with all confidence he swears,
>   As he had seen't or been an instrument
>   To vice you to't, that you have touched his queen
>   Forbiddenly.
> POLIXENES
>   O, then my best blood turn

> To an infected jelly, and my name
> Be yoked with his that did betray the Best!
>
> (1.2.413-418)

Polixenes believes that if he has betrayed the honor of Hermione he is like Judas, who betrayed Christ, "the Best," with a kiss.[9] Therefore, by analogy, Shakespeare likens Hermione to Christ.

When we read Hermione's words in Act III, we find numerous echoes of Christ in His Passion. J. A. Bryant, Jr. expresses this aspect of Hermione's character well:

> Hermione, refusing to fear the death that is offered her as a form of justice, proclaimed a strumpet on every post, and hurried into a place in the open air before she has her strength – all this should suggest readily enough, even to the modern reader, the familiar character of Jesus from Gethsemane to Golgotha.[10]

And Hermione is persecuted to the point of death. Indeed, like Christ, Hermione embraces her death when Leontes threatens her: "Sir, spare me your threats./ The bug which you would fright me with I seek" (3.2.91-92).

Though Hermione's tribulations certainly fall short of Christ's Passion, her suffering is such that Antigonus's description of her appearance in his dream suggests Christ, the "Man of sorrows": "I never saw a vessel of like sorrow" says Antigonus (3.3.20).

The corresponding Biblical reference to Christ is found in the Prophecy of Isaias:

> Despised, and the most abject of men, a man of sorrows, and acquainted with infirmity: and his look was as it were hidden and despised, whereupon we esteemed him not.
>
> (Isaiah, 53.3)

Antigonus's allusions to Christ's Passion, taken alone, would not amount to sufficient basis for seeing Hermione as the Mystical Body of Christ, but they seem clear within the context of so many other identifications.

While these tragic connections pertain to Christ's Passion, the last scene links Hermione to Christ principally through more glorious comparisons. As discussed previously, Hermione takes on roles in the play's final scene that are distinctly Christ-like, with suggestions of both the Resurrection and the Eucharist. By aligning the sorrowful and glorious aspects of Christ's life with the tragic and glorious parts of the allegory, respectively, Shakespeare reinforces the idea that when James I persecutes the Church he is persecuting Christ. A clear Biblical illustration of this idea occurs at the moment of St. Paul's conversion:

> And falling to the ground, he heard a voice saying to him: Saul, Saul, why persecutest thou me? Who said: Who art thou, Lord? And he: I am Jesus whom thou persecutest. It is hard for thee to kick against the goad.
>
> (Acts 9.4)

Saul had not previously met Christ, but he had been persecuting Christians and, by extension, the Church. Shakespeare's development of Hermione thus builds upon this link between the persecution of the Church and the persecution of Christ.

Shakespeare provides another link between Christ and Hermione when Leontes refers to Hermione's statue as "dear stone":

> Chide me, dear stone, that I may say indeed
> Thou art Hermione; or rather, though art she
> In thy not chiding, for she was as tender
> As infancy and grace.
>
> (5.3.24-27)

This "dear stone" reference relates to Christ, as St. Augustine preached in a sermon centuries ago:

> Jesus Christ, making use of a prophetic testimony to assert His authority, called Himself "the Stone." Yea such a stone, "that whosoever shall stumble against it shall be shaken; but on whomsoever it shall fall, it shall grind him to powder." For when this

stone is stumbled against, it lies low; by lying low, it "shakes" him that stumbles against it; being lifted on high, by its coming down it "grinds" the proud "to powder."[11]

Leontes stumbled against the dear stone while he persecuted Hermione. As the play ends, he recognizes the dear stone for what it is.

Although a few references could apply to both Christ and the Church, Shakespeare generally uses references that more clearly indicate only one aspect of Hermione's allegorical character at a time. Interestingly, though, Antigonus's description of his dream unites the two different aspects of Hermione's character:

> To me comes a creature,
> Sometimes her head on one side, some another;
> I never saw a vessel of like sorrow,
> So filled and so becoming. In pure white robes,
> Like very sanctity, she did approach.
>
> (3.3.18-22)

As discussed above, Antigonus says that he "never saw a vessel of like sorrow," which refers to Christ in His Passion as the Man of Sorrows. Next, the fact that Hermione appears in "pure white robes" calls to mind the description of the Church from St. John's Apocalypse:

> Let us be glad and rejoice, and give glory to him; for the marriage of the Lamb is come, and his wife has prepared herself. And it is granted to her that she should clothe herself with fine linen, glittering and white. For the fine linen are the justifications of saints.
>
> (Apocalypse 19, 7-8)

Antigonus links the pure white robes to the holiness of the saints when he adds that Hermione approached "like very sanctity."

Finally, when Antigonus says Hermione is "so filled and so becoming," he expresses the same basic idea that Pope Pius XII used to describe the Mystical Body of Christ:

> This communication of the Spirit of Christ is the channel through which all the gifts, powers and extraordinary graces found superabundantly in the Head as in their source flow into all the members of the Church, and are perfected daily in them according to the place they hold in the Mystical Body of Jesus Christ. Thus the Church becomes, as it were, the filling out and the complement of the Redeemer, while Christ in a sense attains through the Church a fullness in all things.[12]

The Mystical Body is full in the sense that all the superabundant gifts, powers and extraordinary graces of Christ flow through it. And yet it is in a state of "becoming" until the end of time, when the final number of the elect will be complete.[13]

Pope Pius XII also cites St. Paul's letter to the Ephesians for the image of how the Mystical Body of Christ increases in holiness and "integrity of life" over time:

> But doing the truth in charity, we may in all things grow up in him who is the head, even Christ: From whom the whole body, being compacted and fitly jointed together, by what every joint supplieth, according to the operation in the measure of every part, maketh increase of the body, unto the edifying of itself in charity.
>
> (Ephesians, 4.15-16)

Thus, the Mystical Body of Christ is, like Antigonus says of Hermione, "so filled and so becoming."

Why would Shakespeare have portrayed Hermione as the Mystical Body of Christ? As we saw above, King James I derided the fact that the Catholic Church considers itself the Mystical Body of Christ. However, the king steadfastly believed that he faithfully followed Christ. By presenting Hermione as both the Church and Christ through the unifying doctrine of the Mystical Body of Christ, Shakespeare leads us to the conclusion that one cannot reject the Catholic Church without rejecting Christ.

Flora, The Blessed Virgin Mary, and Florizel

From a Catholic perspective, the allegory described thus far lacks at least one key element: a meaningful role for the Blessed Virgin Mary. Of Mary's place in English Catholicism, Eamon Duffy writes:

> Devotions to Mary proliferated in late medieval England as elsewhere in Christian Europe, and indeed Englishmen were encouraged to think of their country as being in a special way "Mary's Dowry," a notion propagated, for example, by the custodians of the shrine at Walsingham. Her cult came second only to that of Christ himself, and towered above that of all other saints.[14]

We can even see importance of Mary from the words of James I in his *Premonition*:

> For the Blessed Virgin Marie, I yeeld her that which the Angel Gabriel pronounced of her, and which in her Canticle shee prophecied of herselfe: that is, that shee is blessed among women, and that all generations shall call her blessed. I reverence her as the Mother of Christ, whom of our Saviour tooke his flesh, and so the Mother of God, since the Divinitie and Humanitie of Christ are inseparable. And I freely confesse, that shee is in glory both above the Angels and men, her owne Sonne (that is both man and God) onely excepted.[15]

So although James I elsewhere mocks Catholic devotion to Mary on the basis that "in heaven shee is in eternall glory and joy, never to bee interrupted with any worldly businesse,"[16] he revered her as the Mother of God, above the angels and men in glory.

Given Mary's importance to the Church and England, we would expect her to have a role in the allegory. But how would Shakespeare honor her? He could have had the characters praise or pray to the Virgin Mary. Indeed, as John Henry de Groot notes, other Shakespeare plays honor Mary in this way:

> In ways sometimes unnecessary to the plot or the dramatic situation, Shakespeare sometimes seems to pay tribute to the intercessory

powers of the Virgin Mary. For example, in *All's Well that Ends Well*, the Countess of Rousillon expresses her displeasure with Bertram's desertion of his wife by exclaiming: "What angel shall/ Bless this unworthy husband? He cannot thrive,/ Unless her prayers, whom heaven delights to hear,/ And loves to grant, reprieve him from the wrath/ Of greatest justice."[17]

Without naming Mary at all, Shakespeare thus allows the Countess of Rousillon to pay tribute to her in *All's Well that Ends Well*. In *The Winter's Tale*, though, the only apparent reference to Mary is in an exclamation from Clown: "Marry, will I" (3.3.131). We should not expect to find any more overt reference to Mary in the play as that might have exposed the allegory.

Instead of honoring Mary openly, Shakespeare could have a character represent her allegorically. Though this could potentially give Mary a greater role in the allegory, it presents great difficulty for a Catholic author (or playwright).

Fr. Papali indirectly provides some sense of why it is difficult to portray the Blessed Virgin Mary in a work of fiction:

> It is said that a certain sculptor presented to Pope Pius IX a statue in white marble representing the Immaculate Conception. The aged Pontiff scanned it long with his keen eyes and at length spotted a faint streak of discolourment about its base. He would not accept the gift, it was not "immaculate." The Church of God has displayed this same scrupulous solicitude through the ages in all matters relating to Our Blessed Lady. Everything about her must be pure and divine. Nothing must be said or thought about her that implies the least stain or imperfection.[18]

If everything about Mary must be pure and divine, how can one portray her in an allegory without falling short of that standard? A dramatist may need to tread lightly when portraying any virtuous or noble person, but the challenge is magnified tremendously when the person being portrayed is Mary, who was born without original sin.

Panel from the Wilton Diptych (from the 14th century)

We can see this difficulty when we consider that some scholars have argued that there is reason to see Perdita as the Blessed Virgin Mary.[19] Perdita has many exemplary virtues but some aspects of her role and behavior in *The Winter's Tale* naturally seem incompatible with Mary. Indeed, although all of the characters necessarily deviate from their allegorical roles from time to time in the play, none of the storyline suggests Perdita could represent the Mother of Christ – she corresponds to Mary only in terms of her innocence and how others praise her. Moreover, she flirts with, and intends to marry, Florizel. This type of behavior is normal for most women, but it hardly fits the Blessed Virgin Mary. If Pope Pius IX rejected a statue of Mary because it had a faint streak of discoloration at the base, how can we accept Perdita as Mary?

Shakespeare provides the ingenious solution by allowing Perdita to temporarily step out of her primary allegorical role:

FLORIZEL
>These your unusual weeds to each part of you
>Does give a life; no shepherdess, but Flora
>Peering in April's front. This your sheepshearing
>Is as a meeting of the petty gods,
>And you the queen on't.

PERDITA
>   Sir, my gracious lord,
>To chide at your extremes it not becomes me
>Oh, pardon that I name them! Your high self,
>The gracious mark o'th'land, you have obscured
>With a swain's wearing, and me, poor lowly maid,
>Most goddesslike pranked up. But that our feasts
>In every mess have folly, and the feeders
>Digest it with a custom, I should blush
>To see you so attired, swoon, I think,
>To show myself a glass.
>   (4.4.1-14)

Perdita and Florizel have donned costumes for a sheep shearing – for this festive occasion, Perdita has become "Flora." We can see from these lines that she is quite modest, unused to her "goddesslike" attire. She later says, "Methinks I play as I have seen them do/ In Whitsun pastorals. Sure this robe of mine/ Does change my disposition" (4.4.133-135). Thus Shakespeare allows Perdita – as Flora – to honor the Blessed Virgin Mary in much the same way a child would honor a saint he or she portrays for an All Saints Day party.

Shakespeare develops the idea of Flora as the Blessed Virgin Mary by identifying her with several attributes of Mary. None of these identifications is necessarily definitive, but taken together they provide an unmistakable connection. The first link to Mary is the name that Florizel gives Perdita: Flora. The name Flora, meaning flower goddess, has a connection with Mary because she is so often associated with flowers. Chaucer called Mary "glorious virgine, of alle floures flour" (the flower of flowers). As we shall see, she is also identified with many specific flowers. In the 12th century, for instance, St. Bernard referred to Mary as "the rose of charity, the lily of chastity, the violet of humility and the golden gillyflower of heaven."[20] And in the Litany of Loreto, she is the *Rosa Mystica*, the Mystical Rose.

Florizel adds to the connection by declaring that the sheep shearing is a meeting of petty gods, over which Flora is the queen. This fits the Catholic conception of Mary as the Queen of Heaven and Earth, an example of which we can see in Pope Sixtus IV's 1476 apostolic constitution on the Immaculate Conception:

> While in an examination of devout deliberation we are thoroughly investigating the distinguished marks of merit, by which the Queen of Heaven, the glorious Virgin Mother of God, is preferred to all in the heavenly courts.[21]

Even King James I's words from the *Premonition* support this: "shee is in glory both above the Angels and men, her owne Sonne (that is both man and God) onely excepted."

Later in the scene, Florizel expands upon his praise for Perdita using similar imagery:

> Each your doing,
> So singular in each particular,
> Crowns what you are doing in the present deeds,
> That all your acts are queens.
>
> (4.4.143-146)

Earlier he called her queen over a meeting of petty gods and here he says all of her acts are queens. Fr. Cyril Papali expresses this same idea about Mary when he writes, "She is the only creature of whom it can be said that every one of her actions was so perfect that from her part it could not have been more perfect."[22] A wonderful consequence of this is that Mary never ceased to grow in grace during her lifetime. As Fr. Reginald Garrigou-Lagrange, O.P. writes:

> Since it appears that Mary's initial fullness of grace surpassed that of all the saints, her subsequent progress cannot but exceed our powers of description. Nothing held her back, neither the consequences of original sin, nor any venial sin, neither negligence, nor distraction, nor imperfection. She was like a soul which, having taken the vow always to do the most perfect thing, proved completely faithful to it.[23]

This perpetual increase in grace is, in a sense, reflected in Florizel's image of crowns.

Shakespeare provides his audience with an earlier indication of Perdita's grace as the character Time opens Act IV by saying that Perdita is "now grown in grace/ Equal with wond'ring" (4.1.24-25). Although some readers take "grace" to relate to her fine manners, the allegorical context lends itself to another reading. At the Annunciation, the angel Gabriel greeted Mary by saying, "Hail, full of grace, the Lord is with thee" (Luke 1.28). At that point, Mary was full of grace, and yet she continued to grow in grace, as explained above. Within the allegorical reading, Shakespeare conveys the same thing about Perdita (and Flora).

Perdita responds to Florizel's praise by calling herself a "poor lowly maid." We can see in these humble words a reflection of the words Mary spoke at the *Annunciation*, when Gabriel the Archangel announced to her that she would conceive Jesus: "Behold the handmaid of the Lord; be it done to me according to thy word" (Luke 1.38). St. Bernard describes this sublime juxtaposition of honor and humility by saying of Mary, "she is chosen to be the mother of God, and she calls herself a handmaid."[24]

Later in the scene, Perdita's foster-father (Shepherd) prompts her to welcome guests to the sheep shearing. She responds with lines that further call to mind the Annunciation:

> Sir, welcome.
> It is my father's will I should take on me
> The hostess-ship o'th'day.
>
> (4.4.70-72)

In the literal meaning of the play, there is little reason Shakespeare has Perdita consent to her father's will. From an allegorical perspective, though, these lines have profound meaning. As Fr. Papali describes, Mary's consent to God's will was a necessary aspect of the Annunciation:

> By the Annunciation, God was not merely giving her a chance to take an intelligent and meritorious part in the Incarnation. He was so placing it in her hands that, if she had withheld consent, that fact would not have taken place. It was completely conditioned by her will. St Bernard had good reason to exclaim: The Angel awaits your reply, O Lady, and we too, miserably cast down by a death sentence, await a word of mercy from thee. Behold the price of our salvation is in thy hands. We shall soon be free if only thou wilt consent."[25]

St. Bernard says that the "price of our salvation" depended upon Mary consenting to do God's will. So Perdita's consent to do her father's will not only mirrors Mary's humility but also her decision to allow the Word of God to become flesh in her womb.

Purity is another key aspect of Perdita's character and she inspires the same virtue in Florizel. Describing how "the gods themselves" transformed for the sake of love, Florizel compares his transformation to a poor humble swain for the sheep shearing:

> Their transformations
> Were never for a piece of beauty rarer,
> Nor in a way so chaste, since my desires
> Run not before mine honor, nor my lusts
> Burn hotter than my faith.
>
> (4.4.31-35)

Florizel says that although Perdita's beauty is rare, his desire for her is chaste. This of course indicates Florizel's virtue, but more particularly Perdita's purity.

As St. Alphonsus de Liguori describes in *The Glories of Mary*, the Blessed Virgin Mary had these same qualities to a preeminent degree:

> She was most beautiful, I repeat, but without injury to those who looked upon her, for her beauty put to flight impure emotions, and suggested even pure thoughts, as St. Ambrose attests: "So great grace she had, that she not only preserved her own virginity, but also conferred a remarkable gift of purity on those who beheld her."[26]

Catholics revere Mary for all of her virtues, but her purity and chastity shine forth in a special way. By emphasizing these virtues in Perdita, Shakespeare gives us further reason to believe that he intended to link her (through her Flora character) to Mary.

Another aspect of Mary's life is her immense sorrow in sharing in the sufferings of Jesus. Catholics honor Mary through devotion to her seven dolors: the prophecy of Simeon, the flight into Egypt, the loss of the Child Jesus in the temple, the meeting of Jesus and Mary on the Way of the Cross, the crucifixion and death of Jesus, the taking down of the body of Jesus from the Cross, and the burial of Jesus. The first of these dolors gave Mary a foreshadowing of those that would follow:

> And Simeon blessed them, and said to Mary his mother: Behold this child is set for the fall, and for the resurrection of many in Israel, and for a sign which shall be contradicted; and thy own soul a sword shall pierce, that, out of many hearts, thoughts may be revealed.
>
> (Luke 2.34-35)

THE WINTER'S TALE AND HIDDEN CATHOLIC ENGLAND | 183

As Fr. Frederick Faber describes, from that moment, "a clear and detailed vision of all her sorrows, especially the whole Passion, was with its minutest circumstances instantaneously impressed upon her soul."[27]

The seven dolors of Mary

Shakespeare has the Third Gentleman describe Perdita's sorrow upon learning of Hermione's death:

> One of the prettiest touches of all,
> and that which angled for mine eyes – caught the
> water, though not the fish – was when, at the relation
> of the Queen's death, with the manner how she came
> to't bravely confessed and lamented by the King,
> how attentiveness wounded his daughter; till, from
> one sign of dolor to another, she did, with an "Alas" I
> would fain to say, bleed tears, for I am sure my heart
> wept blood.
> (5.2.83-88)

Perdita grieves for the fate of Hermione, who represents Christ in her sufferings and apparent death.

Perdita's attentiveness to Hermione's death and "how she came to't" move her from "one sign of dolor to another." This corresponds to Mary's many sorrows, especially the Passion of Christ. Moreover, these sorrows "wound" Perdita, which resembles Simeon's prophecy that a sword shall pierce Mary's soul.

Perdita's sorrow brings to mind one of the Church's hymns to honor Mary's sorrows, the *Stabat Mater* from the thirteenth century:

> At the cross her station keeping, stood the mournful Mother weeping, close to Jesus to the last.
> Through her heart, His sorrow sharing, all His bitter anguish bearing, now at length the sword has passed.
> Oh, how sad and sore distressed was that Mother highly blessed, of the sole-begotten One.
> Christ above in torment hangs, she beneath beholds the pangs of her dying glorious Son.
> Is there one who would not weep, whelmed in miseries so deep, Christ's dear Mother to behold?
> Can the human heart refrain, from partaking in her pain, in that Mother's pain untold?

The Third Gentleman is sure his heart "wept blood" at seeing Perdita move from "one sign of dolor to another."[28] We can see in this an echo of Eamon Duffy's description of the *Stabat Mater*: "the Virgin's grief is presented, not as an end in itself, but as a means of arousing and focusing sympathetic suffering in the heart of the onlooker."[29]

Given that Shakespeare seems to model Perdita's sorrow after Mary's, we must wonder why he describes her as bleeding tears. The description of Perdita's tears is similar to the story of a portrait of the Blessed Virgin Mary that miraculously bled tears of blood in a town near Milan in 1583:

> Two peasant farmers, Gerolamo De Ferri and Alessandro Ghioldi, had stopped in the church at Rho on April 24, 1583, to pray before the ancient image of Our Lady of Sorrows . . . Being familiar with the image, they were surprised to see that the eyes of the Madonna were swollen as though the image had been crying. Thinking that they might be mistaken at the change, they drew near the portrait. At that moment, tears of blood started to drip from the eyes.[30]

Although Catholics may freely choose to not believe such stories, St. Charles Borromeo (the great archbishop of Milan) investigated the story and declared the miracle to be authentic. At the very least, then, it is plausible that Shakespeare would have known of this instance in which Mary's image reportedly bled tears.

Shakespeare has Perdita further honor Mary through the flowers and herbs in her garden. In her book on *Mary's Flowers*, Vincenzina Krymow describes the historical background of "Mary Gardens":

> Early Christians, and especially those of the Middle Ages, kept the memories of Mary alive through legends. They saw her attributes in flowers and herbs that grew around them and named them after her. Likening Mary to the "garden enclosed" of the Song of Solomon, they envisioned her in a garden, sometimes called a Paradise Garden, and dedicated gardens to her. These special gardens were filled with the flowers and herbs that reminded them of her.[31]

This practice of developing so-called Mary Gardens fits with the idea we have already seen that Mary is associated with flowers.[32]

Mary's Garden (from the 15th century)

In her dialogue with Polixenes, Perdita names fifteen types of herbs and flowers: (1) rosemary, (2) rue, (3) carnations, (4) streaked gillyvors, (5) hot lavender, (6) mints, (7) savory, (8) marjoram, (9) marigold, (10) daffodils, (11) violets, (12) pale primroses, (13) bold oxlips, (14) crown imperial, and (15) "lilies of all kinds,/ The Flower-de-luce being one." Perdita's garden does not include all of these flowers, but the fact that she names them leads us to wonder at their possible significance.

Indeed, most of these flowers and herbs are found in Mary Gardens. Although there is no infallible compendium of Mary Gardens from Shakespeare's time, we can find reliable meanings for many of the flowers and herbs that Shakespeare refers to in the play. The following chart sets forth common meanings for thirteen of those that Perdita names.

Flora's Flowers and Common Christian Meanings
Rosemary: Mary's tree. "Mary hung the linens of the Holy Child on the rosemary bush to dry, and afterwards it became aromatic and evergreen, with little blue flowers springing from its branches."[33]
Rue: Herb of grace.[34]
Carnations: Mary's love of God. "The carnation was considered an attribute of the Virgin Mary as early as the thirteenth century."[35]
Streaked gillyvors: Another name for carnations. Among the flowers named by St. Bernard as representing Mary.
Lavender: Mary's drying plant. "Lavender was said to be one of the plants most loved by the Blessed Virgin because it represented purity, cleanliness and virtue."[36]
Mints: "In Christian symbolism, the mint became the herb of the Virgin Mary because of its lovely fragrance."[37]
Savory: St. Joseph's flower.[38]
Marjoram: Mary's bedstraw.[39]
Marigold: Mary's gold. "Tradition says that Our Lady used the golden blossoms as coins and that her garments were adorned with the flowers."[40]
Daffodils: Mary's star.[41]
Violets: Our Lady's modesty. Among the flowers named by St. Bernard as representing Mary.[42]
Pale primroses: "The primrose was an attribute of the Virgin Mary according to a fifteenth-century poem, 'Rosarium': Gratulare, o Maria/ Florum veris primula."[43]
Lilies of all kinds (the flower-de-luce): Mary's purity. "There is a legend that the archangel Gabriel held a lily in his hand at the Annunciation – after Mary touched the flower, which had been scentless, an exquisite fragrance arose from it."[44] The fleur-de-lis in particular has close associations with Mary.

Of the fifteen flowers and herbs Perdita mentions, only two lack common associations with Mary: crown imperial and bold oxlips. Given that Shakespeare masks the allegory in so many different ways, we should consider whether he intended meanings for these remaining flowers that may seem less evident at first glance. Hidden meanings seem particularly likely because Perdita pairs these two flowers.

The crown imperial brings to mind Mary's crown of glory and dignity in heaven. Seeing this connection between the crown imperial and Mary's heavenly crown requires us to disregard the common botanical symbolism and instead think about everyday meanings of the words themselves.

What, then, could bold oxlips represent? Oxlips could mean what it sounds like, "ox lips." And for an example of bold oxlips, we can look at how St. Albert described one of his students: "you call him a Dumb Ox; I tell you that this Dumb Ox shall bellow so loud that his bellowings will fill the world."[45] The student, St. Thomas Aquinas, boldly wrote (and bellowed) many things about the Blessed Virgin Mary that theologians still cite today. Indeed, in his encyclical proclaiming the queenship of Mary, Pope Pius XII cited St. Thomas Aquinas in saying that Mary's dignity is "all but divine": "the Blessed Virgin, from the fact of her being the Mother of God, has a certain infinite dignity deriving from the infinite good that is God."[46] Thus we can say that the two flowers Perdita mentions that lack common associations with Mary may actually have an uncommonly wonderful association with Mary when considered together: from the lips of the Dumb Ox we have one of the boldest supports for Mary's crown in heaven.

Perdita's fifteen flowers and herbs also bring to mind the fifteen mysteries of the rosary. Perdita ends her list of flowers and herbs by saying that she lacks some "to make you garlands of" (4.4.128). Because the word rosary means "garland of roses," we have good reason to believe that Shakespeare intended this connection as well.

We thus have several indications that Shakespeare intended the connection between Perdita's Flora and the Blessed Virgin Mary. Once

Shakespeare makes this connection, we may apply the praise for Perdita to both the Catholic Church and the Blessed Virgin Mary, which is reasonable as they are often praised in the same terms. The *Song of Songs*, for instance, has been applied to both the Catholic Church and the Blessed Virgin Mary. Venerable Bede's work on the *Song of Songs* focuses on the Church, and so he writes:

> Now the church is called the "fairest among women" because it is obvious that while the churches of Christ throughout the world may be as fair as the spiritual flower of fertile women, fairer still is the whole catholic church, which includes all of them within its own members.[47]

Other interpretations naturally consider the Blessed Virgin Mary as the "fairest among women." With this in mind, we can see that the following exchange regarding Perdita could apply to both the Church and Mary:

SERVANT
                    This is a creature,
  Would she begin a sect, might quench the zeal
  Of all professors else, make proselytes
  Of who she but bid follow.
PAULINA
                  How? Not women!
SERVANT
  Women will love her that she is a woman
  More worth than any man; men, that she is
  The rarest of all women.
                  (5.1.106-112)

Certainly this praise applies to the Blessed Virgin Mary, who is the Mother of Christ and was conceived without sin, making her "the rarest of all women." And, following Venerable Bede, we can see that the Catholic Church, as the Spouse of Christ, is also the "rarest of all women."

We should also reflect on why Perdita refers to "Whitsun pastorals": "Methinks I play as I have seen them do/ In Whitsun pastorals" (4.4.133-134). Whit Sunday is another name for Pentecost Sunday, which commemorates the Holy Spirit descending upon Mary and Christ's disciples. In his chapter on Whit Sunday, Dom Guéranger writes:

> First of all, we look for Mary; for her who now, more than ever, is full of grace. . . . Here is a new mission opened for Mary. The Church is born; she is born of Mary. Mary has given birth to the bride of her Son; new duties fall upon the Mother of the Church. Jesus has ascended into heaven, leaving Mary upon the earth, that she may nurse the infant Church. Oh! How lovely and yet how dignified, is this infancy of our dear Church, cherished as she is, fed, and strengthened by Mary! But this second Eve, this true Mother of the living, must receive a fresh infusion of grace to fit her for this new office: therefore it is that she has the first claim to, and the richest portion of, the gifts of the Holy Ghost. Heretofore, He overshadowed her and made her Mother of the Son of God; now He makes her the Mother of the Christian people. . . . From this day forward, she acts as Mother of the infant Church; and when, at length, the Church no longer needs her visible presence, this Mother quits the earth for heaven, where she is crowned Queen; but there, too, she exercises her glorious title and office of Mother of men.[48]

Mary became mother of the Church on Pentecost, or Whit Sunday. Because Mary is mother of the Church, it stands to reason that the Church would want to learn from, and imitate, Mary in loving God. In her role as Flora, Perdita, who represents the Catholic Church in England, imitates Mary. Fittingly, then, Perdita refers to Whitsun pastorals, the festivities that would commemorate the day Mary became mother of the Church.

As a final point regarding the meaning of Flora, we should consider why Florizel says Flora is "peering in April's front." Given the many connections between Perdita's Flora and the Blessed Virgin Mary, it would seem incongruent for Shakespeare to have included such a detail with no association with Mary. For the likely meaning we can turn to "I syng of a mayden," a fifteenth century poem that Eamon Duffy describes as "firmly rooted in the worship and teaching of the Church about Mary."[49] The poem in a modernized English version reads as follows:

> I sing of a maiden that is matchless,
> King of all kings for her son she chose.
> He came as still where his mother was
> As dew in April that fell on the grass.
> He came as still to his mother's bower
> As dew in April that falls on the flower.
> He came as still where his mother lay
> As dew in April that falls on the spray.
> Mother and maiden there was never, ever one but she;
> Well may such a lady God's mother be.

This glorious poem celebrates the Annunciation, where Christ "came as still to his mother's bower as dew in April that falls on the flower." The Blessed Virgin Mary is likened to a flower, receiving the April dew, representing Christ. In the context of all the connections between Flora and Mary, it would seem hard to believe that Shakespeare did not intend this one as well. As if to remove all doubt, though, Shakespeare has Polixenes address Flora as "gentle maiden" during their discussion of the flowers in her garden (4.4.85).

Englishmen thought of their country as "Mary's Dowry." Shakespeare has Perdita, who represents the Catholic Church in England, honor Mary as Flora. James I honored Mary with his words, but believed that she had little concern for man now that she is in heaven. From what we have seen, it seems that Shakespeare certainly disagreed: the play not only honors her virtues and role in salvation history; it also incorporates the Catholic devotions that originate from a firm belief that Mary is our great advocate in heaven with Jesus.

Perdita's role as Flora also leads us to consider how Florizel fits within the allegory. His name indicates zeal for Flora ("flora-zeal"). Because Flora represents the Blessed Virgin Mary, we can see that his name has the allegorical meaning of "zeal for Mary."

What is Florizel's function within *The Winter's Tale*? He loves and honors Perdita, and brings her back to Sicilia at the direction of Camillo. Allegorically, then, he loves and honors Mary and brings the Catholic Church, and devotion to Mary, back to England at the direction of the pope. This description fits that of the many men who became priests and, through their missions, brought Catholicism back to England during Shakespeare's lifetime. Thus Florizel has a priestly function.

Shakespeare provides a few additional clues that Florizel has a priestly vocation. One key to recognizing this lies in interpreting the love between Florizel and Perdita as chaste. Catholic priests are "married to the Church." This follows the same sense in which the Church is considered to be the "Bride of Christ." Because Perdita represents the Catholic Church in England, it is fitting that her "spouse" be a priest who brings her there. Florizel also describes his devotion to Perdita using language a priest might use to describe his devotion to the Church.

Indications of Florizel's Priestly Vocation	
Florizel: I'll be thine, my fair,/ Or not my father's. For I cannot be/ Mine own, nor anything to any, if/ I be not thine. (4.4.42-45)	*Ordination imposes a certain mark on the priest's soul, dedicating him to divine worship.*[50]
Perdita: How often said my dignity would last/ But till 'twere known? *Florizel:* It cannot fail but by/ The violation of my faith. (4.4.478-480)	*Florizel ties the preservation of Perdita's honor to his faith.*
Florizel: So call it, but it does fulfill my vow;/ I needs must think it honesty. Camillo,/ Not for Bohemia nor the pomp that may/ Be thereat gleaned, for all the sun sees or/ The close earth wombs or the profound seas hides/ In unknown fathoms, will I break my oath/ To this my fair beloved. (4.4.489-495)	*Florizel speaks of his vow and his oath, referring to his devotion to Perdita. His language is cryptic in the literal meaning but makes sense in the allegorical meaning, especially if he is in a religious order.*

The way in which Florizel and Perdita travel to Sicilia also resembles the way in which missionary priests brought the Catholic Faith to England at the time of the play. Camillo directs Florizel and Autolycus to exchange garments so that Florizel may go undetected. He then instructs Perdita on her disguise:

> Fortunate mistress – let my prophecy
> Come home to ye! – you must retire yourself
> Into some covert. Take your sweetheart's hat
> And pluck it o'er your brows, muffle your face,
> Dismantle you, and, as you can, disliken
> The truth of your own seeming, that you may –
> For I do fear eyes – over to shipboard
> Get undescried.
>
> (4.4.651-658)

Camillo "fears eyes" that might recognize Florizel and Perdita. This is the same reason that missionary priests disguised themselves and the Faith that they brought to England. It is, indeed, the same reason Shakespeare went to such great lengths to disguise the Catholic allegory within *The Winter's Tale*.

Shakespeare gives us another possible indication of Florizel's priesthood when Florizel says "I bless the time/ When my good falcon made her flight across/ Thy father's ground" (4.4.14-16). Although the literal reading of this suggests that the falcon flew across Bohemia, Perdita's father is Leontes. So within the allegory we can consider whether the falcon made her flight across Sicilia, representing England. Read in this way, the passage brings to mind Fr. John Gerard's accounts of how he evaded detection on his mission to England in the late 1500s:

> Whenever I saw anybody in the fields I went up to him and asked my usual question about the falcon, concealing all the time my real purpose, which was to avoid the village and public roads and get away from the coast where I knew watchers guarded the thoroughfares and kept out strangers.[51]

Fr. Gerard would pretend to be looking for his falcon when he encountered people in the fields who might otherwise question his activities. We can imagine him telling them his falcon had flown across their land, which is what Florizel tells Perdita.

Seeing Florizel as a missionary priest helps us understand one last connection between Flora and the Blessed Virgin Mary: the somewhat complicated way in which Shakespeare seems to pay tribute to the fact that England is considered "Mary's Dowry."

> Shepherd
> >Take hands, a bargain!
> And, friends unknown, you shall bear witness to't.
> I give my daughter to him and will make
> Her portion equal his.
> Florizel
> >Oh, that must be
> I'th'virtue of your daughter. One being dead,
> I shall have more than you can dream of yet;
> Enough then for your wonder.
> >>(4.4.383-389)

Shepherd gives Perdita to Florizel in marriage and says he will make "her portion equal his." By "her portion," Shepherd means Perdita's dowry.

As T.E. Bridgett relates in his book on Our Lady's Dowry, England was known throughout Europe by this title in the fourteenth century, if not earlier:

> 'The contemplation of the great mystery of the Incarnation,' wrote Thomas Arundel, Archbishop of Canterbury, in 1399, 'has drawn all Christian nations to venerate her from whom come the first beginnings of our redemption. But we English, being the servants of her special inheritance and her own Dowry, as we are commonly called, ought to surpass others in the fervor of our praises and devotions.'[52]

Given the many indications that Flora represents Mary, any discussion of a dowry for Perdita should lead us to suspect that Shakespeare has "Mary's Dowry" in mind. That being the case, we can assume that England is the dowry of Perdita (and Flora) in the allegory. If England is Perdita's dowry, and her dowry is equal to Florizel's, then that would suggest that Florizel's portion was also England. In what sense, though, could that make sense in the allegory?

In the literal reading, when Florizel suggests that he will have great fortunes upon the occasion of "one being dead," the "one" that would die apparently is his father, Polixenes. Upon the Bohemian king's death, Florizel would receive the large inheritance. Although this is a reasonable reading and the one most apparent to the audience, the meaning hinges upon who is signified by "one," and that is indeterminate despite the contextual presumption that it is Polixenes. As we saw earlier, it was similarly apparent to the audience that Leontes was identifying Polixenes as Florizel's "holy father" when, in fact, a closer reading suggests Shakespeare intended Camillo as the "holy father." In other words, there is precedent in the play for us to think that the "one" might not be Polixenes even though that interpretation fits the literal meaning. In addition, soon after Florizel appears to boast of a large inheritance he unhesitatingly renounces it: "From my succession wipe me, father" (4.4.483). This gives us reasonable basis for questioning the apparent literal interpretation.

Surely, though, Florizel is not referring to Perdita as the "one." Such would be tantamount to an eager anticipation of his bride-to-be's death. What if Shakespeare instead intended the allegorical reading in which Florizel is considering his own death? If Florizel means that upon *his* death, he will "have more than you can dream of yet; enough then for your wonder," we can imagine that he is alluding to the glory in heaven awaiting martyrs.

In Question 95, Article 1 of the *Summa Theologica*, St. Thomas Aquinas answers the question of "whether any gifts should be assigned as dowry to the blessed":

> I answer that, without a doubt the blessed when they are brought into glory are dowered by God with certain gifts for their adornment, and this adornment is called their dowry by the masters. Hence the dower of which we speak now is defined thus: "The dowry is the everlasting adornment of the soul and body adequate to life, lasting forever in eternal bliss." The description is taken from a likeness to the material dowry whereby the bride is adorned and the husband provided with adequate support for his wife and children.

In light of St. Thomas's answer, we can see the sense in which Florizel might be referring to his future saintly death when he says he "shall have more than you can dream of yet; enough then for your wonder."

It remains to see how this could connect to England. For that we could look to any of several English martyrs, but the words of St. Robert Southwell seem particularly apt:

> When England was Catholic, she had many glorious confessors; it is for the honour and benefit of our country that it should be well stored with a number of martyrs; and we have now, God be thanked! such martyr-makers in authority, as mean, if they have their will, to make saints enough to furnish all our churches with treasure, when it shall please God to restore them to their true honours . . . The kingdom of heaven, says St. Augustine, requireth no price but thyself. It is well worth all thou art; give thyself and thou shalt have it. Oh, thrice happy you are that are now in the last step of this glory![53]

He wrote this "Epistle of Comfort" as a young missionary priest in England. The missionary priests knew that they faced martyrdom if they were captured. Indeed, St. Robert Southwell was executed at Tyburn in 1595.[54] These priests sought martyrdom with eagerness because they wanted to honor God and save souls in England. The saint goes so far as to thank God for the "martyr-makers in authority."

Perdita and Florizel end the play in Sicilia, which represents England. As Leontes says, they are betrothed by the direction of the heavens (5.3.152-153). As it seems probable that Shakespeare intended Florizel as a priest (to be married to the Catholic Church in England, Perdita), we can see that England represents almost certain martyrdom for Florizel. According to St. Thomas Aquinas, this martyrdom will result in a dowry of eternal bliss. We can thus see that Shepherd spoke truly when he said that Florizel's dowry and Perdita's (as Flora) would be equal: representing Mary, Flora's dowry is England; and Florizel's dowry is England because in trying to bring the Catholic Church (Perdita) to it he will find martyrdom that would give him more glory than we can dream of yet.

The Oracle and Providence

Whereas the preceding chapters have attempted to illustrate parts of the allegory in great detail, this chapter instead provides a comparatively rough outline of Shakespeare's vision of Providence in the play. This is one of the most purely spiritual aspects of *The Winter's Tale*, and there is a sense in which it seems to reveal Shakespeare's faith even more than the rest of the allegory.

Providence has many attributes – some of which we will explore here – but we can see its essence in the words of Fr. Reginald Garrigou-Lagrange, O.P.:

> Providence is the conception in the divine intellect of the order of all things to their end; and the divine governance as St. Thomas observes, is the execution of that order.[55]

God, the Heavenly Father, cares for, and governs, all of His creation. And He does so with unfathomable benevolence. To see this we need only reflect on Christ's words from the Sermon on the Mount:

> Consider the lilies of the field, how they grow: they labour not, neither do they spin. But I say to you, that not even Solomon in all his glory was arrayed as one of these. And if the grass of the field, which is today, and tomorrow is cast into the oven, God doth so clothe: how much more you, O ye of little faith? Be not solicitous therefore, saying, what shall we eat: or what shall we drink, or wherewith shall we be clothed? For after all these things do the heathens seek. For your

Father knoweth that you have need of all these things. Seek ye therefore first the kingdom of God, and his justice, all these things shall be added unto you. Be not solicitous for tomorrow; for the morrow will be solicitous for itself. Sufficient for the day is the evil thereof.

(Matthew 6.26-34)

We can see echoes of this Providence throughout the play, even though some of the references are ostensibly non-Christian:

Providence in The Winter's Tale

Camillo: Swear this thought over/ By each particular star in heaven and all/ By all their influences. (2.1.423-425)

Hermione: There's some ill planet reigns./ I must be patient till the heavens look/ With an aspect more favorable. (2.1.106-108)

A Lord: Please you t' accept it, that the Queen is spotless/ I' th' eyes of heaven. (2.1.132-133)

Hermione: If powers divine/ Behold our human actions, as they do,/ I doubt not then but innocence shall make/ False accusation blush and tyranny/ Tremble at patience. (3.2.28-32)

Leontes: Apollo's angry, and the heavens themselves/ Do strike at my injustice. (3.2.146-147)

Mariner: In my conscience,/ The heavens with that we have in hand are angry/ And frown upon 's.
Antigonus: Their sacred wills be done! (3.3.4-7)

Paulina: There is none worthy,/ Respecting her that's gone. Besides, the gods/ Will have fulfilled their secret purposes;/ For has not the divine Apollo said,/ Is't not the tenor of his oracle,/ That King Leontes shall not have an heir/ Till his lost child be found? (5.1.34-40)

Leontes: The blessed gods/ Purge all infection from our air whilst you/ Do climate here! (5.1.168-170)

Leontes: This' your son-in-law/ And son unto the King, whom, heavens directing,/ Is trothplight to your daughter. (5.3.151-153)

These lines make it clear that Shakespeare purposefully emphasized the role of Providence. Of these references to divine oversight of human affairs, only Paulina's reference to the oracle serves as an important plot point. The others are certainly beautiful but Shakespeare could have omitted them without sacrificing the literal or allegorical meanings of the play. He therefore must have wanted *The Winter's Tale* to tell us something about Providence.

As explored earlier, the oracle represents the Catholic Church within the allegory, each being a source of truth. Shakespeare also uses the oracle as an instrument and mouthpiece of Divine Providence. The decree of the oracle sets a single precondition for Leontes to have an heir – Perdita, who represents the Catholic Church in England, must be found:

> Hermione is chaste, Polixenes blameless,
> Camillo a true subject, Leontes a jealous tyrant,
> his innocent babe truly begotten; and the king shall
> live without an heir if that which is lost be not found.
>
> (3.2.132-135)

With these words the entire remainder of the play depends upon finding Perdita. The central role of the oracle in the play points to the central role of the Catholic Church in Providence.

In his letter on the Mystical Body of Christ, Pope Pius XII writes:

> Christ has need of his members. First, because the person of Jesus Christ is represented by the Supreme Pontiff, who in turn must call on others to share much of his solicitude lest he be overwhelmed by the burden of his pastoral office, and must be helped daily by the prayers of the Church. Moreover as our Saviour does not rule the Church directly in a visible manner, He wills to be helped by the members of His Body in carrying out the work of redemption. That is not because He is indigent and weak, but rather because He has so willed it for the greater glory of His spotless Spouse. Dying on the Cross He left to His Church the immense treasury of the Redemption, towards which she contributed nothing. But when those graces come to be distributed,

not only does He share this work of sanctification with His Church, but He wills that in some way it be due to her action.[56]

So Christ established the Church and wills that it shares in His work of sanctifying souls. Within the Catholic allegory, Shakespeare logically places great weight on the role of the oracle because it corresponds with the great role of the Church in Providence.

The decree of the oracle also frames several ways in which Providence works in the play. All depends on finding Perdita, and Leontes and others must cooperate with God's will to find her. We know this because the oracle gives a conditional prophecy: the king will "live without an heir *if* that which is lost be not found." And because the drama of *The Winter's Tale* proceeds through a series of moral decisions, we should understand that the fulfillment of the oracle depends not upon random chance but *predominantly* upon moral choices.

As we have seen, Leontes takes a few significant steps before he finds Perdita: he undergoes sixteen years of penance, he then recalls Camillo from Bohemia, and finally he chooses to follow Paulina's counsel regarding remarriage. Paulina and Camillo certainly assist Leontes along the way, but the Sicilian king caused the play's tragic moments and bears primary moral responsibility for the actions that lead to Perdita's restoration. Once Leontes has, in a sense, cooperated with these divine requirements, the oracle is fulfilled and Perdita is found.

Finding Perdita depends not only on the works of virtuous characters but also the misdeeds of Antigonus and Autolycus. When Leontes orders Antigonus to abandon Perdita, he does not identify where she is to be abandoned. By having Antigonus choose Perdita's destination, Shakespeare allows the most unfortunate character in the play to inadvertently perform a deed necessary for the joyful ending. We see this in Third Gentleman's description of the end of Antigonus and his followers:

> Wrecked the same instant of their
> master's death and in the view of the shepherd; so that

all the instruments which aided to expose the child
were even then lost when it was found.
(5.2.70-73)

Shakespeare identifies Antigonus and his followers as "instruments," suggesting that they are instruments of Divine Providence even though they committed an evil act in abandoning Perdita. As St. Thomas Aquinas writes:

> If evil were completely excluded from things, much good would be rendered impossible. Consequently it is the concern of Divine Providence, not to safeguard all beings from evil, but to see to it that the evil which arises is ordained to some good.[57]

So, too, with Autolycus who brings Shepherd and Clown to Polixenes's ship. He scarcely acts through pure motives:

> If I had a mind to be honest, I see Fortune
> would not suffer me; she drops booties in my mouth
> I am courted now with a double occasion: gold, and a
> means to do the Prince my master good, which who
> knows that may turn back to my advancement? I
> will bring these two moles, these blind ones, aboard him.
> (4.4.834-840)

Because only Shepherd and Clown can positively identify Perdita, Autolycus's selfish act has an important role in fulfilling the oracle's decree.

And whereas Antigonus dies an accursed death, Autolycus returns to Sicilia for the play's joyful ending. Like Judas, Antigonus despairs and fails to repent for his sins before dying. Like the Prodigal Son, Autolycus acknowledges his past sins and makes at least some attempt at reform.

Shakespeare also makes it clear that his vision of Providence is intimately connected with the work of Christ. For those familiar with Christian doctrines, this notion likely comes as no surprise. And yet

Shakespeare gives us a uniquely stunning portrayal once Perdita is found. The moment in which the oracle's prophecy is realized seems somewhat muted in comparison with the last scene, but arguably provides the greatest expression of joy and marvel in the play. First Gentleman relates the response of Camillo and Leontes when they realize Perdita's identity:

> I make a broken delivery of the business,
> but the changes I perceived in the king and
> Camillo were very notes of admiration. They seemed
> almost, with staring on one another, to tear the cases of
> their eyes. There was speech in their dumbness, language
> in their very gesture. They looked as they had
> heard of a world ransomed, or one destroyed. A notable
> passion of wonder appeared in them, but the wisest
> beholder, that knew no more but seeing, could not say
> if the importance were joy or sorrow; but in the extremity
> of the one it must needs be.
>
> (5.2.10-20)

First Gentleman describes Camillo and Leontes as full of wonder, experiencing the extremity of joy or sorrow. They appear "as they had heard of a world ransomed, or one destroyed."

These lines allude to the joy of Christ's redemption, and in particular a concept explained by St. Thomas Aquinas: "As Christ destroyed our death by His Death, so He restored our life by His resurrection."[58] There is both great joy and great sorrow in this. St. Augustine expands upon this idea in his commentary on Psalm 95:

> Men were held captive under the devil and served the demons, but they were redeemed from captivity. For they could sell themselves, but they could not redeem themselves. The Redeemer came, and gave the price; He poured forth his blood and bought the whole world. Do you ask what He bought? See what He gave, and find what He bought. The blood of Christ is the price. How much is it worth? What but the whole world? What but all nations?[59]

Shakespeare clearly intended the allusion to Christ's ransom, but how does it apply to the finding of Perdita? By finding Perdita, Camillo and Leontes witness the fulfillment of the oracle's prophecy and a sublime working of Providence, but we can imagine them expressing gratitude and awe without referring to the work of Christ.

Here Shakespeare calls our attention to his lesson on Providence. The oracle supplies the script for the second part of the play: all will end well if Perdita is found. When Leontes and Camillo discover Perdita's identity, the oracle is fulfilled. First Gentleman does not describe them as praising the oracle or making any other pagan gestures. Instead, he describes Leontes and Camillo as recognizing Christ's redemptive work. And like many who contemplate Christ's work of redemption, they were moved to the extremes of joy and sorrow.

This is a vision of Divine Providence that is perhaps worth far more than the literal and allegorical meanings of the play of themselves: the Church plays the central role in God's Providence; we must cooperate with God's will; even evil has a role in Providence, and today's wicked man may yet save his soul; and every grace and every bit of good in this world has its meritorious cause in the redemptive work of Christ. All of this provides great consolation to Catholics throughout the ages, and one can imagine that those in Shakespeare's England needed this vision more than most. As Fr. Oswald Tesimond wrote in his narrative of the Gunpowder Plot:

> The attitude of the majority of Catholics, and up to point even of all, is something very obvious to anyone who remembers the great fervor which they show in spiritual matters, that is, in their recourse to the sacraments, their continued prayers in perfect resignation of their wills to the will of God. All the time they encouraged one another to expect relief from Divine Providence alone as they waited on God with true patience and fortitude, and painfully made their way through hard times.[60]

Without trust in Divine Providence, the painful journey of Catholics in Shakespeare's England almost certainly would have been impossible.

With a deep trust in Divine Providence, though, even the most unsupportable burdens could, when it mattered most, become light enough to carry cheerfully.

Hermione's Yoke (and *Agnus Dei*)

One of the more obscure aspects of Hermione's role in the play involves three seemingly unconnected descriptions of her being "about the necks" of Polixenes, Perdita, and Leontes. Each instance is subtle enough to escape notice, but Shakespeare's repetition of the theme calls for a second look.

The first instance occurs in Act I, as Leontes's irrational suspicion of Hermione has completely taken hold of his mind:

> LEONTES
>   Were my wife's liver
> Infected as her life, she would not live
> The running of one glass.
> CAMILLO
>   Who does infect her?
> LEONTES
> Why, he that wears her like her medal, hanging
> About his neck, Bohemia.
>   (1.2.303-307)

We may read this exchange to mean simply that Polixenes is physically close to the Sicilian queen, and that Hermione shows him some affection. Interestingly, though, Shakespeare attributes the action to Polixenes: he wears Hermione, rather than Hermione hanging around his neck.

Hermione is next around the neck of Perdita, at least indirectly. When, in Act V, the three gentlemen discuss the realization that Perdita is the lost heir of Leontes, the Third Gentleman describes one proof of her identity as the "mantle of Queen Hermione's, her jewel about the neck of it" (5.2.34-35). From a plot standpoint, there is no way that Hermione could have been physically about the neck of Perdita when the Shepherd found her in Bohemia, but Hermione's mantle would go about her daughter's neck.

Finally, after Hermione's statue has come to life, she hangs about the neck of Leontes:

> POLIXENES
>   She embraces him.
> CAMILLO
>   She hangs about his neck.
>   If she pertain to life, let her speak too.
>   (5.3.112-114)

Camillo generally is an eloquent character, but his response that "she hangs about his neck" adds little to Polixenes's lines other than a clarification regarding the precise positioning of Hermione's embrace. It would suffice for him simply to reply, "If she pertain to life, let her speak too." But Shakespeare's choice to have Camillo deliver this arguably superfluous line establishes an essential counterpoint to Leontes's criticism in Act I that Hermione hangs about the neck of Polixenes.

Even if the play simply featured three instances of different characters being about the necks of other characters, we might find that intriguing. We can find even further significance in the fact that only Hermione is about the necks of others in the play. And the imagery is something of a litmus test for which royal characters are virtuous: both Polixenes and Perdita are good characters when Hermione is about their necks; Leontes is a bad character when he criticizes Hermione being about Polixenes's neck; Leontes is a good character in the end when she is about his neck. Thus, within the allegory, Hermione is "about the necks" only of the royal characters (including Perdita) who embrace her as the true queen, the Mystical Body of Christ. If we believe that Shakespeare intended this coincidence, surely we should believe that he intended a particular meaning. Each of two possible allegorical meanings harmonizes the three references to Hermione being about the necks of those who embrace her as the true queen.[61]

The first possible meaning requires us to consider the "yoke of Christ." In the Gospel of St. Matthew, Christ describes his yoke:

> Come to me, all you that labour and are burdened, and I will refresh you. Take up my yoke upon you, and learn of me, because I am meek, and humble of heart: and you shall find rest to your souls. For my yoke is sweet, and my burden light.
> (Matthew 12.28-30)

So the yoke of Christ is about the neck of Christians who seek to do His will.

Because Hermione represents the Mystical Body of Christ, her yoke is that of both Christ and the Catholic Church. When Henry VIII rejected the Catholic Church, he cast off the yoke of the papacy. In so doing, he almost certainly would *not* have believed he had cast off the yoke of Christ. However, from the Catholic perspective the yoke of Christ and the yoke of the papacy are inseparable – it is hard to imagine Catholics would have jeopardized their freedom and lives otherwise. Catholics in Shakespeare's England hoped that James I would eventually take on the yoke of the papacy that Henry VIII threw off.

Hermione hangs about the neck of Leontes only after he has undergone penance and awakened his faith. Within the allegory this represents the English monarch accepting the yoke of Christ, and the Church, because Hermione represents the Mystical Body of Christ.

It is worth noting that James I apparently had some sensitivity to the question of whether he accepted the yoke of Christ, despite his adamant claims of orthodoxy. In his *Basilicon Doron*, the widely published letter to his son before he became king of England, he complains of the opposition he faced from ministers in Scotland:

> Some of them would sometimes snapper out well grossley with the trewth of their intentions, informing the people, that all Kings and Princes were naturally enemies to the libertie of the Church, and could never beare the yoke of Christ: with such sound doctrine fed they their flockes[62]

These last words regarding "sound doctrine" showcase his penchant for biting sarcasm and indicate how much the implication of not bearing the yoke of Christ stung him. It seems to have been as much of a source of conflict for James I as the idea of Hermione being about the neck of Polixenes was for Leontes. The allegorical symbolism of Hermione's yoke therefore seems particularly timely.

The second possible meaning behind Hermione being about the neck of Polixenes, Perdita, and Leontes requires us to see her as a "medal." In particular, the *Agnus Dei* may well have been the "medal" Shakespeare had in mind when Hermione is about the necks of Polixenes, Leontes, and Perdita.

Agnus Dei means the "Lamb of God," representing Christ. The Biblical basis for this is from the words of St. John the Baptist upon seeing Christ:

> The next day, John saw Jesus coming to him, and he saith: Behold the Lamb of God, behold him who taketh away the sin of the world. This is he, of whom I said: After me there cometh a man, who is preferred before me: because he was before me.
>
> (John 1.29-30)

St. John the Baptist calls Jesus the "Lamb of God" who takes away the sins of the world.

Agnus Dei is also the name of the Catholic wax medallions that were traditionally blessed by the popes and distributed to the faithful (a practice that Pope Paul VI ended during his papacy in the 1970s). The Catholic Encyclopedia explains its significance:

> The name *Agnus Dei* has been given to certain discs of wax impressed with the figure of a lamb at stated seasons by the Pope. They are sometimes round, sometimes oval in diameter. The lamb usually bears a cross or flag, while figures of saints or the name and arms of the Pope are also commonly impressed on the reverse. These *Agnus Deis* may be worn suspended round the neck, or they may be preserved as objects of devotion.[63]

So within the allegory, the *Agnus Dei* truly would be like Hermione's medal about the neck of Polixenes, Perdita, and Leontes, for Hermione represents the Mystical Body of Christ.

This correlation between Hermione and the *Agnus Dei* makes especial sense when we consider a peculiarity of the dialogue mentioned above:

CAMILLO
                    Who does infect her?

LEONTES
    Why, he that wears her like her medal, hanging
    About his neck, Bohemia.
                                            (1.2.305-307)

Why does Shakespeare refer to the medal as "her medal" and not "a medal"? The *New Variorum* version of the play notes a suggestion from 1780 that "*her* was inadvertently repeated by the compositor."[64] Seeing Hermione as the Mystical Body of Christ allows us to avoid this conclusion that we have inherited an error in the play: the *Agnus Dei* would be *her* medal.

Did the *Agnus Dei* have any significance in Shakespeare's England? Fr. Gerard's *The Condition of Catholics under James I* certainly suggests it did. Here he describes the laws in place under Queen Elizabeth I:

> Whosoever shall bring into any dominions of England . . . any token or tokens, thing or things, called by the name of *Agnus Dei*, or any crosses, pictures, beads, or any such like, from the Bishop or See of Rome, or from any person or persons authorized from the said Bishop or See to consecrate or hallow the same . . . shall incur the penalties, pains, and forfeitures provide by the statute of praemunire, which are the loss of all his lands and goods and perpetual imprisonment.[65]

Leontes's anger that Hermione is about the neck of Polixenes thus takes on even greater meaning in light of the law against having the *Agnus Dei*. Moreover, James I wrote disparagingly of the Agnus Dei in his

Premonition: "For their Sorcery consider of their Agnus Dei, that will slocken fire."[66]

Finally, the *Agnus Dei* has special importance in connection with the martyrdom of St. Cuthbert Mayne, the first martyr from the Douai seminary. Alice Hogge relates Mayne's confrontation with Richard Grenville, "a ruthless naval adventurer with no love of Catholicism":

> When Grenville ripped open Mayne's doublet he found about his neck an Agnus Dei case. Agnus Deis were small wax discs made from the Easter candles, impressed with an image of the paschal lamb and blessed by the Pope. They had been outlawed by Parliament in 1571. The penalty for possessing one was death.[67]

Without a doubt, then, the *Agnus Dei* about the neck of Catholics had tremendous significance in Shakespeare's England.

With three seemingly insignificant lines about Hermione being about the neck of Polixenes, Perdita, and Leontes, Shakespeare thus creates yet another hiding spot in *The Winter's Tale* for the struggles and hopes of Catholics in England. Given that one may miss this hidden gem and still have abundant illustrations of the allegory throughout the play, one may reasonably wonder how many more hiding spots remain undiscovered.

Catholic Englishman's Tale

As we saw earlier, Perdita's description of the "bastard slip" in her garden mirrors the language that Thomas Stapleton used in his 1565 preface to Venerable Bede's *The History of the Church of England*. As it seems almost certain that Shakespeare intended the connection to Stapleton's preface, it is well worth looking at it greater detail here.

Addressing Elizabeth I, Stapleton writes:

> In this history your highness shall see in how many and weighty points the pretended reformers of the church in your Grace's dominion have departed from the pattern of that sound and Catholic faith planted first among Englishmen by holy St. Augustine our

apostle, and his virtuous company, as described truly and sincerely by Venerable Bede.[68]

Thomas Stapleton wrote his preface to Venerable Bede's work to highlight the ways in which the church under Queen Elizabeth I differed from the Catholic Church that England had known since Christianity had first been introduced in England. The logic he uses is straightforward and persuasive. For practicing Catholics, continuity with past beliefs and practices has always been a mark that identifies the Catholic Church as the true Church. Because the church in England had broken with the timeless beliefs and practices of the Catholic Church, it could not possibly be correct. To Stapleton, the Protestant churches were thus like "bastard slips" grafted onto the true Church.

Stapleton goes on to enumerate several specific points of departure between Catholicism and the church under Elizabeth I. Not surprisingly, the allegory within *The Winter's Tale* features many of these differences:

1. **Mass**: Stapleton writes that "our apostles said Mass. . . . Nothing is more horrible in the sight of Protestantism than Mass. In the Mass is the external sacrifice offered to God the Father the blessed body and blood of Christ himself. . . . This seemeth an extreme blasphemy to Protestants." In *The Winter's Tale*, Shakespeare presents a few allusions to the Catholic Mass, including the pivotal scene in which Hermione is brought to life. Speaking of Hermione's statue, Leontes says, "Would you not deem it breathed? And that those veins/ Did verily bear blood?" (5.3.64-65). This suggestion that Hermione's apparently lifeless body truly bears blood matches the Catholic principle Stapleton defends: that the actual body and blood of Christ is consecrated at the Mass.
2. **Propitiatory Sacrifice**: Stapleton writes, "This sacrifice [of the Mass] is taught to be propitiatory. Protestants abhor such doctrine." In *The Winter's Tale*, Paulina's cryptic lines in allegorical the Mass scene point to the propitiatory nature of the

Mass: "Stir, nay, come away,/ Bequeath to death your numbness, for from him/ Dear life redeems you" (5.3.101-103).

3. **Confession:** Stapleton writes that Bede's book witnesses to "confession of sins made to the priest" whereas "the sacrament in the faith of Protestants of our country is abolished." In *The Winter's Tale*, Leontes unambiguously (and favorably) refers to the Catholic sacrament of penance when he says that the priestlike Camillo has cleansed his bosom (1.2.235-237).

4. **Penance:** Stapleton writes, "satisfaction and penance for sin enjoined . . . which in like manner the court of Protestants admit not." In *The Winter's Tale*, Leontes undergoes voluntary penance, expressing to Paulina that she was right to tell him his sins called for great penance (3.2.207-243).

5. **Eucharistic Adoration:** Stapleton writes, "reverence of the blessed Sacrament thought no superstition in our primitive church." In *The Winter's Tale*, the allegorical Mass scene features a few examples of Leontes and Perdita adoring the statue of Hermione. Perdita asks Paulina to allow her to kneel before the statue, and tells her to "not say 'tis superstitious" (5.3.42-44).

6. **Reverence for Relics:** Stapleton writes, "of relics of holy men, of the reverence used towards them and of miracles wrought by them the history is full. . . . Nothing is more vile in the sight of Protestants, than reverence of Christians." In *The Winter's Tale*, Paulina tells her husband, Antigonus, that his hands will be forever "unvenerable" if he commits the sin of following Leontes's command to dispose of Perdita. The clear implication is that the bodies of those who die without sin (the saints) would be venerable.

7. **Sign of the Cross:** Stapleton writes, "blessing with the sign of the Cross, accounted no superstition but practiced for godly and good, in our primitive church. . . . In the devotion of Protestants it is esteemed for magic." In *The Winter's Tale*, Shepherd tells his son, Clown, "now bless thyself" (3.3.110).

8. **Christian Burial**: Stapleton writes, "solemnities of Christian burial Protestants despise and set light by, terming it a . . . heathen superstition. The devotion of our primitive church was to be buried in monasteries, churches and chapels." In *The Winter's Tale*, Shepherd fears that he may die an unholy death, in which "Some hangman must put on my shroud and lay me/ Where no priest shovels in dust." (4.4.459-460). The corollary is that Shepherd wanted to die a holy death and receive a proper burial.

9. **Chastity**: Stapleton writes, "in our primitive church the vow of chastity both of men and women was thought godly and practiced. Such vows now are broken, and esteemed damnable." In *The Winter's Tale*, the chastity of Perdita and Florizel shines forth as a truly honorable virtue.

10. **Holy Vestments**: Stapleton writes, "altar cloths and holy vestments the profane faith of the Protestants admitteth not. Our primitive church used them." In *The Winter's Tale*, Dion's report of the ceremonies at the oracle (representing Mass at St. Peter's in Rome) highlights the great splendor of the vestments: "the celestial habits –/ Methinks I so should term them – and the reverence/ Of the grave wearers." (3.1.4-6)

11. **Papal Authority**: Stapleton writes, "the final determination of spiritual causes in our primitive church rested in the See Apostolic of Rome. . . . How far that See is now detested by the sober religion of Protestants all men do see." In *The Winter's Tale*, papal authority is allegorically represented in both Camillo and the oracle. In each case, such authority is opposed by Leontes during his madness and praised by him when he regains sanity.

Again, while one might reasonably doubt some of these correlations considered in isolation, the presence of so many correlations within the same play makes it difficult to believe that Shakespeare unwittingly incorporated them. Rather, it seems probable that he intended each of them. More importantly, we can see that Shakespeare clearly takes the Catholic side in each of the dichotomies (between timeless Catholic beliefs and transitory Protestant beliefs).

This does not necessarily mean that Shakespeare intended the connection to Stapleton's work specifically. Indeed, a main thrust of Stapleton's arguments is that faithful Catholics throughout the centuries would have shared his assessment of the religious situation in England. In a very real sense, one of the most compelling defenses of the Catholic Faith is that it has been handed down faithfully through the ages from Christ to the Apostles and their successors. St. Paul set forth the guiding principle while the Church was in its infancy: "But though we, or an angel from heaven, preach a gospel to you besides that which we have preached to you, let him be anathema" (Galatians 1.8). In general, then, the similarities between the allegory and Stapleton's work simply suggest that Shakespeare thought like a faithful and knowledgeable Catholic who saw that Protestantism was not the faith of his ancestors.

Elizabeth I and other Protestants would have rejected Stapleton's clear explication of the ways in which Protestantism deviated from the historical beliefs and practices of English Christians. Then, as today, Catholic beliefs are often considered superstitious or otherwise misguided. Stapleton anticipates the arguments that the miracles in Venerable Bede's history are mere superstitious tales:

> If the Cross of Saint Oswald seem a superstitious tale, how much more fond and fabulous is the tale of one that suffered at Bramford, with a great white Cross, appearing in his breast? Thus if we may compare truth with falsehood, light with darkness, true miracles with light tales, we see as much incredibility, if we look to reason, as great vanity in respect of the matter itself, in the one as in the other. But how far more credit this ancient history of Venerable Bede deserveth than the lying libels of upstart sectaries, it shall (as I have already said) safely appear, if we consider but the author of this history, and the time that he wrote in.[69]

In this passage, Stapleton compares Catholic miracles in Venerable Bede's history with Protestant miracles. Protestants, he says, would ridicule the Catholic miracles as superstitious tales while upholding their own miracles. Using pure reason as a guide, the miracles his Protestant critics would accept scarcely differ in credibility from the Catholic ones they would reject. But, he argues, we should be ready to believe Venerable Bede based on his authority, and that of the Catholic Church.

In *The Winter's Tale*, Paulina tells her audience that if she had only told them Hermione was alive, without showing them, they would hoot at her words as an old tale:

> That she is living,
> Were it but told you, should be hooted at
> Like an old tale; but it appears she lives,
> Though yet she speak not.
> (5.3.116-119)

Her lines about the "miracle" of Hermione being alive resemble the reasoning Stapleton used to defend the Catholic miracles in Venerable Bede's history.[70] It is fitting that Shakespeare brings his play – and the accompanying Catholic allegory – to a close with this lesson that truth is not contingent upon the assent or understanding of the audience.

For those readers who have followed this tale of Shakespeare's religious allegory, it should be clear that *The Winter's Tale* is remarkably Catholic, from beginning to end. If we were to hear such a claim without it actually being demonstrated (as it has been in the preceding chapters), we would justifiably hoot at it as an "old tale." It is certain that Shakespeare knew this quite well, as he went to great lengths to disguise the Catholic allegory. Now that we see it, though, we should rejoice at the splendor of the allegory and Shakespeare's incredible genius in being able to disguise it. And it seems very likely that Shakespeare would want us to contemplate the evident display of Catholic Faith in *The Winter's Tale*. After all, he does have Hermione, Perdita, Camillo, Paulina, Florizel and ultimately Leontes echo the sentiments of so many English martyrs who wanted nothing more than to reestablish the Catholic Faith in England.

A Tale Told Boldly

The previous chapters have described the separate components of the religious allegory by juxtaposing the events and characters of the play with Catholic theology and the history of Shakespeare's England. Although there are other connections and meanings this book has omitted, we can piece together a fairly complete version of the allegory based on what has already been explored. This chapter briefly summarizes the allegory as a tale that Catholics in Shakespeare's England would have understood before and after *The Winter's Tale*, even if they never suspected that Shakespeare had told the same tale in the play.

The first three acts describe the circumstances of Catholics in England at the time the play was first performed. The last two acts reflect the hopes of Catholics for change in England.

We can see the allegory as follows:

Dramatis Personae:[71]
Leontes, King of Sicilia (*King James I*)
Camillo, lord of Sicilia (*St. Peter's successor, Pope Paul V*)
Antigonus, lord of Sicilia (*Archpriest George Blackwell, Judas*)
Flora, Perdita in costume for the sheep shearing (*the Blessed Virgin Mary*)
Florizel, Prince of Bohemia (*missionary priest, with zeal for Mary*)
Hermione, Queen to Leontes (*Catholic Church/Mystical Body of Christ*)
Paulina, wife to Antigonus (*St. Paul figure*)
Mamillius, son to Leontes and Hermione (*Anglican Church*)
Perdita, daughter to Leontes and Hermione (*Catholic Church in England*)
Polixenes, King of Bohemia (*all Catholic monarchs*)
Bear, bear (*St. Robert Bellarmine*)
Oracle at Delphos (Delphi), oracle (*Rome*)

Scene – Partly in Sicilia (*England*), and partly in Bohemia (*Bohemia*)

Catholics in Shakespeare's England looked back on days before Henry VIII when their ancestors knew the Catholic Faith as the only Christian faith. But the "royal necessities" of Henry VIII to find a male heir broke this unity. When the pope would not annul Henry VIII's marriage to Catherine, the king broke his union with the Catholic Church, casting off the yoke of the papacy. Because the religion of the monarch was generally enforced on the subjects, Catholics in England faced a grave dilemma: they could follow their king, which patriotism and loyalty demanded, or they could follow their religious convictions. This difficulty persisted through the years (with relief under Queen Mary) and continued under the reigns of Queen Elizabeth I and King James I.

Even so, Catholics in England had hopes for the conversion of King James I and were willing to endure the trials they faced to see happier days. And then the Gunpowder Plot was discovered. However well Catholics managed the conflict before the Gunpowder Plot, they afterwards faced far greater difficulties in balancing their twin obligations to king and Church.

In the wake of the Gunpowder Plot, James I called for his Catholic subjects to take an Oath of Allegiance, but the Oath required its takers to pronounce arguably heretical claims about the pope's authority. Pope Paul V wrote letters stressing that Catholics could not take the Oath. Archpriest Blackwell, who was in charge of the secular priests in England, initially opposed the Oath but then supported it. St. Robert Bellarmine wrote to Blackwell, encouraging him to resist the Oath, even unto martyrdom. James I responded to the letters of Pope Paul V and St. Robert Bellarmine with his own letters in defense of the Oath.

In his defense of the Oath, James I attacked the Catholic Church, calling it an adulteress rather than the Bride of Christ. He also derided the Catholic doctrine that the Church is the Mystical Body of Christ. The king went to great lengths to reject the authority of the pope and label many other Catholic beliefs as superstitious. The king's attacks on the Church sounded like madness to Catholics in England and beyond.

He accused his Catholic subjects of treason, but their sole crime was adhering to the religion of their ancestors. He also accused them of heresy, and they replied that they maintained the same Faith that had been planted in England over a thousand years ago. The king doubted the blameless Church because he had fallen into heresy.

James I began to suspect all Catholics precisely because, as he thought, they followed the "adulterous" Church's teachings and heeded the pope's guidance in her defense. As James I persecuted Catholics, he claimed that he was proceeding in justice because they were breaking the laws he had established. However, his laws criminalized the practice of the religion that had been England's glory for over a thousand years before Henry VIII, so he could not escape the title of tyrant.

Archpriest Blackwell led some of his fellow Catholics astray by encouraging them to take the Oath, which he defended until his death. Others, however, boldly chose to endure persecution rather than abandoning the Faith by taking the Oath. For these courageous souls, the king's tyranny could not overcome their love for the Catholic Church. Through all their hardships they trusted in God's Providence.

While Catholicism was forced underground in England, some English Catholics fled the country. In Bohemia and other lands, English Catholics could openly practice their religion. They could also pray for the day when they could return home to an England that welcomed the Faith that had been the only Christianity it knew before Henry VIII cast off the yoke of the papacy.

Catholics hoped and prayed that James I would eventually realize the great sins he had committed against the Church. If that were to happen, he would see the need for penance and reconciliation with Rome. After such reconciliation, England would see the restoration of the Catholic Mass as a public form of worship and the establishment of the Catholic Church in England. This would symbolically reunite Saints Peter and Paul, affording primacy to St. Peter and his successors as popes. This Catholic renewal would come about through the heroic efforts of priests from foreign lands such as Bohemia, where St. Edmund Campion had prepared for his martyrdom. These priests would almost certainly have a great zeal for the Church and for the Blessed Virgin Mary. This, truly, would be the greatest joy England could imagine this side of heaven.

A Tale Told Softly

Regarding Mamillius's tale . . .

Under even the best of circumstances, Shakespeare could not simply stage any play he liked. As Northrop Frye observes:

> He had to contend with a vigilant and by no means stupid censorship, and references to contemporary politics, or anything that looked like such references, would probably be pounced on before the play reached the stage. We have some of a censor's comments on what seems to us an utterly harmless play, *Sir Thomas More*, which exists in a manuscript of several different hands, one of which is said by handwriting experts to be Shakespeare's. The censor regards it almost as a revolutionary manifesto, and insists on drastic and extensive changes "and not otherwise at your peril." [72]

Censors would have prevented *The Winter's Tale* from reaching the stage if they detected the religious allegory.

The persecution of Catholics in Shakespeare's England naturally led those who wished to remain loyal to Rome to seek clandestine means of expressing and advancing their faith. Even the martyrs, who eventually mounted the scaffold (or worse) rather than deny their faith, went to great lengths to remain hidden while they could. Fr. John Gerard describes in his *Autobiography of a Hunted Priest* one practice Catholics adopted to conceal their correspondence:

> I obtained [the guard's] leave to write a few lines in charcoal, begging my friends to pray for me. All this he allowed, suspecting nothing at all in my action; but, in fact, on the same sheet of paper I wrote to my friends in orange juice, telling them to reply in the same way if they

received the note, but not to say much at first, and to give the warder a little money.[73]

In this way, his friends would receive the letter on which only insignificant charcoal writing appeared; and holding it to the fire they could read the lines that Fr. Gerard had composed in orange juice. Knowing this, over four hundred years since the time of Fr. Gerard and Shakespeare, we can imagine that had Shakespeare actually wanted to write a play sympathetic to Catholicism, he would likely have done so in a similarly clandestine manner.

One cannot stage a play in charcoal and citrus with the same effect that Fr. Gerard achieved in his correspondence. Perhaps for this reason, Shakespeare gave us this exchange between Hermione and Mamillius:

HERMIONE
        Pray you sit by us
  And tell 's a tale.
MAMILLIUS
  Merry or sad shall 't be?
HERMIONE
  As merry as you will.
MAMILLIUS
  A sad tale's best for winter. I have one
  Of sprites and goblins.
HERMIONE
  Let's have that, good sir.
  Come on, sit down. Come on and do your best
  To fright me with your sprites. You're powerful at it.
MAMILLIUS
  There was a man –
HERMIONE
  Nay, come sit down, then on.
MAMILLIUS
  Dwelt by a churchyard. I will tell it softly;
  Yond crickets shall not hear it.
                        (2.1.22-31)

Mamillius must tell the tale softly, lest the crickets hear it. This, truly, is the most that we can gather with certainty about their conversation, that it must be hidden. Given that the play's title derives from these lines, we may reasonably extend the same conclusion to *The Winter's Tale*.

Beyond this, what does Mamillius's tale mean? We know it involves sprites, goblins, and a man who dwelt by a churchyard, but the meaning appears hidden or disguised. This tale ends with one possible meaning, whose elegance should not necessarily be confused for its validity. Robert and Thomas Wintour (also spelled Winter) were co-conspirators in the Gunpowder Plot. As Joseph Pearce relates, Robert and Thomas Wintour were Shakespeare's distant relatives on his mother's side.[74] As Robert Wintour ascended the scaffold, "he said little and was praying quietly as he went to his death."[75] He was executed in St. Paul's Churchyard. A sad tale's best for Winter; there was a man, dwelt by a churchyard . . .

THE END

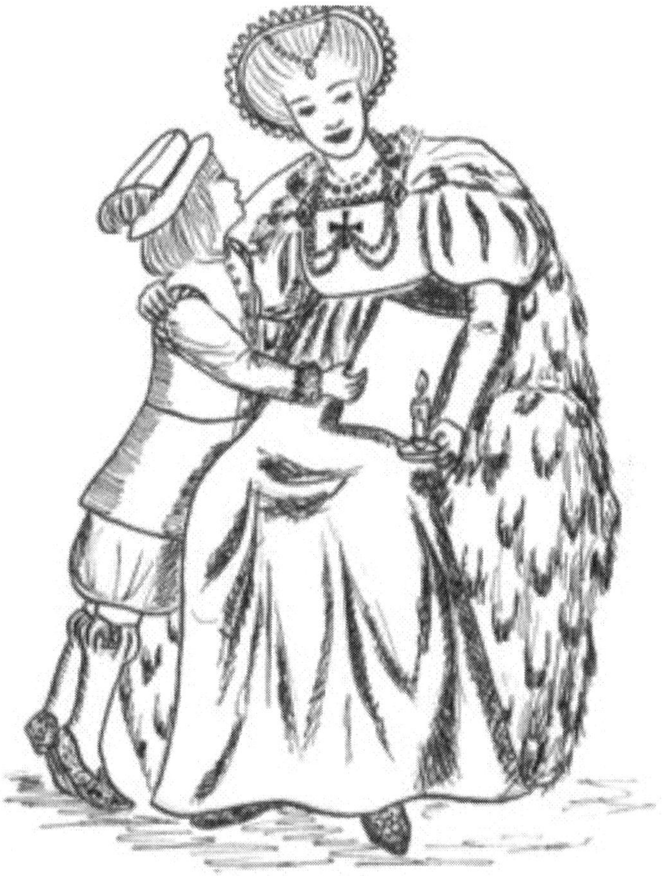

Notes

[1] King James VI & I, 325.

[2] Pope Pius XII, *Mystici Corporis Christi*, 53.

[3] St. Augustine, Letter 185. Newadvent.org/fathers/1102185.htm.

[4] Johann P. Sommervile, ed., *King James VI and I: Political Writings*, 139.

[5] Pope Pius XII, *Mystici Corporis Christi*, 66.

[6] Indefectibility is one of the "three attributes" of the Catholic Church, along with authority and infallibility.

[7] Dr. Ludwig Ott, *Fundamentals of Catholic Dogma*, 296.

[8] Ibid., 53.

[9] Northrop Frye notes that while other Biblical references in the play could be seen as unintentional "Polixenes's reference to Judas Iscariot hardly could be." Northrop Frye, *Northrop Frye on Shakespeare*, 163-164.

[10] Bryant, 212.

[11] Catholic Encyclopedia, *Sermon 41 on the New Testament*.

[12] Pope Pius XII, *Mystici Corporis Christi*, 77.

[13] Some Shakespeare scholars tend to read Antigonus's use of the word "becoming" in the sense of "flattering." But that conflicts with the contradistinction of his word "filled" – Shakespeare intentionally gives us a clear paradox in the literal meaning that is resolved by the allegorical meaning. It also seems to conflict with Antigonus saying of Hermione that he "never saw a vessel of like sorrow."

[14] Eamon Duffy, *The Stripping of the Altars*, 256.

[15] King James VI & I, 302-303.

[16] Ibid.

[17] John Henry de Groot, *The Shakespeares and "The Old Faith"*, 173.

[18] Rev. Cyril Papali, O.D.C., *Mother of God: Mary in Scripture and Tradition*, 16.

[19] As Fr. Peter Milward remarks in his *Shakespeare's Religious Background*, "almost all of the ideal heroines in Shakespeare's plays have their setting not only in the Bible, but more precisely in relation to Mary, the Mother of God." Some scholars see a closer parallel to Mary in Hermione. These critics cite both the ways in which Shakespeare refers to Hermione in terms of grace and the suggestion that the statue of a holy woman would represent Mary.

[20] John S. Stokes, Jr., *The Garden Way of the Rosary*.

[21] Denzinger, number 734.

[22] Rev. Cyril Papali, O.D.C., *Mother of God: Mary in Scripture and Tradition*, 29.

[23] Fr. Reginald Garrigou-Lagrange, O.P., *The Mother of the Saviour*, 76.

[24] St. Bernard of Clairvaux, *Homilies in Praise of the Blessed Virgin Mary*, 54-55.

[25] Papali, 42.

[26] St. Alphonsus de Liguori, *The Glories of Mary*, 263.

[27] Fr. Frederick William Faber, D. D., *The Foot of the Cross: or the Sorrows of Mary*, 80.

[28] As wonderful as this English translation is, the *Stabat Mater* in its original Latin is sublime and many Catholics in Shakespeare's England would have known that version. This is significant because the word for "sorrow" in the Latin version is "dolor," the same word Shakespeare uses. According to the Shakespeare concordance, Shakespeare uses the word "sorrow" 219 times while using the word "dolor" (or "dolour") only 7 times.

[29] Duffy, 259.

[30] Joan Carroll Cruz, *Miraculous Images of Our Lady: 100 Famous Catholic Statues and Portraits*.

[31] Vincenzina Krymow, *Mary's Gardens: Gardens, Legends & Meditations*, 3.

[32] Fr. Papali also points to a Biblical basis for seeing Mary in connection with a garden: "The *enclosed garden* of the Canticles is another symbol that refers to Mary. 'My sister, my spouse, is a garden enclosed, a garden enclosed, a fountain sealed up.'" Papali, 59.

[33] Krymow, 76.

[34] Krymow, 151.

[35] Krymow, 43-44.

[36] Krymow, 119-120.

[37] Mirella Levi D'Ancona, *The Garden of the Renaissance: Botanical Symbolism in Italian Painting*, 232.

[38] "Herbs and Mary," University of Dayton, Mary Gardens Website.

[39] Krymow, 151.

[40] Krymow, 123-124.

[41] Krymow, 150.

[42] Krymow, 31-32.

[43] D'Ancona, 323.

[44] Krymow, 27-28.

[45] G.K. Chesterton, *Saint Thomas Aquinas: "The Dumb Ox,"* 50.

[46] Papali, 48.

[47] The Venerable Bede, *On the Song of Songs and Selected Writings*, 173.

[48] Abbot Guéranger, O.S.B., *The Liturgical Year: Pascal Time Book III*, 283-284.

[49] Eamon Duffy, *The Stripping of the Altars*, 256-257.

[50] *Catechism of the Council of Trent*, 337.

[51] Gerard, *Autobiography of a Hunted Priest*, 11.

[52] T.E. Bridgett, *Our Lady's Dowry, or How England Gained and Lost That Title*, 1.

[53] St. Robert Southwell, *Mary Magdalen's Funeral Tears: The Triumphs over Death; and an Epistle of Comfort*, 197-198.

[54] In his biography of St. Edmund Campion, Evelyn Waugh writes that "A Salesian father, James Gall, an estatic, came to the door of Campion's cell, on the eve of his departure, and inscribed above it *P. Edmundus Campianus Martyr*. Some days before, another father had painted the emblem of martyrdom, a garland of roses and lilies, on the wall at the head of Campion's bed." Waugh, 83.

[55] Fr. Reginald Garrigou-Lagrange, O.P., *Providence: God's loving care for man and the need for confidence in Almighty God*, 27.

[56] Pope Pius XII, *Mystici Corporis Christi*, 44.

[57] St. Thomas Aquinas, *Aquinas's Shorter Summa*, 159.

[58] St. Thomas Aquinas, 309.

[59] St. Augustine, *Enarratio in Psalm 95*.

[60] Francis Edwards, *The Gunpowder Plot: The Narrative of Oswald Tesimond alias Greenway*, 53.

[61] Another meaning suggests itself when we see the picture of James I on page 43 and consider the possible meaning of Hermione's name, ermine. Shakespeare could have intended all three meanings.

[62] *King James VI & I*, 160.

[63] *Catholic Encyclopedia*, *Agnus Dei*.

[64] *New Variorum Edition of Shakespeare: The Winter's Tale*, 113.

[65] Gerard, *The Condition of Catholics under James I*, 322.

[66] *King James VI & I*, 321.

[67] Alice Hogge, *God's Secret Agents: Queen Elizabeth's Forbidden Priests and the Hatching of the Gunpowder Plot*, 61.

[68] Thomas Stapleton, *The history of the Church of Englande. Compiled by Venerable Bede, Englishman. Translated out of Latin in to English by Thomas Stapleton student in divinite*, 3.

[69] Ibid., 9.

[70] Paulina's lines also bring to mind Christ's rebuke of St. Thomas (doubting Thomas): "Jesus saith to him: Because thou hast seen me, Thomas, thou hast believed: blessed are they that have not seen, and have believed." (John 20.29).

[71] Although this list of characters in the allegory appears to fit Shakespeare's apparent intent most closely, writers have noticed different allegorical identities that make sense as well. For instance, Clare Asquith has written persuasively about the connection between Paulina and Magdalen Montague, a Catholic lady in Shakespeare's England who boldly practiced her faith. This certainly fits Paulina, who stayed in Sicilia, while Camillo was forced to Bohemia. If we accept the argument that Shakespeare intended the allegory, accepting that he crafted certain characters with more than one allegorical counterpart does not seem improbable.

[72] Frye, 9.

[73] Gerard, *Autobiography of a Hunted Priest*, 117-118.

[74] Joseph Pearce, *The Quest for Shakespeare: The Bard of Avalon and the Church of Rome*, 151.

[75] Antonia Fraser, *Faith and Treason: The Story of the Gunpowder Plot*, 114.

Bibliography

Robert A. Adams, *Shakespeare: The Four Romances* (New York: W. W. Norton & Company, 1989).

St. Thomas Aquinas, *Aquinas's Shorter Summa* (Manchester: Sophia Institute Press, 2002).

Clare Asquith, *Shadowplay: The Hidden Beliefs and Coded Politics of William Shakespeare* (New York: Public Affairs, 2005).

Roy Battenhouse, "Theme and Structure in *The Winter's Tale*," *Shakespeare Survey 33* (1980).

The Venerable Bede, *On the Song of Songs and Selected Writings* (New York: Paulist Press, 2011).

Sarah Beckwith, *Shakespeare and the Grammar of Forgiveness* (Ithaca: Cornell University Press, 2011).

St. Bernard of Clairvaux, *Homilies in Praise of the Blessed Virgin Mary* (Kalamazoo: Cistercian Publications, 1993).

S. L. Bethell, *The Winter's Tale: A Study* (New York: Staples Press Limited, 1947).

David Bevington, *The Complete Works of Shakespeare (Seventh Edition)* (Boston: Pearson, 2013).

Henry Sebastian Bowden, *Mementoes of the English Martyrs and Confessors for Every Day in the Year* (London: Burns & Oates, 1899).

Henry Sebastian Bowden, *The Religion of Shakespeare: Chiefly from the Writings of the Late Mr. Richard Simpson, M.A.* (London: Burns & Oates, 1899).

T.E. Bridgett, *Our Ladys Dowry, or How England Gained and Lost That Title* (London: Burns & Oates, 1890).

James Brodrick, *Saint Robert Bellarmine: Saint and Scholar* (Westminster: The Newman Press, 1961).

J.A. Bryant, Jr., "Shakespeare's Allegory: The Winter's Tale," *The Sewanee Review* Vol. 63, No. 2 (Apr. – Jun., 1955).

Dom Bede Camm O.S.B., *Witness to the Holy Mass and Other Sermons* (Columbia, Requiem Press, 2004).

Warren H. Carroll, *The Building of Christendom* (Front Royal: Christendom College Press, 1987).

Joan Carroll Cruz, *Miraculous Images of Our Lady: 100 Famous Catholic Statues and Portraits* (Charlotte: TAN Books, 1993).

Clara Longworth de Chambrun, *Shakespeare Rediscovered* (New York: Charles Scribner's Sons, 1938).

G.K. Chesterton, *Saint Thomas Aquinas: "The Dumb Ox"* (New York: Image Books, 1956).

Mirella Levi D'Ancona, *The Garden of the Renaissance: Botanical Symbolism in Italian Painting* (Firenze: Leo S. Olschki, 1977).

John Henry de Groot, *The Shakespeares and "The Old Faith"* (Fraser: Real-View-Books, 1947).

Henry Denzinger, *The Sources of Catholic Dogma* (Fitzwilliam: Loreto Publications, 1955).

Eamon Duffy, *Fires of Faith: Catholic England under Mary Tudor* (New Haven: Yale University Press, 2010).

Eamon Duffy, *The Stripping of the Altars: Traditional Religion in England 1400-1580* (New Haven: Yale University Press, 2005).

R.W. Dyson, *St. Thomas Aquinas Political Writings* (Cambridge: Cambridge University Press, 2002).

Eugene England, "Cordelia and Paulina, Shakespeare's Healing Dramatists," *Literature & Belief 2* (1982).

Francis Edwards, *The Gunpowder Plot: The Narrative of Oswald Tesimond alias Greenway* (London, The Folio Society, 1973).

Fr. Frederick William Faber, D. D., *The Foot of the Cross: or the Sorrows of Mary* (Rockford, TAN Books and Publications, 1978).

Fr. Adrian Fortesque, *The Mass: A Study of the Roman Liturgy* (Fitzwilliam: Loreto Publications, 2003).

Antonia Fraser, *Faith and Treason, The Story of the Gunpowder Plot* (New York: Nan A. Talese, 1996).

Northrop Frye, *Northrop Frye on Shakespeare* (New Haven: Yale University Press, 1986).

Fr. Reginald Garrigou-Lagrange, O.P., *The Mother of the Saviour* (Charlotte: Tan Books, 2012).

Fr. Reginald Garrigou-Lagrange, O.P., *Providence: God's loving care for man and the need for confidence in Almighty God* (Rockford: Tan Books and Publishers, Inc., 1998).

Julia Gasper and Carolyn Williams, "The Meaning of the Name 'Hermione'," *Notes and Queries* (September, 1986).

Fr. John Gerard, S.J., *Autobiography of a Hunted Priest* (Boonville: Preserving Christian Publications, Inc., 2011).

Fr. John Gerard, S.J., *The Condition of Catholics under James I* (London: Longmans, Green & Co., 1871).

Stephen Greenblatt, *Will in the World: How Shakespeare Became Shakespeare* (New York: W. W. Norton & Company, 2004).

Abbot Guéranger, O.S.B., *The Liturgical Year: Time After Pentecost, Book III* (Great Falls: St. Bonaventure Press, 2000).

Joan Lord Hall, *The Winter's Tale: A Guide to the Play* (London: Greenwood Press, 2005).

Donna B. Hamilton, *Shakespeare and the Politics of Protestant England* (Lexington: The University Press of Kentucky, 1992).

Alice Hogge, *God's Secret Agents: Queen Elizabeth's Forbidden Priests and the Hatching of the Gunpowder Plot* (London: Harper Perennial, 2005).

Philip Hughes, *Rome and the Counter-Reformation in England* (Mediatrix Press, 2016).

King James VI & I, *The Workes* (an Unabridged Facsimile of the 1616 Edition Including the Two Workes Appended in 1620) (Miscellany Press, 2008).

Gerard Kilroy, *Edmund Campion: Memory and Transcription* (Burlington: Ashgate Publishing Company, 2005).

G. Wilson Knight, *The Crown of Life: Essays in Interpretation of Shakespeare's Final Plays* (London: Methuen & Co. Ltd, 1948).

Vincenzina Krymow, *Mary's Gardens: Gardens, Legends & Meditations* (Cincinnati: St. Anthony Messenger Press, 1989).

Peter Milward, S.J., *Shakespeare the Papist* (Ave Maria: Sapientia Press, 2005).

Peter Milward, S.J., *Shakespeare's Religious Background* (Bloomington: Indiana University Press, 1973).

Peter Milward, S.J., *The Pattern in Shakespeare's Carpet* (Hyogo: BookWay, 2012).

Thomas More, *The Sadness of Christ* (New York: Scepter Publishers, Inc., 2012).

H. Mutschmann and K. Wentersdorf, *Shakespeare and Catholicism* (New York: Sheed and Ward, 1952).

Dr. Ludwig Ott, Fundamentals of Catholic Dogma (Rockford: Tan Books and Publishers, 1974).

M.D.H. Parker, *The Slave of Life: A Study of Shakespeare and the Idea of Justice* (London: Chatto & Windus, 1955).

W. B. Patterson, King James VI and I and the Reunion of Christendom (Cambridge: Cambridge University Press, 1997).

Joseph Pearce, *The Quest for Shakespeare: The Bard of Avalon and the Church of Rome* (San Francisco: Ignatius Press, 2008).

Robert Persons, *The Judgment of a Catholicke Englishman Living in Banishment for His Religion* (Gainesville: Scholars' Facsimiles & Reprints, 1957).

Reginald Pole, *Pole's Defense of the Unity of the Church* (Westminster, The Newman Press, 1965).

Pope Pius XII, *Mystici Corporis Christi* (Vatican: Libreria Editrice Vaticana, 1943).

Velma Bourgeois Richmond, *Shakespeare, Catholicism, and Romance* (New York: Continuum, 2000).

Thomas Rist, Shakespeare's Romances and the Politics of Counter-Reformation (Lewiston: The Edwin Mellen Press, 1999).

William Roper, *The Life of St. Thomas More* (Long Prairie: The Neumann Press, 2002).

John Saward, John Morrill, and Michael Tomko, *Firmly I Believe and Truly: The Spiritual Tradition of Catholic England* (Oxford University Press, 2013).

Alison Shell, *Shakespeare and Religion* (London: Bloomsbury, 2010).

Richard Simpson, *Edmund Campion: A Definitive Biography* (Charlotte: TAN Books, 2013).

Thomas Stapleton, *The history of the Church of Englande. Compiled by Venerable Bede, Englishman. Translated out of Latin in to English by Thomas Stapleton student in divinite (1565)* (Antwerp 1565).

St. Robert Southwell, *Mary Magdalen's Funeral Tears: The Triumphs over Death and an Epistle of Comfort* (London: Keating & Co., 1822).

Alfred Thomas, *A Blessed Shore: England and Bohemia from Chaucer to Shakespeare* (Ithaca: Cornell University Press, 2007).

Stefania Tutino, *Law and Conscience: Catholicism in Early Modern England, 1570-1625 (Catholic Christendom, 1300-1700)* (London: Routledge, 2016).

John Waterfield, *The Heart of His Mystery: Shakespeare and the Catholic Faith in England under Elizabeth and James* (Bloomington: iUniverse, 2014).

Evelyn Waugh, *Saint Edmund Campion: Priest and Martyr* (Manchester: Sophia Institute Press, 1996).

Ian Wilson, *Shakespeare the Evidence* (New York: St. Martin's Press, 1993)

Printed in Great Britain
by Amazon